Jamaican Cooking Made Easy

Jamaican Cooking Made Easy

Volume I

Third Edition

GetJamaica.Com

iUniverse, Inc.

New York   Lincoln   Shanghai

Jamaican Cooking Made Easy
Volume I

iUniverse books may be ordered through booksellers or by contacting:

iUniverse
2021 Pine Lake Road, Suite 100
Lincoln, NE 68512
www.iuniverse.com
1-800-Authors (1-800-288-4677)

Because of the dynamic nature of the Internet, any Web addresses or links contained in this book may have changed since publication and may no longer be valid.

First Published 2004

ISBN: 978-0-595-47957-3 (pbk)
ISBN: 978-0-595-60053-3 (ebk)

Printed in the United States of America

Get Jamaica.Com

VOLUME I TABLE OF CONTENTS

JAMAICAN COOKING MADE EASY THIRD EDITION

ACKNOWLEDGEMENTS

Worldwide Realtors Company Limited would like to thank the many persons that contributed to publication of the Third Edition of this masterpiece Jamaican cookbook Jamaican Cooking Made Easy. Over 300 Jamaican housewives, cooks and professional Jamaican chefs have worked on the cookbook along with the excellent stenography team from Get Jamaica.Com.

Worldwide Realtors Company Limited would also like to thank Frank Scott Director in charge of technical operations for his service in providing support for our in-house writers in the most rural parts of Jamaica to access rural cooks and chefs and record some of their authentic Jamaican recipes. His service and assistance was much appreciated.

First Published 2004 by
Worldwide Realtors Company Limited
Special Projects Division
Jamaica W.I
Reprinted 2005 and 2006

Text Copyright ©	**Colin Scott—Worldwide Realtors Company Limited**
Photography Copyright ©	**Worldwide Realtors Company Limited**
Book Design and Marketing	**Import Export Services (Subsidiary)**
Publishing & Distribution Rights	**Worldwide Realtors Company Limited**
Electronic Distribution	**Get Jamaica.Com LLC and approved affiliates**

Worldwide Realtors Company Limited would also like to acknowledge several individuals and other affiliated and associate companies that have assisted in making this project a reality. Distribution of this book via the web has now improved and has led to an almost explosion of the Jamaican cuisine. Feel free to build on our Jamaican recipe database which at time of publication stood at 5,412 authentic Jamaican recipes. The Fourth Edition of **Jamaican Cooking Made Easy** is due to be published in June 2009 and will boast just under 2,000 authentic Jamaican recipes. You can submit some of your own recipes to the Fourth Edition on internet at **www.getjamaica.com** home of Get Jamaica.Com.

Special Thanks Go Out To Sandor Panton and the team at

DEDICATION OF JAMAICAN COOKING MADE EASY

This Jamaican cookbook is dedicated to all the Jamaican housewives, cooks and professional chefs who have created one of the most diverse cuisines globally. These Jamaicans have fostered the idea of creativity in preparing Jamaican recipes, whether by necessity in the lack of options or just plain ingenuity. Jamaican cuisine is the most diverse in the world encompassing over 13 distinct different cultures, their cooking techniques and some ingredients that were brought to Jamaica by these traveling immigrants. Combined the dedicated Jamaican cooks and chefs have made the Jamaican cuisine what it is. It is because of these great Jamaicans that this cookbook could have been published.

As every beautiful building has an architect, every machine a mechanic and every masterpiece an artist, so must every recipe have a designer. Not merely just a cook but a designer, dietitian, nutritionist and economist all combined into one person. And blended with all the qualities associated with these professions will be also a liberal sprinkling of idealism and concern a sense of mission akin to that of our founding fathers and mothers.

Such homemakers have found these traditional recipes a stimulating aid in measuring up to the ideals and plans of each individual in meal planning and preparation. An aid not only in that it contains an exciting variety of tempting new dishes but also that the recipes found un this cookbook utilize ingredients that are readily available anywhere in the world that you are. With contributions from over 300 cooks, chefs and homemakers these recipes lead to a nutritional start and finish to every day with great menu suggestions for either that special occasion or just an ordinary meal.

With the authority of a group rather than just one person this collection of recipes from the brilliant collective are therefore dedicated to those who believe that there is good religion in a loaf of bread and good sense in the discipline of health of mind. I hope that this book will be just more than a Jamaican cookbook but a window into the soul and culture of the Jamaican people with understanding the simplicity in our recipe preparations that one might have a greater understanding of just who WE are. I hence officially dedicate this book to

To the many cooks and chefs that contributed recipes.
To Frank and Yvonne Scott, the architects of this movement.
To the staff of Special Projects at the Worldwide Realtors Company Limited designers.
To the Jamaican people who have endured years of hardships to forge such a distinctive culture.

And to
YOU.... The cook, the chef, the homemaker who through you the culture and spirit of Jamaican recipes will continue to live with every recipe that you prepare.

I thank you ALL

Colin Scott.
VP Get Jamaica.Com Limited

AN INTRODUCTION TO JAMAICAN RECIPES AND JAMAICAN FOOD

Before anyone can really answer questions about Jamaican recipes one must understand what it actually means to be Jamaican and what is the culture of Jamaica. But on this particular subject Jamaica's motto is '*Out of many, One people*', this effectively means that Jamaica is made of diverse ethnic groups. Based on Jamaica's history going back as far as the Arawak Indians, the Spanish conquistadores, the French settlers and British plantation overlords who inhabited and governed the islands to throughout the 15th to 19th centuries to the predominantly African, Indian and Chinese freed slaves and indentured laborers who now make up over 90% of the current population. As diverse is the ethnicity of Jamaica so is its culture and by extension its cuisine.

Jamaican recipes that have been passed down through the years have been a mixture of the cuisine from all these ethnic groups coupled with the indigenous Jamaican herbs and spices along with a few brought to Jamaica by the settlers. One's imagination would have to be boundary-less to think of what taste or flavor would be born from a blend of all the recipes brought by settlers throughout the years. So this leads us back to the question 'Are Jamaican recipes really Jamaican? The answer to that question is a resounding YES. Jamaican recipes are a blend of different types of recipes taken from almost every race that one can think of coupled with the Jamaican herbs, spices and seasonings that are grown locally and unique methods of preparation that yield undeniably one of the most savoring flavor and taste in the world today. Jamaican recipes have catapulted the Jamaican culture and cuisine leaps and bounds above almost every other cuisine in the Caribbean and none other is as celebrated globally.

Among these recipes are our famous Jamaican Jerk Chicken, Pork and Fish recipes, Ackee and Salt fish recipe, Callaloo, Breadfruit, Rice and Peas recipes, Cassava Cakes (Bammies) recipes, Stewed Peas recipe, Jamaican Style Curry Goat recipe, Jamaican blue mountain coffee, Jamaican patties, Johnny cakes and festival recipes, Jamaican peppered shrimps recipe, Escoveitched Fish recipe and a host of other recipes. These are what we like to call distinctly Jamaican recipes. Another notable about Jamaican cuisine is the alcoholic and non-alcoholic drink recipes. In most countries once asked about Jamaica one will mention either or all of the following, Bob Marley, Rum and Red Stripe Beer. The latter of rum and Red Stripe Beer being two of the most potent alcoholic beverages on the island. Rum from Appleton Estate is brewed to perfection along with Red Stripe Beer that keeps the taste of the isle alive to the very last drop. But there's so much more to Jamaican Drink Recipes, non-alcoholic Jamaican beverages sometimes double as an aphrodisiac and a potent drink designed to improve male and or female stamina. These boiled herbs are blended together to give rise to things such as Strong Back Roots and Four Man Strength Roots. The names of these Jamaican drink recipes are self-explanatory. Jamaica has found a way to export the taste of Jamaica in exporting the sauces that accompany many of the meals and bottling and selling the Jamaican drink recipes.

GetJamaica.Com is the largest source of Jamaican cooking and Jamaican food techniques globally, with over 300 recipes and you can learn much more by visiting the website www.getjamaica.com.

Jamaican
Breakfast
And
Appetizer
Recipes

MONTEGO BAY MANNISH WATER
A special goat meat appetizer popular across Jamaica.

INGREDIENTS
1 lb Jamaican yam
¼ tsp salt
¼ tsp black pepper
¼ tbsp dried thyme leaves
½ tbsp scotch bonnet pepper diced
2 lg green bananas boiled and chopped
½ cup chopped carrots
¼ cup chopped escallion
4½ cups water
2 lb goat head meats
2 chochos, peeled and finely chopped

PREPARATION
1. Chop goat head meat finely and place in water.
2. When it reaches a boil add all other ingredients to the pot.
3. Reduce heat, cover, and simmer 45 to 55 minutes, or until yam, chocho and bananas are soft.
4. Serve hot.

NEGRIL WRAPPED CHICKEN RECIPE
A favorite chicken recipe on the hip strip in Negril

INGREDIENTS
½ pound chicken
½ tsp Jamaican Appleton V/X rum
1½ tsps soy sauce
½ tsp jerk sauce
½ tsp June plum sauce
½ tsp ketchup
¼ tsp salt
¼ tsp sesame oil
3 stalks escallions diced

PREPARATION
1. Cut chicken meat into thin slices.
2. Cut 6-inch sheets of aluminum foil.
3. Mix chicken meat with all ingredients.
4. Place slices of chicken on each sheet of foil.
5. Wrap to form sealed triangular packets.
6. Heat oil in frying pan and deep fry the foil-wrapped packets over high heat for about 15 minutes or until the chicken is prepared.
7. Remove and drain.

Cooking Tip
Some Jamaican appetizers and breakfast recipes can sometimes be interchanged. However Jamaican appetizer recipes are to be used as a taster, to prepare the guest for what is coming in the main course and dessert. While the appetizer is designed for this purpose, breakfast recipes are designed as an entire meal; leaving no room for any other meal to follow until late afternoon or evening.

DORREEN'S SPECIAL CHICKEN NUGGETS
Doreen's favorite chicken nugget recipe with two new ingredients.

INGREDIENTS
1 stalk escallion minced
1 tbsp onion powder
1 tbsp garlic powder
1tbsp all spice (pimento)
¼ tsp paprika
½ cup dry bread crumbs
1 tbsp diced scotch bonnet pepper
½ tsp cinnamon
¼ cup dried thyme leaves
¼ tsp scotch bonnet pepper minced
2 lb boneless chicken breasts **
¼ cup vegetable oil

PREPARATION
1. In large bowl, combine all dry ingredients with the bread crumbs, thyme and pepper.
2. Dip chicken in bread crumb mixture, coating well.
3. In large skillet, heat ½ inch vegetable oil and cook chicken over medium heat turning once, until done; drain on paper towels.

KINGSTON CHICKEN CANAPES
A cold recipe but loved as a great appetizer

INGREDIENTS
½ cup creamed cheese
¼ cup sour cream
2 cups cubed chicken breast
½ tsp allspice
¼ tsp onion powder
¼ tsp scotch bonnet pepper

PREPARATION
1. Fry the chicken cubes in a large frying pan for 15 to 20 minutes.
2. Remove the prepared cubes and drain any remaining oil from them.
3. Mix cheese, sour cream and dry spices together.
4. Place the chicken cubes in the mixture and then keep chilled.
5. Just before serving, spread on butter
6. Serve with crackers.

**—Boneless chicken breasts are are one of the most convenient meats available in your supermarket. There are so many recipes for chicken breasts on our website *www.getjamaica.com*.

COCKTAIL BEEF PATTY RECIPE
A special beef patty recipe that is almost synonymous with the Jamaican recipe.

INGREDIENTS
6 Jamaican patty crusts
1½ cups ground beef
1 tsp salt
¼ tsp dried thyme leaves
1 lg tomato chopped
½ tbsp scotch bonnet pepper diced
2 stalk escallion chopped
1 lg onion finely chopped
2 tbsp soy sauce
¼ tsp sugar
½ tsp allspice

PREPARATION
1. Sauté escallion, onions, thyme, pepper and chopped tomato in a frying pan.
2. Add beef mince in frying pan and fry until minced is cooked.
3. Add soy sauce, sugar, salt and allspice.
4. Ensure that the beef is wet when placing it on the patty crust.
5. Place at least 3 tablespoons of filling on each circle then fold and crimp with a fork the corners.
6. Brush a small amount of oil on each patty.
7. Place in the oven then bake for approximately 45 minutes at 375 Degrees.

MIDDLE QUARTERS SHRIMP PATTY RECIPE
The town of Middle quarters in St. Elizabeth is the home of the Jamaican shrimp and the Shrimp Patty.

INGREDIENTS
6 Jamaican patty crusts
1½ cups peeled and de-veined shrimp
¼ tsp salt
¼ tbsp scotch bonnet pepper diced
½ stalk escallion chopped
1 tbsp curry powder
¼ tsp sugar
½ tsp allspice

PREPARATION
1. Sauté escallion and pepper in a frying pan.
2. Add shrimp in frying pan and fry until shrimp is cooked.
3. Add curry powder, sugar, salt and allspice.
4. Continue to stir and allow to simmer until shrimp are well cooked.
5. Ensure that the curry shrimp is wet when placing it on the patty crust.
6. Place at least 3 tablespoons of filling on each circle then fold and crimp with a fork the corners.
7. Brush a small amount of oil on each patty.
8. Place in the oven then bake for approximately 45 minutes at 375 Degrees.

Cooking Tip
When preparing these recipes **<u>don't use too much curry</u>** it will not only drown out the taste of the recipe but also make it inedible.

JAMAICAN BANANA FRITTERS
Banana fritters are a popular banana recipe.

INGREDIENTS
¼ tsp salt
¼ tsp baking powder
1 egg beaten
2¼ cup flour
1 tbsp margarine
1½ cups crushed ripe bananas

PREPARATION
1. Sift flour with baking powder and salt. Add the egg to the crushed bananas and to the flour mixture.
2. Mix until you have a medium batter and fry each tablespoon amount in at least ½ inch vegetable oil.
3. Serve hot.

WHITEHOUSE LOBSTER PATTY RECIPE
The town of Whitehouse Westmoreland, is a major fishing town in Jamaica with the most divine lobster patties.

INGREDIENTS
6 Jamaican patty crusts
1½ cups chopped lobster meat
¼ tsp salt
¼ tbsp scotch bonnet pepper diced
½ stalk escallion chopped
1 tbsp curry powder
¼ tsp sugar
½ tsp allspice

PREPARATION
1. Sauté escallion and pepper in a frying pan.
2. Add chopped lobster meat in frying pan and fry until lobster is cooked.
3. Add curry powder, sugar, salt and allspice.
4. Continue to stir and allow to simmer until lobster is well cooked.
5. Ensure that the curry lobster is wet when placing it on the patty crust.
6. Place at least 3 tablespoons of filling on each circle then fold and crimp with a fork the corners.
7. Brush a small amount of oil on each patty.
8. Place in the oven then bake for approximately 45 minutes at 375 Degrees.

Cooking Tip
Jamaican patty recipes are very flexible and can be made using fish, chicken, pork and beef fillings.

SPANISH TOWN ACKEE PATTY RECIPE
Another great patty recipe from the old capital with many variations including the callaloo patty.

INGREDIENTS
6 Jamaican patty crusts
30 Ackee pods or 1 can of Ackees
½ lb salt fish
¼ tsp salt
¼ tsp black pepper
4 tomatoes chopped
3 stalks escallion finely chopped
2¼ cup water
2 tbsp margarine
1 lg chopped onion

PREPARATION
1. Soak salt fish overnight, then boil and flake salt fish and set aside.
2. Fry the bacon strips and set aside.
3. Boil ackees after removing pink and seeds (not necessary if canned ackees) for 20 minutes and drain.
4. Sauté onions, tomatoes, escallion, then add ackees, bacon and salt fish stirring softly.
5. Add black pepper and salt and sauté for just another five minutes.
6. Ensure that the ackee filling is wet when placing it on the patty crust.
7. Place at least 3 tablespoons of filling on each circle then fold and crimp with a for the corners.
8. Brush a small amount of oil on each patty.
9. Place in the oven then bake for approximately 45 minutes at 375 Degrees.

> **Cooking Tip**
> Eating **uncooked ackee is a very dangerous**. Ackee has been known to induce vomiting and before you prepare this recipe ensure that the ackee is well cooked.

JAMAICAN PATTY CRUST
A popular Jamaican recipe that is filled with various beef, chicken, fish and seafood fillings.

INGREDIENTS
1 lb flour
1 tsp salt
1¼ baking powder
½ cup vegetable shortening
2½ cups iced water
tomato coloring
annatto coloring
¼ tsp allspice

PREPARATION
1. Mix and sift salt and flour and add baking powder.
2. Add water and colorings to flour mixture and make firm dough.
3. Shape each pieces into circles and allow to sit until filling is ready.

COOLIE TOWN CURRIED ACKEE
In Coolie Town, curry is used for just about anything, including the curried ackees.

INGREDIENTS
8 Ackee pods or ½ can of Ackees
¼ tsp salt
¼ tsp black pepper
4 tomatoes chopped
1 onion finely chopped
3 stalks escallion finely chopped
¾ cup coconut milk
2 tbsp margarine
¼ tsp Jamaican hot sauce
1 tbsp curry powder

PREPARATION
1. Boil ackees in salted water unless using canned ackees.
2. Sauté onions, tomatoes, escallion and curry powder in butter.
3. Add the coconut milk and bring to a mild boil then add the ackees.
4. On a low flame continue to cook until the ackees have absorbed the curry sauce.
5. Add black pepper and salt and let cook for another 5 minutes.
6. Serve hot.

ST. THOMAS COCONUT TOAST
St. Thomas has both crawfish and coconut trees in abundance.

INGREDIENTS
½ cup condensed milk
6 slices of hard dough bread (remove ends)
1 tsp salt
¼ tsp nutmeg
1 dry coconut with meat extracted

PREPARATION
1. Grater the coconut meat and ensure that the meat is edible and add salt and nutmeg.
2. Cut bread into strips place in the condensed milk and dip in grate coconut.
3. Remove and place on baking sheet and bake at 375 Degrees for 5-7 minutes

JAMAICAN BANANA FRITTERS
Banana fritters are a popular banana recipe.

INGREDIENTS
¼ tsp salt
¼ tsp baking powder
1 egg beaten
2¼ cup flour
1 tbsp margarine
1½ cups crushed ripe bananas

PREPARATION
1. Sift flour with baking powder and salt. Add the egg to the crushed bananas and to the flour mixture.
2. Mix until you have a medium batter and fry each tablespoon amount in at least ½ inch vegetable oil.
3. Serve hot.

BOSCOBEL CALLALOO FRITTERS
A Jamaican fritter recipe that is the rave for many vegetarians.

INGREDIENTS
¼ tsp salt
¼ tsp baking powder
1 egg beaten
2 tomatoes chopped
1 stalk escallion finely chopped
2¼ cup flour
1 tbsp margarine
1 lg chopped onion
2 cups callaloo chopped

PREPARATION
1. Sauté onions, tomatoes and escallion in margarine the add chopped callaloo and steam for 10 minutes.
2. Sift flour with baking powder and salt. Add the egg to the callaloo and to the flour mixture.
3. Mix until you have a medium batter and fry each tablespoon amount in at least ½ inch vegetable oil.
4. Serve hot.

PORTMORE CRAB BACKS
On any given Sunday you can see Portmore residents with bags catching large land crabs. This is a delicious Portmore recipe.

INGREDIENTS
¼ tsp salt
¼ tsp black pepper
3 slices of hard dough bread
2 tomatoes chopped
3 stalks escallion finely chopped
1 cup milk
2 tbsp margarine
1 lg chopped onion
½ cup bread crumbs
8 large crabs

PREPARATION
1. After boiling crabs extract crabmeat from claws and clean crab backs and reserve the shells.
2. Soak the bread slices in milk and add onion, escallions, tomatoes, black pepper, salt and crabmeat.
3. After mixing well place the crab mixture in the crab back shells.
4. Preheat the oven to approximately 375 Degrees then add crab backs for 20 minutes.
5. Serve hot.

Cooking Tip
Processed crab meat can be used in this recipe however, ensure that the meat is fresh and has not past it's best before date. Any meat in a tin that has passed the best before date **SHOULD NOT BE USED**. This spells trouble as especially red meats such as corned beef carry very dangerous bacteria that can cause very painful symptoms and in extreme cases death. Use up to par meat and foods when preparing your recipes.

JAMAICAN ONION AND CHICKEN FLAUTAS
A special treat for onion lovers

INGREDIENTS
3 medium onions chopped
2 cup de-boned chopped chicken cubes
¼ cup Jamaican Jerk Sauce
2 stalks Escallion chopped
¼ tsp cinnamon
¼ cup vegetable oil
½ cup creamed cheese
3 patty crust—sold in some stores

PREPARATION
1. Heat about ½ oil in small skillet until hot but not smoking.
2. Quickly fry chicken cubes in oil until done and drain on paper towels.
3. Combine cheese, chicken, Jamaican jerk sauce, onions, escallion and cinnamon; mix well.
4. Spoon 1 tbsp chicken mixture on each patty dough.
5. Roll tightly; secure with wooden pick and place seam-side down on baking sheet.
6. Bake in preheated oven at 400'F. about 18-20 minutes or until crisp.
7. Serve warm

JAMAICAN CHICKEN PUFFS
A children's favorite chicken recipe.

INGREDIENTS
4 tbsps butter
½ cup boiling water
½ cup flour
2 eggs
½ cup cheese grated
2 cups chicken cubes cooked
¼ cup onions diced
¼ cup garlic diced
¼ tbsp allspice (pimento)

PREPARATION
1. Melt butter in boiling water then add flour; stir vigorously.
2. Cook and stir until mixture forms a ball that doesn't separate and forms a dough.
3. Remove from heat and cool slightly. Preheat oven to 400 Degrees.
4. Add egg; beat vigorously until smooth. Stir in cheese.
5. Drop dough onto greased baking sheet, using 1 level tsp dough for each puff.
6. Bake for 20 minutes. Remove from oven; cool and split.
7. Finely chop cooked chicken, pimiento, garlic and onions.
8. Combine with remaining ingredients. Fill each puff with 2 tsps.
9. Serve warm

Cooking Tip
When making gravy for Jamaican chicken recipes ensure that the gravy is not too dark as chicken is white meat.

SPICY CHICKEN PATE
A spicy Jamaican appetizer

INGREDIENTS
1½ cup chicken breast, cooked, minced
¾ cup cheese, softened
1 medium chopped onion
1 tsp Jamaican Appleton V/X rum
1 tbsp mayonnaise
2 tbsp lemon juice
¼ tsp minced scotch bonnet pepper
¼ tsp nutmeg
¼ tsp paprika
2 stalks parsley

PREPARATION
1. Combine chicken, cheese, onion, rum, mayonnaise, lemon juice, pepper and nutmeg in an electric blender and puree until smooth.
2. Transfer mixture to a 2 cup mold coated with cooking spray.
3. Cover, and chill overnight. Sprinkle with paprika. Garnish with parsley sprigs.
4. Serve with Jamaican coconut toast or unsalted crackers.

SPECIAL CHICKEN SATAY
A favorite low fat Jamaican recipe, preferred by most women on a diet.

INGREDIENTS
7 chicken breast halves
¼ cup unsweetened pineapple juice
¼ cup low sodium soy sauce
2 tbsps brown sugar
½ tsp scotch bonnet pepper diced
2 garlic cloves crushed
2 tbsps wine vinegar
1 tbsp water
1 sweet pepper diced
vegetable cooking spray

REPARATION
1. Place chicken in a zip top plastic bag.
2. Combine pineapple juice and all dry ingredients and pour over chicken.
3. Seal bag and marinate in refrigerator for 1 hour.
4. Soak skewers in warm water for at least 5 minutes.
5. Combine soy sauce, vinegar, water and scotch bonnet pepper in blender and puree until smooth.
6. Drain chicken and discard marinade. Thread chicken onto skewers.
7. Cut sweet pepper square diagonally in half, forming triangles.
8. Place one triangle on the end of each skewer.
9. Place half of skewers on rack of broiler pan coated with cooking spray.
10. Broil 5 inches from heat 4 minutes on each side or until chicken is done.

PORTLAND CHICKEN SATAY
A great satay appetizer recipe using skewers.

INGREDIENTS
1 lb chicken breasts or thighs, de-boned and skinned

1 tsp ginger root, grated

1 clove garlic, minced

1 tsp curry powder

1 pinch salt

1 pinch black pepper

1 tsp vegetable oil

PREPARATION
1. Cut chicken into strips.
2. Combine marinade all ingredients. Add chicken and chill covered for 30 minutes or more.
3. Soak skewers in boiling water for at least 5 minutes.
4. Thread chicken onto skewers.
5. Grill chicken for at least 15 minutes or until golden brown.

Cooking Tip
Prepare curry by cooking or burning the curry in a frying pan then adding seasoning and then the meat.

WESTMORELAND CHICKEN WITH CURRY SAUCE
A favorite of the residents of coolie town in Westmoreland Jamaica. One of the bets Jamaican curry recipes.

INGREDIENTS
2 tbsp vegetable oil

4 chicken thighs, de-boned cut in ½ inch squares

2 garlic cloves diced

1 tbsp curry paste

1 cup coconut cream

1 tbsp jerk sauce

2 tsp brown sugar

½ cup basil leaves

1 tbsp thyme leaves

PREPARATION
1. Pre-heat frying pan over medium high heat then add oil.
2. When oil is hot add chicken and stir-fry until lightly browned.
3. Remove to a bowl; set aside. Add garlic to frying pan and lightly brown.
4. Reduce heat and add curry paste then fry gently.
5. Stirring for 1 minute add coconut cream stirring constantly until smooth.
6. Add jerk sauce, basil and thyme leaves and the chicken.
7. Simmer together for 5-10 minutes or until chicken is done.
8. Add the basil leaves; stir together for 2-3 minutes.
9. Serve hot

OCHO RIOS CHICKEN FINGERS
A sweet Jamaican chicken fingers recipe served up on the North Coast

INGREDIENTS
1 lb chicken tenders
¼ cup Jerk Sauce
½ cup milk
1 cup cornmeal
½ cup Jerk-BQ Sauce

PREPARATION
1. Remove silver skin from chicken tenders and place in a deep bowl.
2. Add Jerk sauce and milk to cover.
3. Let marinate for 1 hour and shake excess liquid off chicken and dredge in corn flour.
4. Fry in oil until golden brown and crispy.
5. Serve with Jamaican Jerk-BQ Sauce.

JAMAICAN COOLIE CURRIED CHICKEN TRIANGLES
A favorite Jamaican recipe for the Indian population in Jamaica

INGREDIENTS
½ cup diced chicken Breast
½ cup chopped onions
2 tbsp flour
½ tsp salt
1½ tsp curry powder
½ cup evaporated milk
¼ cup chopped escallion
½ cup melted butter
Prepare dough
1 cup Mango chutney

PREPARATION
1. In a medium skillet, cook chicken in butter until no longer pink.
2. Stir in flour, salt and curry powder and cook for 1 minute.
3. Gradually add milk stirring until mixture comes to a boil and thickens.
4. Remove from heat. Stir in onions and escallions.
5. Place dough on a flat surface and brush lightly with melted butter.
6. Use a rolling pin flatten the dough and cut into squares.
7. Spoon 1 tablespoon of filling onto short end of each strip.
8. Fold one corner of strip diagonally over filling so short edge meets the long edge, forming a right triangle.
9. Repeat process with remaining strips. Brush top of each triangle with butter.
10. Place on baking sheet. Bake in preheated 375 degree oven for 10-12 minutes, until golden brown.
11. Serve with mango chutney

JAMAICAN COCONUT CHICKEN
A perfect blend of coconut and Jamaican chicken

INGREDIENTS
2 cups sweetened coconut flakes
¼ cup flour
2 eggs
1 lb boned and skinned chicken breast halves
½ cup vegetable oil
3 tbsp honey
3 tbsp orange marmalade
1 tbsp soy sauce

PREPARATION
1. Place coconut in medium sized bowl, place flour in a second bowl and lightly beat eggs in a third bowl.
2. Dip chicken pieces in flour, then egg, and then roll in coconut flakes.
3. Place on a baking sheet. Pour enough oil into skillet to reach a depth of ½ inch.
4. Heat over medium heat. When hot add chicken with slotted spoon, 6 pieces at a time.
5. Cook 4-6 minutes until cooked through and light golden, turning once.
6. Adjust heat as needed to prevent over browning. Drain on paper towel.
7. To prepare sauce, combine all ingredients in small bowl.

Cooking Tip
Coconuts must be fresh to capture the true taste of this recipe. Add a few sliced tomatoes to heighten the taste.

HOT AND CRISPY GOLDEN JAMNUGGETS
A simple Jamaican chicken nuggets recipe which will leave you feeling hot!

INGREDIENTS
½ cup dry bread crumbs
¼ cup grated cheese
2 tsps Jamaican red fire dry seasoning
1 tsp salt
6 boneless skinless chicken breast cut in 1 inch squares
½ cup melted butter

PREPARATION
1. Combine all dry ingredients.
2. Dip chicken in butter; roll in crumb mixture.
3. Place in a single layer on an un-greased baking pan.
4. Bake at 400 degrees for 12-15 minutes or until juices run clear.

jamaican callaloo steamed
with raw vegetables and
fried plantains. ©

jamaican crab cakes ©

SPICY GRILLED CHICKEN ROLL-UPS IN ROTI
A spicy hot recipe just for those who love hot peppers

INGREDIENTS
1 lb boneless skinless chicken breasts
1 pinch salt
1 pinch black pepper
2 tsp vegetable oil
2 tsp lime juice
1 garlic clove, minced
¼ cup Wincarnis wine
8 cooked roti
¼ cup chopped escallions
½ cup sour cream

PREPARATION
1. Cut chicken breasts in half lengthwise.
2. Salt and pepper chicken, then combine oil, lime juice and garlic; marinate chicken for 30 minutes.
3. Remove from marinade. Grill or barbecue chicken** 10 to 12 minutes, turning once, until chicken is just cooked or sauté in nonstick skillet 10 to 12 minutes.
4. To make each roll-up, spread 1 tbsp cheese on lower third of Roti.
5. Lay 1 chicken strip across; sprinkle with a little escallion.
6. Fold in sides of roti; roll up tightly.
7. Wrap in foil and when serving, warm on grill. or barbecue for 8 to 10 minutes.

JAMAICAN CHICKEN BALLS
A great appetizer recipe served without fear of too much grease.

INGREDIENTS
½ lb cream cheese
2 tbsp mayonnaise
1 cup chopped cooked chicken cubes
1 tbsp mango chutney
½ tsp salt
1 tbsp curry powder
½ cup grated coconut

PREPARATION
1. Beat together cream cheese and mayonnaise.
2. Add chicken, chutney, salt and curry powder.
3. Shape into walnut sized balls and roll in coconut.
4. Serve with a glass of wine.

**—This recipe works best if you barbeque the chicken. We tried both techniques and the recipes tended to be more dry when grilled. The meat should have some texture to it when tasting and eating.

ST. ANN CHICKEN CAKES
In the parish of St. Ann these are the best chicken cakes in the country

INGREDIENTS
2 lb Chicken legs
1 cup cracker crumbs
¼ cup mayonnaise
¼ cup chopped escallions
2 tbsp lemon juice
½ tsp salt
1 tbsp Vegetable oil
½ tbsp allspice (pimento)
½ tbsp dried thyme leaves

PREPARATION
1. Poach chicken. When chicken is cool enough to handle, remove skin then pull meat off bones, and tear into fine shreds.
2. Mix together chicken, ½ cup of cracker crumbs, mayonnaise, escallions, allspice lemon juice, and salt.
3. Form into 8 patties ½ inch thick and coat with remaining crumbs.
4. Heat half the oil in a non-stick frying pan over medium-high heat.
5. Cook cakes 2-4 minutes per side, adding remainder of oil if necessary.

JAMAICAN SPICY CHICKEN WONTONS
A Chinese favorite with an added Jamaican twist

INGREDIENTS
1 lb ground raw chicken or pork
½ cup shredded carrot
¼ cup finely chopped celery
1 tbsp soy sauce
1 tbsp Jamaican Appleton V/X rum
2 tsp cornstarch
2 tsp grated ginger
½ pack wonton wrappers
2 tbsp melted butter
¼ cup June plum sauce

PREPARATION
1. In a medium skillet cook and stir ground chicken or pork till no pink remains; drain.
2. Stir in carrot, soy sauce, sherry, cornstarch, and gingerroot; mix well.
3. Spoon 1 rounded tsp of the filling atop a wonton wrapper.
4. Lightly brush edges with water. To shape each wonton, carefully bring 2 opposite corners of the square wonton wrapper up over the filling and pinch together in the center.
5. Carefully bring the 2 remaining opposite corners to the center and pinch together.
6. Pinch together edges to seal. Place wontons on a greased baking sheet.
7. Repeat with remaining filling and wonton wrappers. Brush wontons with melted margarine or butter.
8. Bake in a 375 degree oven for 8 to 10 minutes or till light brown and crisp.
9. Serve with plum sauce.

Cooking Tip
Never use too much Jamaican rum inside any one recipe. Rum is meant to enhance the flavor of the recipe not dominate the taste.

JAMAICAN JERK AND SPICY CHICKEN KEBABS
Kebabs are a favorite especially in the Middle East, we have added a new Jamaican jerk twist to the recipe.

INGREDIENTS
3 chicken breasts skinned and boned
1 tsp salt
½ tbsp allspice (pimento)
1 small lemon juiced
6 tbsps plain yogurt
½ stalk ginger peeled and grated
3 cloves garlic crushed
2 stalks escallion chopped finely
2 large sweet peppers
½ cup unsalted melted butter
1 sliced cucumber for garnish

PREPARATION
1. Cut each breast in half lengthwise and then cut each half crosswise into three or four equal pieces.
2. Lay the pieces in a single layer on a platter.
3. Sprinkle the salt and the juice from the lemon over them and rub into the chicken. Set aside for 20 minutes.
4. Put the yogurt in a small bowl. Beat it with a fork or whisk until it is smooth and creamy.
5. Add the ½ ginger, ½ garlic and 1 escallion stalk. Stir into mix.
6. Make a paste out of the left ginger, garlic and escallion and ¼ cup of water in a food processor.
7. Add the paste to the yogurt mixture.
8. After the chicken has sat around for 20 minutes, hold a sieve over the chicken pieces and pour the yogurt mixture into the sieve and push through as much as you can with a rubber spatula.
9. Mix well with the chicken pieces and refrigerate for 6-24 hours, in an airtight container.
10. Preheat over to maximum temperature .
11. Thread the chicken pieces on skewers.
12. Brush the chicken with half the melted butter and put in the over for about 7 minutes.
13. Take out the baking tray and skewers. Turn the chicken pieces over and brush with the rest of the butter.
14. Bake for another 8-10 minutes. Serve with thick slices of cucumbers.

MONTEGO BAY HOT CHICKEN STRIPS
A hot and spicy version of a old favorite chicken strips recipe

INGREDIENTS
1 cup mayonnaise
¼ cup onion minced
1 cup crackers crushed
½ tbsp minced scotch bonnet pepper
2 lbs chicken breast
Jamaican jerk sauce

PREPARATION
1. Combine mayonnaise and onion.
2. In another bowl, combine the crackers and scotch bonnet peppers.
3. Dip strips into mayonnaise mixture, then into the pepper mixture.
4. Place in a single layer on a large greased baking sheet.
5. Bake at 425~ for 15 to 18 minutes or until juices run clear.
6. Combine sauce ingredients and serve with strips.

JAMAICAN SOUTH COAST CHICKEN TRIANGLES
This is a favorite appetizer recipe on Jamaica's south coast

INGREDIENTS
2 skinless boneless chicken breast cooked, shredded and chopped
½ cup grated cheese
1 sweet pepper finely chopped
6 tomatoes peeled, seeded and chopped
2 stalks escallion chopped
½ tsp allspice
½ tsp cinnamon
½ lb dough
½ cup melted butter
2 tbsps vegetable oil
1 tin whole kernel sweet corn
2 onions finely chopped
1 pinch salt
1 pinch black pepper

PREPARATION
1. Cut dough crosswise into 5 equal sections.
2. Then cut the dough into 4 sections to make triangles.
3. In a medium bowl place the chicken, cheese, sweet peppers, tomatoes, escallion, allspice and cinnamon.
4. Mix the ingredients together well.
5. Preheat the oven to 400 °for each section of the dough, separate the pieces and lay them out flat on a large surface.
6. Brush all the pieces with the melted butter. Turn them over and brush the other side.
7. Place a teaspoon of the chicken mixture at one end of each piece of dough.
8. Fold the bottom left corner over the filling so that the bottom edge lines up with the side edge.
9. On an oiled baking sheet, place the triangles and bake them for 20 minutes, or until they are a golden brown.
10. Serve the triangles with the corn on the side.

KINGSTON SWEET-N-SOUR MEATBALLS
A sweet tasting recipe heightened with the use of our favorite Get Jamaica Sauce.

INGREDIENTS
1 lb lean ground beef
½ tsp salt
1 cup soft bread crumbs
1 pinch black pepper
1 egg beaten
1 tbsp cooking oil
¼ cup onion minced
½ cup Get Jamaica Sauce®
2 tbsps milk
1 clove garlic minced

PREPARATION
1. Combine first 8 ingredients form into 40 bite size meatballs.
2. Brown lightly in oil. Cover; cook over low for 5 minutes. Drain.
3. Take get Jamaica sauce and pour over meatballs.
4. Heat, stirring occasionally and allow to simmer 10 to 12 minutes until sauce is thickened, basting occasionally.
5. Serve with the Jamaican side dish of your choice.

JERK-BQ CHICKEN APPETIZERS
A landmark recipe using both the renowned jerk and barbeque recipes

INGREDIENTS
3 lb Chicken wing drums
¼ cup coarsely chopped garlic*
2 stalks escallion chopped finely*
½ tsp allspice (pimento)*
¼ cup onion minced*
1 tsp curry powder*
¼ tsp chopped scotch bonnet pepper*
1 tbsp brown sugar
¼ tsp salt
3 tbsp Jamaican jerk sauce
½ cup coconut milk
2 garlic cloves minced
2 stalks escallion minced
½ cup vinegar
½ cup ketchup
½ tbsp brown sugar
3 stalks lettuce
2 twigs parsley

PREPARATION
1. Preparing the marinade ingredients* in a blender until smooth.
2. Marinate chicken and refrigerate overnight.
3. Grill over hot coals until done, brushing frequently with coconut milk.
4. Serve garnished lettuce and parsley

DIPPING SAUCE:
Use other dry ingredients combine with ketchup, vinegar and other dry ingredients and place in blender. Remove and then bring the mixture to a boil and then serve with drums.

> **Cooking Tip**
> It is actually the jerk seasonings that deliver the great Jamaican jerk taste. Ensure you use fresh seasonings every time you cook meals.

JAMAICAN CORNED BEEF CHEESE BALL
An easy to make appetizer recipe with corned beef and cheese

INGREDIENTS
½ cup cream cheese
1 small tin corned beef
1 small onion diced
2 tbsp melted butter

PREPARATION
1. Sauté corned beef and onions in 2 tablespoons butter.
2. Combine beef with creamed cheese.
3. Roll into ball, then roll in remaining chipped beef.

JAMAICAN JERK TURKEY TENDERS
A favorite of the American chef as a great appetizer recipe

INGREDIENTS
1¼ lb fresh turkey tenderloin
1¼ cup soft bread crumbs
¼ tsp salt
½ tsp black pepper
½ tsp minced scotch bonnet pepper
¼ cup egg whites
2 tbsp low fat evaporated milk
1 tsp paprika
½ cup vegetable oil

PREPARATION
1. Cut turkey tenderloins or chicken breasts into 6 slices by cutting across the turkey carefully with sharp knife.
2. Pound tenders to ¼ inch thickness. Slit around edges to keep from curling.
3. Blend ½ cup of the oat bran cereal with salt and pepper and coat tenders.
4. Whip egg whites lightly with milk. Blend remaining ¾ cup oat bran with paprika.
5. Dip meat into egg whites, then into oat bran paprika mixture.
6. Place on baking rack and allow 5 minutes to dry.
7. Heat vegetable oil in large frying pan until hot.
8. Brown tenders 2-3 pieces at a time for 3 minutes per side, or until crusty and brown.
9. Drain well and serve with a low-fat dip.

JAMAICAN HERBED CHICKEN PATE
This is a perfect blend of Jamaican herbs used to marinate chicken.

INGREDIENTS
2 lb skinned/boned breast chicken
½ cup escallion chopped
¼ cup onion minced
¾ cup unsalted butter
3 cups eggs whites only
1½ tsp salt
¼ tsp black pepper
¼ tsp grated nutmeg

PREPARATION
1. Cut chicken into ½ inch pieces. Puree with salt and pepper in processor in 2 batches to very smooth paste.
2. Refrigerate until well chilled, at least 1 hour.
3. Melt butter in heavy small skillet over low heat. Add escallions and onions and brown.
4. Combine half of chicken with half of escallion and onion mixture in processor.
5. Puree until smooth. Add egg whites and process until smooth.
6. Transfer to bowl. Sprinkle with grated nutmeg.
7. Repeat with remaining chicken and refrigerate until well chilled.

JAMAICAN CRAB FRITTERS
A favorite appetizer especially with Jamaican fish meals.

INGREDIENTS
1¾ cups all-purpose flour
1½ cups warm water
2 tbsps vegetable oil
2 tsps baking powder
½ cup escallion chopped
¼ cup onions chopped
¼ tsp scotch bonnet pepper diced
¼ tsp salt
1 lb crabmeat
¾ cup white breadcrumbs
4 large egg whites
3 tbsps chopped fresh parsley
½ cup vegetable oil

PREPARATION
1. Mix the first eight (8) ingredients in a medium bowl to blend.
2. Let the batter stand for 1 hour at room temperature.
3. Mix the crabmeat, bread crumbs, two of the egg whites and the parsley in a large bowl.
4. Season with salt and pepper. Divide the mixture into mounds and press each mound firmly into a ball.
5. Roll each crabmeat ball in flour shake off excess.
6. Immediately before frying, beat the remaining egg whites in a small bowl to stiff peaks.
7. Fold the egg whites into the batter.
8. Heat the oil in a deep fryer or heavy saucepan to 360F. Dip the crab balls, one at a time, into the batter, coating completely.
9. Carefully lower into the oil. Repeat with the remaining crab balls, cooking until pale and golden brown.
10. Use a slotted spoon to transfer the fritters to paper towels and drain. Do not overcrowd the fryer or saucepan when making these crab fritters.

JAMAICAN CHICKEN PINWHEELS
A great Jamaican appetizer recipes

INGREDIENTS
1 tsp basil leaves
½ tsp seasoned salt
¼ tsp seasoned pepper
¼ tsp garlic powder
4 chicken breast halves, skinned, boned
4 slices ham
2 tbsp lemon juice
¼ tsp paprika
3 stalks lettuce
2 tomatoes, peeled and cooked

PREPARATION
1. Combine basil, seasoned salt and pepper, garlic powder and set aside.
2. Place chicken between sheets of plastic wrap, pound to ¼ inch thickness.
3. Lightly sprinkle seasonings over each chicken breast, top with slice of ham.
4. Roll up, beginning with longest side.
5. Place rolls seam side down in baking dish. Drizzle with lemon juice, sprinkle with paprika.
6. Bake in preheated 350F oven 20-25 minutes. Chill.
7. Slice into ¼ inch rounds, arrange on lettuce leaf line platter, garnish with cherry tomatoes.

JAMAICAN CREAMY CHICKEN ROLL-UPS
A creamy blended Jamaican recipe

INGREDIENTS
3 oz creamed cheese
4 stalks chopped escallions
½ cup minced onion
1 cup grated cheese
½ cup sour cream
4 thighs cooked and de-boned
½ cup melted butter
3 crescent rolls

PREPARATION
1. Mix everything together in food processor until well mixed and pasty.
2. Take crescent roots, separate & roll out thin.
3. Place 2 tablespoons in center of each roll and roll up.
4. Brush with melted butter.
5. Bake at 350 for 25 min. May use as appetizer or have several for "finger-food" dinner.

JAMAICAN CHICKEN FINGERS IN JUNE PLUM SAUCE
A sweet chicken appetizer recipe using June plum sauce

INGREDIENTS
3 lb chicken breasts, skinless and boneless
1½ cup milk
2 tbsp lemon juice
2tsp Worcestershire sauce
1 tsp soy sauce
1 tsp paprika
1 tsp black pepper
1garlic clove minced
4 cups seasoned bread crumbs
¼ cup minced escallion
4 tbsp melted butter
1 cup June plum preserves

PREPARATION
1. If the breasts are whole, split them. Cut each chicken breast half crosswise into ½ inch strips.
2. In a large bowl, combine buttermilk, 1 tsp of the lemon juice, Worcestershire, soy sauce, paprika, pepper, and garlic.
3. Add chicken strips and toss to coat. Cover and marinate at room temperature for 1 hour, or refrigerate overnight.
4. Preheat oven to 350F. Drain chicken well. In a large shallow bowl, toss bread crumbs with escallions to mix.
5. Roll chicken in crumbs to coat. Arrange in a single layer on a greased baking sheet. Drizzle melted butter over chicken fingers.
6. Bake for 35 minutes.
7. Meanwhile, in a non aluminum saucepan, combine June plum preserves and remaining 1 teaspoon of lemon juice. Melt over low heat, stirring, until smooth.
8. Serve chicken fingers hot or warm, with plum sauce for dipping, on the side.

JAMAICAN APPETIZER CHEESE BALL
A great cheese ball recipe that is a great starter for any main course meal

INGREDIENTS
½ cup creamed cheese
½ cup blue cheese, crumbled
½ cup cheddar cheese, shredded
¼ tsp garlic powder
¼ tsp salt
½ cup peanuts chopped
¾ cup parsley chopped

PREPARATION
1. Place the cream cheese, blue cheese, cheddar cheese, garlic powder, and salt in a mixer bowl and beat at low speed just until well mixed.
2. Stir in the pecans and currants. Taste and adjust seasoning.
3. Refrigerate the cheese mixture for 30 minutes or until slightly firm, then shape into a ball.
4. Roll in the chopped parsley to coat well.
5. Cover with plastic wrap and refrigerate until ready to serve.
6. Let stand at room temperature for about 30 minutes before serving.
7. Place on a platter surrounded with crackers and apple wedges.

Cooking Tip
Try not to overuse garlic powder in recipes, it is not the most favorite ingredient and can over power the taste of other ingredients.

JAMAICAN BACON CHEESE BALL
A Jamaican treat for bacon lovers

INGREDIENTS
1 lb bacon
¼ tsp allspice
¾ cup cream cheese softened
½ cup cheddar cheese shredded
¼ tsp onion powder
¼ tsp garlic powder
1 tsp Worcestershire sauce
chopped peanuts

PREPARATION
1. Cook bacon; drain and crumble.
2. Combine with rest of ingredients (except nuts) and form into ball.
3. Roll in nuts.
4. Serve with crackers

JAMAICAN CHEESE STRAW RECIPE
A Jamaican cheese straw recipe to die for.

INGREDIENTS
1 cup flour
½ tsp salt
½ tsp ginger powdered
¼ cup melted butter
¼ cup shredded cheese
¼ tsp onion powder
¼ tsp allspice
¼ cup minced escallions
2½ tbsps cold water

PREPARATION
1. Place flour, ginger, onion powder, allspice and salt in food processor.
2. Cut butter into small cubes and add to processor, blend until pastry resembles coarse meal.
3. Add shredded cheese and escallion and process until just blended.
4. Sprinkle water over flour mixture, and process until dough is moistened holds together when pinched with fingers.
5. Gather dough into a ball on lightly floured board, and roll out to ¼ thick.
6. Cut into strips 3 long and 1½ wide.
7. Freeze unbaked on baking sheets. Do not thaw before baking.
8. Bake on un greased sheet at 400-degrees until lightly browned and crisp.

JAMAICAN MINI CHEESECAKES
These are mini muffin cakes that have a distinct Jamaican flavor

INGREDIENTS
3 cups cheddar cheese
2 cups cottage cheese
½ cup mayonnaise
¼ lb Canadian bacon
1 tsp chives
¼ tsp salt
¼ tsp white pepper
2 tsp unsalted butter
pimiento strips
4 stalks escallions chopped
4 bags savory crackers

PREPARATION
1. Combine cheddar, cottage cheese, mayonnaise, Canadian bacon, chives, salt, pepper, and butter in a food processor.
2. Process until smooth and well blended pour into an un greased mini-muffin pan cover and chill for 48 hours.
3. Unfold onto a serving platter or individual serving plates garnish as desired serve slightly chilled or at room temperature, with assorted savory crackers to the side.

JAMAICAN HAM AND CHEESE BALL
A perfect blend of Jamaican ham and cheese

INGREDIENTS
1 cup ground ham
1 tsp Worcestershire sauce
½ cup cream cheese
½ tsp lemon juice
¼ cup shredded cheddar
¼ tsp Onion powder
1 tsp Tabasco sauce

PREPARATION
Mix all ingredients, chill and serve.

JAMAICAN SHRIMP-CHEESE ROLL
A favorite in the parish of St. Elizabeth Jamaica, otherwise known as shrimp country

INGREDIENTS
1½ cup shredded cheese
¼ tsp black pepper
1 cup cooked shrimp
1 pack crescent rolls
¼ cup minced onions
¼ of a clove of garlic
¼ cup escallions
¼ tsp scotch bonnet pepper diced
1 tbsp melted butter
2 eggs
1 egg yolk
½ tsp salt

PREPARATION
1. In large bowl, stir together cheese, shrimp, onion, escallion, garlic, scotch bonnet pepper, salt, pepper, and eggs and set aside.
2. Unroll crescent roll dough onto lightly floured surface. Pinch together perforations on both sides of dough.
3. Fold in half crosswise and with a lightly floured rolling pin, roll out to 14x9 inch rectangle.
4. Brush with butter and spread cheese-shrimp mixture in a 2 inch strip along 1 long edge of dough.
5. Roll up as a jelly roll. Firmly pinch seam and ends together, then moisten slightly with water and smooth lightly.
6. Lift roll onto un greased cookie sheet. Brush with egg-yolk mixture.
7. Bake in preheated oven 400F for 25 minutes or until golden brown.
8. Cool on rack 20 minutes. With sharp knife, cut in ½ inch slices.

Cooking Tip
Pre-heating the oven is very important, often ignored by many cooks, it allows the food not to cool but to baked as a constant temperature.

HELLSHIRE APPETIZER CRAB BALLS
A Hellshire beach favorite of how to prepare crab meat

INGREDIENTS
½ lb crab meat
1½ cup bread crumbs, soft
1 egg
2 tbsp Jamaican seafood sauce
2 tbsp mayonnaise
2 tbsp escallion, minced
½ tsp scotch bonnet pepper diced
¼ cup onion chopped
1 tbsp fresh parsley, chopped
1 pinch black pepper
1 cup potato chips, crushed

PREPARATION
1. In large bowl, combine crab meat, bread crumbs, beaten egg, Jamaican seafood sauce, mayonnaise, escallions, onion, scotch bonnet pepper, parsley and black pepper.
2. Cover and chill at least 1 hour. Form mixture into balls using a rounded tsp for each.
3. Roll in crushed chips place on baking sheet.
4. Bake in 425 degree oven for 10 to 12 minutes until hot and golden brown.
5. Serve immediately with additional Jamaican seafood sauce for dipping.

BACON-WRAPPED SHRIMP WITH CREAMED CHEESE
A great triple combo appetizer Jamaican recipe.

INGREDIENTS
24 large shrimp peeled and de-veined
12 bacon slices cut crosswise
6 tbsp unsalted butter
¼ cup creamed cheese
¼ cup escallions minced
¼ cup onions minced
½ cup mayonnaise
½ cup sour cream
1 tbsp fresh lemon juice
Jamaican seafood sauce
1 pinch black pepper

PREPARATION
1. Wrap 1 bacon strip around 1 shrimp and secure with a toothpick.
2. Repeat with remaining shrimp, water chestnuts and bacon.
3. Melt 3 tablespoons butter in heavy large skillet over high heat.
4. Add half of shrimp and cook until bacon browns and 2½ minutes per side.
5. Transfer to large gratin dish. Repeat with remaining butter and shrimp.
6. Preheat broiler. Beat cream cheese in medium bowl until smooth.
7. Add remaining ingredients and beat until blended.
8. Season with salt. Spoon Jamaican seafood sauce over shrimp.
9. Broil until top is golden brown.

Cooking Tip
Shrimp normally does not have a flavor, a Jamaican fish sauce is used to enhance the taste of the shrimp or lack thereof.

JAMAICAN COCONUT BEER BATTER SHRIMP
A great blend recipe between Red Stripe Beer, coconut and shrimp.

INGREDIENTS
1 tbsp scotch bonnet pepper diced
¼ tsp salt
1 tsp paprika
½ tsp black pepper
¼ tsp garlic powder
¼ tsp onion powder
¼ tsp dried thyme
2 eggs
¾ cup flour
½ cup Red Stripe Beer
½ tbsp baking powder
1½lbs medium shrimp, peeled and de-veined.
vegetable oil for frying
3 cups grated coconut

PREPARATION
1. Thoroughly combine the ingredients for the seasoning mix in a small bowl and set aside.
2. Mix ½ cup of the flour, paprika, black pepper, garlic powder, onion powder, dried thyme, baking powder, eggs, and beer together in a bowl, breaking up all lumps until it is smooth.
3. Combine the remaining flour with 1½ tsps. of the seasoning mix and set aside.
4. Place the coconut in a separate bowl.
5. Sprinkle both sides of the shrimps with the remaining seasoning mix.
6. Then hold shrimp by the tail, dredge in the flour mixture, shake off excess, dip each in batter and allow excess to drip off.
7. Coat each shrimp with the coconut and place shrimp on a baking sheet.
8. Heat deep fryer to 350. Drop each shrimp into the hot oil and cook until golden brown about ½ to 1 minute on each side. Do not crowd the fryer.
9. Drain on paper towels and serve immediately.

JAMAICAN CRAB AND PEAR COCKTAIL
The Jamaican avocado pear is a popular choice and even more so in this crab recipe

INGREDIENTS
1 cup cooked crab meat
2 avocado pears peeled & chopped
½ tsp scotch bonnet pepper minced
¼ cup tomato chopped
¼ cup lime juice
2 tbsps vegetable Oil
2 tbsps onion chopped
2 tbsps chopped escallion
1 clove garlic chopped
¾ tsp salt
1 pinch black pepper
1½ cups lettuce finely chopped
3 lemon wedges

PREPARATION
1. Mix all ingredients except lettuce and lime wedges.
2. Place ¼ cup of lettuce on edge of 6 serving dishes.
3. Divide the crabmeat mixture among the dishes and garnish with lime wedges.

JAMAICAN CRAB CLAW FINGERS
Crab fingers are enjoyed as a starter recipe

INGREDIENTS
2 lbs jumbo crab claws
3 eggs
1 pint milk
1½ cups corn flour
1 cup flour
1 tsp black pepper
2 tsps salt
1 tbsp onion powder
1½ tbsps garlic powder
3 tbsps paprika
¼ cup chopped parsley
¼ cup escallions chopped fine

PREPARATION
1. Remove crabmeat from claws.
2. Make egg wash with eggs and milk.
3. Mix remaining ingredients except crab meat.
4. Add crab meat and allow to dry to make a dough.
5. Let rest for 30 minutes then remove small amount to form fingers.
6. Fry fingers to brown in hot oil.
7. Serve with a Jamaican seafood sauce.

MONTEGO BAY FRIED CRABS
Montegonians are not avid crab lovers but this recipe is to die for.

INGREDIENTS
½ cup onion chopped
2 tbsps margarine
½ cup creamed cheese
4 tomatoes drained and cut up
4 lettuce leaves shredded
¼ cup escallions chopped
1½ lb crabmeat
¼ cup sour cream
1 pack savory crackers

PREPARATION
1. In saucepan, sauté onions in margarine.
2. Add creamed cheese and tomatoes, stir until both are well mixed.
3. Place crackers on serving platter, cover with lettuce, cheese spread mixture and crabmeat.
4. Top with sour cream.

JAMAICAN CRAB WON TONS WITH PORT ROYAL SEAFOOD SAUCE

This is a favorite from a chef in the little town of Port Royal.

INGREDIENTS
SAUCE
¼ cup Pickappepa sauce
1 tbsp cornstarch
½ tsp salt
½ tsp scotch bonnet pepper
½ tsp ginger grated
1 tsp lime juice
2 garlic cloves, minced
1½ tbsp honey
½ cup escallion chopped
1 tbsp melted butter
4 tbsp onion, chopped finely
½ cup creamed cheese
2 tbsp lemon juice
2 tbsp breadcrumbs, dry
½ lb crabmeat, flaked, cooked
24 won Ton wrappers
1 cup vegetable oil

PREPARATION
1. Mix all pickapeppa sauce, cornstarch, salt, scotch bonnet pepper, ginger, lime juice, garlic and honey in a saucepan.
2. Bring to a boil over medium high heat. Lower heat and cook until clear and thickened.
3. Put melted butter in sauté pan. Sauté onions until transparent.
4. Cut cream cheese into small chunks. Reduce heat to low, and add cream cheese until it softens then add lemon juice to blend.
5. Remove pan from heat and stir in breadcrumbs, cooked crab and escallion.
6. Place 1-2 teaspoon filling in each won ton wrapper and seal according to package directions.
7. Place single layer of wontons in hot oil and fry 2-3 minutes until golden brown.
8. Drain on paper bags or paper towels, and serve immediately Port Royal Seafood Sauce

ROCKY POINT CRAB BALLS

Another sweet recipe from the fishermen of Rocky Point.

INGREDIENTS
1 lb crabmeat
3 tbsps self-rising flour
1 each egg
¼ tsp scotch bonnet pepper diced
1 tbsp minced onion
1 tbsp mayonnaise
1 tbsp Jamaican fish seasoning

PREPARATION
1. Put crabmeat in bowl, removing shell pieces.
2. Add all ingredients and mix gently until blended.
3. Form into balls and deep fry until golden.

JAMAICAN CRAB HORS D'OEUVRES
These are great party hors d'oeuvres to kick off a party

INGREDIENTS
1 lb crabmeat cooked
8 oz Cream cheese, softened
1 pinch salt and black pepper
¼ cup onion minced
¼ cup escallion minced
¼ tsp scotch bonnet pepper minced
3 sprigs of parsley

PREPARATION
1. Gently mix crab with cream cheese, being careful not to break the pieces.
2. Add in seasonings to the mixture.
3. Shape into a balls, sprinkle with parsley, chill, and serve with crackers.

JAMAICAN CRAB TARTS
A tasty recipe loved by party goers as an appetite builder.

INGREDIENTS
3 cups cookie dough
3 lg eggs, beaten
1½ cup milk
¾ cup cheese, grated
2 tbsp cream cheese
1 tbsp onion, minced
¼ cup parsley, chopped
½ cup carrots, shredded
1 lb regular crabmeat cooked
½ tsp nutmeg grated
¼ tsp black pepper
1 pinch salt
pastry for 2 crust pie

PREPARATION
1. Roll out cookie dough thinly and cut into 2 diameter circles with a cookie cutter.
2. Lightly press dough circles into oiled tart shells. Prick dough with fork.
3. Bake for 5-7 minutes at 450 degrees. Remove from oven. Set aside.
4. Mix together remaining ingredients to make filling and spoon into tart shells, filling ½ inch over top of shells.
5. Bake for 25 minutes at 375 degrees or until a toothpick inserted comes out clean.

JAMAICAN CROCKED SHRIMP
A healthy and hearty shrimp recipe served with saltine crackers.

INGREDIENTS
2 cups water
1 cup dry white wine
2 lemons sliced
3 cloves garlic, chopped
1 tbsp black pepper
2 cups raw shrimp unpeeled
1 cup cream cheese softened
¼ cup unsalted melted butter
1 tbsp fresh lemon juice or to taste
2 small escallions minced
salt and black pepper to taste
water crackers for serving
cucumbers thinly sliced, for serving

PREPARATION
1. Combine water, white wine, lemon juice, garlic and black pepper in saucepan and bring to boil over high heat.
2. Bring the liquid to a boil; then cover it partway and let it boil for 10 minutes.
3. Reduce heat to medium-low, stir in the shrimp still in their shells and simmer for 3 minutes.
4. Let the shrimp cool in the liquid and then chill them, covered, overnight.
5. Drain and peel the shrimp. In a food processor, combine the cream cheese, escallions, butter and lemon juice and process until smooth.
6. Drop in the shrimp and use on-off pulses to chop it finely. Leaving a bit of shrimp texture is fine.
7. Transfer the mixture to large bowl, stir in the scallions and season with the salt and pepper.
8. Cover the bowl tightly with plastic wrap and chill it overnight.
9. Let the shrimp sit for 1 hour at room temperature before serving it with water crackers and thin-sliced cucumbers.

DUNNS RIVER FALLS CRAB MELT RECIPE
A recipe that was taken from several chefs out at the Dunn's River Beach

INGREDIENTS
2 cups crabmeat
¼ cup cheese
¼ cup mayonnaise
¼ tsp black pepper
12 melba toast rounds
½ cup escallion chopped
¼ cup onion chopped

PREPARATION
1. In small bowl, with fork, mix crabmeat, cheese, mayonnaise, escallion, onion, and black pepper.
2. Spread 1 heaping tsp crabmeat mixture on each Melba toast round.
3. Place on cookie sheets; sprinkle with ½ tsp coarsely ground black pepper.
4. If not serving right away, cover and refrigerate.
5. Broil canapés about 3 minutes or until cheese melts.
6. Top each canapé with a sprigs of parsley.

JAMAICAN VEGETABLE AND SHRIMP COCKTAIL
A strong Jamaican appetizer recipe

INGREDIENTS
1 cup water
¼ cup lime juice
1 clove garlic finely chopped
2 tsp salt
½ tsp black pepper
24 raw shrimp
1 avocado pear peeled And chopped
½ tsp scotch bonnet pepper diced
¼ cup tomato chopped
2 tbsps onion chopped
2 tbsps carrot finely chopped
2 tbsps escallion finely chopped
2 tbsps vegetable Oil
1½ cups lettuce finely shredded
lemon wedges

PREPARATION
1. Heat water, lime juice, garlic, salt and pepper to boiling in a 4-quart Dutch oven; reduce heat.
2. Simmer uncovered until reduced to ½ cup.
3. Add shrimp. Cover and simmer 3 minutes.
4. Immediately remove shrimp from liquid with slotted spoon; place in bowl of iced water.
5. Simmer liquid until reduced to 2 tablespoon cool.
6. Mix reduced liquid, shrimp and remaining ingredients except shredded lettuce and lemon wedges in a glass or plastic bowl .
7. Cover and refrigerate at least 1 hour. Just before serving place ¼ cup lettuce on each of 6 serving dishes.
8. Divide shrimp mixture among dishes.
9. Garnish with lemon wedges.

Cooking Tip
Shrimp normally does not have a flavor, a Jamaican fish sauce is used to enhance the taste of the shrimp or lack thereof.

JAMAICAN PLANTAIN CHIPS
This plantain recipe is like the well known Jamaican potato chips and just as delicious.

INGREDIENTS
3 green Jamaican plantains peeled
½ tbsp garlic powder
¼ tsp salt
¼ cup vegetable oil

PREPARATION
1. Slice the Jamaican plantains as in making potato chips.
2. Fry until crisp and season with Jamaican garlic and salt.

JAMAICAN DEVILLED CRABS
A devilled crab recipe is the best crab recipe on the Jamaican south coast

INGREDIENTS
6 large live crabs
2 tbsp flour
1 tbsp melted butter
1 tsp Worcestershire sauce
1 pinch salt & pepper
1 cup creamed cheese
¼ tsp scotch bonnet pepper diced
1 tsp parsley, minced
4 eggs, hard boiled, mashed
½ cup bread crumbs

PREPARATION
1. Cover crabs with boiling salt water and boil for 30 minutes. Drain off the water, break off all claws, separate the shells and remove the spongy fingers and the stomach, which is found under the head.
2. Pick out all the meat and set aside. Clean the upper shells of the crabs thoroughly.
3. Melt the butter and add the flour and blend. Stir in cream and cook until mixture thickens, stirring constantly.
4. Add the parsley, mashed egg yolks, seasonings and crab meat. Fill the shells with this mixture and cover with bread crumbs.
5. Bake at 350-F for 10 minutes or put in a frying basket and plunge into hot oil until golden brown.

JAMAICAN CURRIED SHRIMP APPETIZER BUNDLES
Curried recipes are a favorite in Jamaica and curried shrimp is a popular choice.

INGREDIENTS
¼ cup yogurt
¼ cup coconut flakes
¼ cup peanuts, chopped
1 tsp curry powder
¼ tsp ginger
1 cup Shrimp
6 dough sheets
½ cup melted butter

PREPARATION
1. In small mixing bowl, stir together yogurt, coconut, finely chopped peanuts, curry powder, and ginger.
2. Gently stir in shrimp. Preheat oven to 375.
3. Unfold dough. Place one sheet of dough on a waxed-paper-lined cutting board.
4. Cover remaining sheets with a damp paper towel. Keep covered to prevent drying.
5. Generously brush with butter. Top with another sheet of dough, then brush with more butter.
6. Repeat with a third sheet of dough and butter.
7. Using a sharp knife, cut the stack of dough sheets into twelve 4" squares.
8. Place about 2 tsp filling in the center of each square.
9. For each bundle, bring the 4 corners together pinch and twist slightly.
10. Repeat with remaining dough and butter.
11. Arrange bundles on un greased baking sheet. Bake 18-20 minutes, until golden.

JANGA (CRAWFISH) AND SHRIMP COCKTAIL
A sweet recipe sometimes called Janga rundown

INGREDIENTS
½ cup hot pepper sauce
1 tbsp lemon or lime juice
½ cup Ketchup
½ cup parsley, chopped fine
1 Jamaican hot sauce
1 tbsp Worcestershire sauce
½ cup boiled crawfish
½ cup boiled shrimp
½ tsp salt

PREPARATION
1. Combine all ingredients to make sauce and pour over crawfish or shrimp, or dip the crawfish or shrimp in the sauce.
2. Place the mixture in a sauce pan and fry over medium heat for 5-10 minutes.
3. Serve with saltine crackers.

JAMAICAN FRIED SHRIMP BALLS
A great recipe of fried shrimp.

INGREDIENTS
1 lb Fresh shrimp
¼ cup chopped onions
¼ cup escallion chopped
½ cup bamboo shoots chopped fine
¼ tsp fresh chopped ginger
1 tsp salt
1 tbsp Jamaican Appleton white rum
2 tsp cornstarch
¼ cup egg white
1 cup deep frying oil

PREPARATION
1. Prepare shrimp by cleaning thoroughly and removing shell, legs and de-vein.
2. Mince the shrimp. Combine all of the ingredients except oil.
3. Use a teaspoon of the mixture and shape into balls.
4. Heat oil in a deep pot or skillet and deep fry shrimp balls until Golden Brown.
5. Remove from oil and place onto paper towels to drain excess oil.
6. Serve Hot

Cooking Tip
Curry shrimp is an excellent recipe however try not to overcook the shrimp they cook within 15-18 minutes.

RED STRIPE BEER AND GARLIC MARINATED SHRIMP
A perfect blend between Red Stripe Beer and garlic

INGREDIENTS
1 lb fresh or frozen shrimp
¾ cup Red Stripe Beer
1 tbsp vegetable oil
2 tsps escallions chopped
½ tsp scotch bonnet pepper diced
¼ tsp salt
2 garlic cloves, crushed
½ cup melted butter
3 lemon wedges

PREPARATION
1. Peel shrimp. De-vein. Mix remaining ingredients in shallow glass pan. Stir in shrimp.
2. Cover and refrigerate at least 1 hour. Set oven control to broil.
3. Remove shrimp from marinade. Place shrimp on rack in broiler pan.
4. Broil shrimp about 4 inches from heat about 5 minutes, turning once and brushing with marinade, until shrimp are pink.
5. Serve with melted margarine or butter and lemon wedges

HERBED SHRIMP IN BEER AND BATTER
A Jamaican herb seasoned meal

INGREDIENTS
2 lb Peeled raw shrimp
1½ cup Red Stripe Beer
2 cloves garlic, minced
2 tbsp escallion chopped
2 tbsp parsley, snipped
1½ tsp salt
½ tsp scotch bonnet pepper
Shredded lettuce
2 onions, finely chopped
¼ tsp allspice (pimento)

PREPARATION
1. Combine all ingredients except lettuce in a bowl.
2. Cover, Refrigerate 8 hours or overnight; stir occasionally.
3. Drain, reserve marinade.
4. Broil shrimp 4 inches from heat until cooked and tender. Brush occasionally with marinade.
5. Serve shrimp on shredded lettuce.

Cooking Tip
Be careful how much Scotch Bonnet pepper you use it can quickly make a meal inedible. The high peppery taste will overpower all other seasonings and spoil your recipe.

BLUE MOUNTAIN SAUTEED PLANTAIN RECIPE
A popular plantain recipe served as Jamaican side dish.

INGREDIENTS
4 ripe Jamaican plantains
½ cup Butter or Margarine Optional
2 Jamaican cloves
2 sticks Jamaican Cinnamon
2 tbsp brown sugar

PREPARATION
1. Peel ripe Jamaican plantains and slice.
2. Heat butter or margarine and add spices.
3. Sauté at medium heat with spices until browned
4. Sprinkle with brown sugar

JAMAICAN GRILLED SEAFOOD KABOBS**
A perfect blend of different seafood meats seasoned with authentic Jamaican herbs.

INGREDIENTS
1 lb large shrimp (de-veined)
1 lb large mushrooms
¼ cup honey
8 wooden skewers
¼ cup cooked jumbo shrimp
¼ cup cooked lobster
¼ cup cooked crawfish
½ cup Jamaican bar-b-q sauce
2 lb fresh fruit as garnish
3 large green sweet peppers

PREPARATION
1. Combine the Jamaican bar-b-q sauce and honey in a bowl and mix well.
2. Place alternating groups of shrimp, lobster, crawfish and sweet peppers on the skewers.
3. Place completed kabobs in a baking pan.
4. Spoon the marinade over the kabobs and allow to set for a few hours in the refrigerator.
5. Grill over direct heat for 7 to 8 minutes or until the shrimp have turned pink, turning frequently to prevent burning.
6. Baste with marinade and use a covered grill to ensure a smoky flavor.
7. Garnish with fresh fruit.

**—Kebab (*also translated as kabab, kebap, kabob, kibob*) refers to a variety of grilled/broiled meat dishes on a stick or skewer. Jamaicans love kebabs and this appetizer recipe uses a mixture of meat recipes.

JAMAICAN LAYERED SHRIMP APPETIZER
A layered Jamaican shrimp recipe

INGREDIENTS
2½ cup water
¾ lb unpeeled medium-size fresh shrimp
½ cup cream cheese softened
½ cup sour cream
¼ tbsp onion salt
¼ tsp scotch bonnet pepper diced
1½ tsp Worcestershire sauce
¾ tsp lemon juice

PREPARATION
1. Bring water to a boil; add shrimp, and cook 3 to 5 minutes or until shrimp turn pink.
2. Drain well; rinse with cold water. Chill. Peel and de-vein shrimp.
3. Chop two-thirds of shrimp, leaving remaining shrimp whole. Cover and chill chopped and whole shrimp.
4. Beat cream cheese at medium speed of an electric mixer until creamy.
5. Add sour cream, onion salt, and red pepper, beating until smooth. Spread mixture onto serving platter, shaping into a 5-inch circle.
6. Cover and chill at least 30 minutes.
7. Add Worcestershire sauce and stir well and spread over cream cheese round.
8. Sprinkle chopped shrimp over mixture; top with whole shrimp.
9. Garnish with fresh parsley sprigs and lemon slices.

JAMAICAN SHRIMP TERIYAKI
A great tasting Jamaican shrimp appetizer

INGREDIENTS
½ cup soy sauce
2 tbsp sugar
1 tbsp vegetable Oil
1½ tsp cornstarch
1 garlic crushed
1 tsp minced fresh ginger root
2 tbsp water
2 lb medium sized raw shrimp

PREPARATION
1. Bend soy sauce, sugar, oil, cornstarch, garlic, ginger and water in small saucepan.
2. Simmer, stirring constantly, until thickened, about 1 minute cool.
3. Coat shrimp with sauce drain off excess.
4. Place on rack of broiler pan.
5. Broil 5 inches from heat source 3 to 4 minutes on each side, or until shrimp are opaque and cooked.
6. Serve immediately with wooden picks.

aican shrimp steamed
n appetizer. ©

JAMAICAN SHRIMP ROLLS
A shrimp roll recipe that is a delicious recipe.

INGREDIENTS
1lb medium shrimp, unpeeled
2 cups bean sprouts
10 rice papers cut into halves or quarters
1 lg leaf lettuce, leaves separated and trimmed
½ fresh pineapple, peeled, eyes removed, halved, cored

PREPARATION
1. Cook shrimp in salted, boiling water for 2 to 3 minutes, or until pink and firm to the touch. Drain and cool.
2. Peel and de-vein shrimp, or serve them in their shells and let diners peel them at the table.
3. Blanch bean sprouts in boiling water for 1 minute. Drain and refresh with cold water.
4. Moisten rice papers in warm water for 10 to 20 seconds, or until softened.
5. Place a lettuce leaf inside each piece of softened rice paper.
6. Fill with a few shrimp, a little pineapple, bean sprouts and tomato.
7. Roll up the bundles.

SKEWERED SHRIMP AND TOMATOES
A great mixture of tomatoes and shrimp covered with allspice.

INGREDIENTS
½ cup Jamaican Seafood sauce
½ tsp Worcestershire sauce
1 tbsp fresh orange juice
4 short skewers
¾ pound jumbo shrimp—peeled and de-veined
1 orange sliced thin
8 tomatoes
Non-stick cooking spray

PREPARATION
1. Mix Worcestershire sauce with Jamaican seafood sauce and orange juice.
2. Thread shrimp onto skewers, alternating with orange slices and tomatoes and ending with shrimp.
3. Spray grill rack and place it on grid over coals. Mop shrimp simply with marinate and grill kabobs 2 minutes.
4. Turn and mop kabobs. Grill 2 minutes longer or until shrimp are white in color and just firm to touch. Do not over grill or shrimp will become tough.
5. Place one kabob on each plate and pass remaining marinating sauce.

> **Cooking Tip**
> You can substitute bananas with plantains in almost any recipe except Jamaican drink recipes. The Jamaican plantain and Jamaican banana only have a slightly different taste.

PORT MARIA BAKED SWEET PLANTAIN RECIPE
This delicious Jamaican plantain recipe is a favorite Jamaican side dish recipe and can be served like Jamaican yams.

INGREDIENTS
4 very ripe plantains (black)
1 cup (low fat) milk
½ cup brown sugar
4 tbsp. margarine

PREPARATION
1. Peel Jamaican plantains place them in a baking dish and pour the milk and sugar over them.
2. Spread one tbsp. of margarine over the top of each Jamaican plantain.
3. Bake at 400 Degrees for about ½ hour.

JAMAICAN BARBEQUED PLANTAIN WITH BEEF
This is a great plantain recipe that uses ripened plantains cooked with beef.

INGREDIENTS
4 very ripe plantains (black), peeled
½ cup of seasoned (cooked) ground beef
4 slices of white cheese
4 strips of guava

PREPARATION
1. On a hot grill, place the peeled Jamaican plantains for about 7 minutes.
2. Turn and grill for 7 more minutes so that each side is cooked evenly. Once golden brown, use a small knife to slice the plantains lengthwise down the middle.
3. Stuff them with cheese and Jamaican guava and with the cooked ground Jamaican beef.
4. Place the plantains back in the grill for 2 more minutes or until the cheese is melted.

OCHO RIOS PLANTAIN RECIPE
This is a favorite plantain recipe prepared by some cooks and chefs in Ocho Rios.

INGREDIENTS
4 ripe plantains
2 cups of milk
1 cup of sugar
½ cup butter
¼ cup of vermouth
1 tsp. vanilla
¼ tsp. cinnamon

PREPARATION
1. Mash the Jamaican plantains in a bowl.
2. Add the milk, sugar, butter, Vermouth and vanilla. Mix well.
3. Grease a frying pan with oil and warm it up.
4. Pour the plantain mixture into the pan.
5. Cook on very low heat until fully cooked.
6. Sprinkle with ground Jamaican cinnamon.

DARLISTON DOUBLE FRIED JAMAICAN PLANTAIN RECIPE
A savory and delicious plantain recipe.

INGREDIENTS
4-5 ripe Jamaican plantains
¼ cup vegetable oil
¼ tsp salt
3 garlic cloves (chopped finely)
¼ cup Jamaican chicken broth

PREPARATION
1. Heat Jamaican chicken broth in a small saucepan.
2. Add garlic. Let it sit until the plantain is finished.
3. Peel plantain. Cut into ½ inch slices and heat 2 inches of oil in a heavy duty frying pan.
4. Fry plantain a little at a time until it is slightly golden.
5. Remove, drain on paper towels then take a glass and flatten the plantain.
6. Return to frying pan and fry until golden. Remove and drain.

CLARENDON SWEET POTATO CHIPS RECIPE
Jamaican sweet potato chips are the most popular Jamaican sweet potato recipe.

INGREDIENTS
2 medium sweet potatoes
1 cup ice water
¼ cup vegetable oil
¼ tsp salt

PREPARATION
1. Peel Jamaican sweet potatoes and cut in half lengthwise then slice very thin with a knife.
2. Place slices in a medium bowl and cover with ice water; chill for 1 hour.
3. Lift from water and drain on paper towels.
4. Heat oil to about 375° in deep fryer or about 1 inch deep in an electric skillet or deep skillet on stovetop.
5. Fry sweet potato slices in one-layer batches for a minute or two, or until golden brown.
6. Lift sweet potato chips out with slotted spoon and drain on paper towels.
7. Sprinkle sweet potato chips with salt before serving.

JAMAICAN MORNING PORRIDGE
Jamaicans love porridge recipes and nothing beats a great porridge in the morning

INGREDIENTS
4½ cups water
1½ cups oatmeal
½ cups dried fruit (apples and bananas)
¼ tsp nutmeg
¼ tsp allspice
¼ cinnamon
½ cup milk

PREPARATION
1. Bring water and fruit to a boil.
2. Slowly add cereal and spices to boiling water while stirring. Then add milk and continue stirring.
3. Reduce heat to low, cook, stirring frequently, 15 to 30 minutes.

ST. BESS RICE PORRIDGE

Rice is grown in parts of St. Elizabeth and the cooks there have learnt how to make the best rice porridge.

INGREDIENTS

1 cup white rice
¼ tsp salt
2¼ cup water
1 tbsp margarine
½ cup raisins
1 tsp cinnamon

PREPARATION

1. Combine all ingredients in 2 to 3-quart saucepan. Bring to a boil; stir once or twice.
2. Reduce heat, cover, and simmer 45 to 55 minutes, or until rice is tender and liquid is absorbed.
3. Fluff with fork.
4. Serve with milk or cream, honey or brown sugar, and fresh fruit.

> **Cooking Tip**
> Jamaican porridge recipes are not to be served cold, they are rather distasteful.

ST. MARY BANANA PORRIDGE

Banana is the main staple of St. Mary and they make a mean Banana porridge recipe.

INGREDIENTS

1 cup crushed ripe bananas
¼ tsp salt
2¼ cup water
1 tbsp margarine
½ cup raisins
1 tsp cinnamon

PREPARATION

1. Combine all ingredients in 2 to 3-quart saucepan. Bring to a boil; stir once or twice.
2. Reduce heat, cover, and simmer 45 to 55 minutes, or until mixture is thick.
3. Serve with milk or cream, honey or brown sugar, and fresh fruit.

JAMAICAN SOLOMON GUNDY OR SALAMANGUNDI

A Jamaican recipe that has its origins from before 1900 as an authentic Jamaican recipe.

INGREDIENTS

¼ tsp Appleton white rum
2 tbsp margarine
1 lg chopped onion
1 tbsp vinegar
2 red herrings cooked
1 scotch bonnet pepper diced

PREPARATION

1. Flake the flesh off the red herrings and set aside.
2. Add peppers, onion and other ingredients to herring and place in a food processor and puree.
3. Pour in a jar and keep the paste refrigerated.
4. Serve hot.

JAMAICAN HOMINY PORRIDGE
A sweet hominy porridge recipe.

INGREDIENTS
½ cup hominy corn
6 cups water
2 cinnamon leaves
¼ tsp salt
¼ cup flour
2 cups coconut milk
1 tsp. grated nutmeg
½ cup condensed milk
½ cup evaporated milk

PREPARATION
1. After soaking corn in water overnight, place corn in the water in which it has been soaked
2. Add cinnamon leaves and salt in a saucepan and bring to a boil.
3. Simmer for 1½ hours. Mix the flour into a smooth paste with a little of the coconut milk.
4. Add the rest of the coconut milk to the paste.
5. Pour paste into saucepan. Stir well. Bring porridge back to boiling point. Add nutmeg.
6. Simmer for five minutes. Add condensed and evaporated milk. Cook for five minutes more.
7. Serve hot.

NEGRIL FIRE ACKEE AND MACKEREL TOSS
If you love ackees and love pepper then this recipe is for you.

INGREDIENTS
1½ cup ackee, boiled
1 onion chopped
1 sweet pepper, chopped
3 tomatoes, diced
1 stalk of escallion chopped
1 clove garlic, minced
¼ tsp dried thyme
1 scotch bonnet pepper diced
½ tsp curry powder
2 tbsp vegetable oil
1 cup canned mackerel steaks

PREPARATION
1. Heat oil in a large skillet.
2. Add curry, onion, thyme, and garlic tossing continuously.
3. Add remaining vegetables, adding ackees last. Keep tossing until flavors are released and blended.
4. Add mackerel and cover and allow to heat through for approximately one minute.
5. Garnish with one teaspoon finely chopped sweet pepper and a sprinkle of black pepper.

> **Cooking Tip**
> Jamaican ackee and mackerel rarely make a good combination unless well spiced, bear this in mind when preparing this recipe.

JAMAICAN SWEET POTATO FRITTERS RECIPE
A sweet fritters recipe to remember

INGREDIENTS
2 cups mashed sweet potatoes
½ cup flour
½ tsp salt
1 tsp baking powder
4 tsp melted butter
2 eggs
1 cup milk
1 tbsp sugar

PREPARATION
1. Combine melted butter with Jamaican sweet potatoes, sugar, milk and egg yolks.
2. Sift flour, measure and sift with baking powder and salt. Add to the first mixture.
3. Beat egg whites until stiff peaks form; fold into the batter.
4. Drop by teaspoonfuls into hot deep fat, at 365° and fry in batches until browned.
5. Remove with slotted spoon to paper towels or brown paper to drain.

KINGSTON ACKEE AND SALTFISH
The flagship Jamaican breakfast and the Jamaican National dish

INGREDIENTS
30 Ackee pods or 1 can of Ackees
½ lb salt fish
¼ tsp salt
¼ tsp black pepper
4 tomatoes chopped
3 stalks escallion finely chopped
2¼ cup water
2 tbsp margarine
1 lg chopped onion
8 strips of bacon (optional)

PREPARATION
1. Soak salt fish overnight, then boil and flake salt fish and set aside.
2. Fry the bacon strips and set aside.
3. Boil ackees after removing pink and seeds (not necessary if canned ackees) for 20 minutes and drain.
4. Sauté onions, tomatoes, escallion, then add ackees, bacon and salt fish stirring softly.
5. Add black pepper and salt and sauté for just another five minutes.
6. Serve hot.

Cooking Tip

Salt fish is very tasty but you must boil the salt fish well and remove the fine bones as this will result in a very salty dish and very difficult to eat because of bones. Place salt fish in boiling water until it becomes flaky, then remove and easily pick out the bones. Set aside and allow to cool first before cooking.

JAMAICAN DUMPLINGS OR JOHNNY CAKES
Jamaican dumpling recipe best served with any Jamaican breakfast recipe.

INGREDIENTS
1 cup all purpose flour
¼ tsp salt
1 tbsp sugar
1¼ cup water
¼ cup milk
1 tbsp margarine
1 cup vegetable oil
½ tsp allspice

PREPARATION
1. Mix all ingredients with the exception of the milk and water.
2. Add a little water and milk until a dough is formed.
3. Knead the dough well and separate into balls
4. Preheat frying pan and deep fry each ball.
5. Remove from pot drain and serve.

KINGSTON CORNMEAL DUMPLINGS
Jamaican cornmeal dumplings are a viable substitute for fried dumplings.

INGREDIENTS
½ cup flour
½ cup cornmeal
¼ tsp salt
½ tsp baking powder
2 cups water
¼ cup milk
¼ cup margarine

PREPARATION
1. Sift flour, cornmeal, salt and baking powder.
2. Rub in margarine, then add enough water to make a firm dough.
3. Knead lightly and make into balls and cook in boiling water.

JAMAICAN ORANGE EGGS
A perfect blend between Jamaican orange and eggs.

INGREDIENTS
2 oranges
¼ tsp salt
½ tsp black pepper
¼ cup flour
1 egg beaten
¼ cup margarine

PREPARATION
1. Juice both oranges and set aside then season the egg with salt and pepper and add orange juice.
2. Melt margarine in sauce pan and add egg mixture and scramble using a fork and serve hot.

OCHO RIOS MACKEREL RUNDOWN (DIP AND FALL BACK)
This is another popular Jamaican breakfast recipe prepared for guests on the North Coast.

INGREDIENTS
1 lb salted mackerel
1¼ cups coconut milk
1 lg onion diced
½ tbsp cane vinegar
1 tomato finely chopped
½ tsp scotch bonnet pepper diced
½ tbsp lime juice

PREPARATION
1. Clean the mackerel with lime juice and soak fish in boiling water to remove some salt.
2. Place coconut milk in Dutch pan and bring to boil, then add tomato, onion, vinegar and peppers and sauté.
3. Flake the fish and add to the Dutch pot and allow to simmer stirring constantly for 5—10 minutes under a low flame.
4. Serve hot with boiled dumplings and boiled green bananas

JAMAICAN CALLALOO AND SALTFISH
This is also one of the most popular Jamaican breakfast dishes and a must have recipe for all chefs.

INGREDIENTS
½ lb salt fish
¼ tsp salt
¼ tsp black pepper
4 tomatoes chopped
3 stalks escallion finely chopped
1¼ cup water
2 tbsp margarine
1 lg chopped onion
8 strips of bacon (**optional**)
2 bundles of callaloo or 1 bag of chopped callaloo

PREPARATION
1. Soak salt fish overnight, then boil and flake salt fish and set aside.
2. Fry the bacon strips and set aside.
3. Wash callaloo well, drain then chop finely (not necessary if canned ackees).
4. Sauté onions, tomatoes and escallion in butter then add water.
5. Add callaloo and steam under low flame by covering being careful not to let the water dry out.
6. When fully steamed add bacon and salt fish stirring softly.
7. Add black pepper and salt and steam for another five—ten minutes.
8. Serve hot.

PORT ROYAL SALT FISH FRITTERS
A popular recipe also called 'Stamp and Go' it is a perfect blend of Jamaican seasonings and salt fish.

INGREDIENTS
½ lb salt fish
2 cups water
½ lb flour
¼ tsp black pepper
2 tomatoes chopped
3 stalks escallion finely chopped
2 tbsp margarine
1 lg chopped onion
2 cloves of garlic finely chopped
½ tsp scotch bonnet pepper diced

PREPARATION
1. Soak salt fish overnight, then boil and flake salt fish and set aside.
2. Sauté onions, tomatoes, escallion, garlic and pepper in butter then add to flaked salt fish.
3. Mix baking powder and flour and add codfish and seasonings to it.
4. Add small amounts of water stirring until you have a medium batter.
5. Remove and fry in saucepan in ½ inch oil until golden.
6. Serve hot.

FAITHS PEN SALTFISH BALLS
This recipe was taken from a chef who plies his trade in St. Ann the famous travelers halt called Faiths Pen.

INGREDIENTS
½ lb salt fish
¼ tsp salt
¼ tsp black pepper
4 tomatoes chopped
¼ tsp scotch bonnet pepper
3 stalks escallion finely chopped
2 cups diced raw potato
¼ cup margarine
1 lg chopped onion
2 eggs beaten well
¼ cup bread crumbs

PREPARATION
1. Soak salt fish overnight, then boil and flake salt fish and set aside.
2. Sauté onions, tomatoes and escallion in butter and set aside.
3. Boil potatoes until extremely soft then add sautéed seasonings and salt fish and crush well.
4. Form the mixture in light balls dip in egg and then breadcrumbs.
5. Fry in oil until golden brown.
6. Serve hot.

ST. BESS PEPPER SHRIMP
The perfect peppered shrimp recipe from the home of the Jamaican shrimp.

INGREDIENTS
2 tsp salt
2 tsp cane vinegar
2 cloves garlic chopped
3 stalks escallion finely chopped
¾ cup salad oil
2 tbsp margarine
2 scotch bonnet peppers diced
3½ cups medium shrimp still in shells

PREPARATION
1. place all ingredients except shrimp and vinegar in a large pot and bring to boil.
2. Add shrimps and stir for at least 8 minutes.
3. Add vinegar and allow to continue cooking for another 8-10 minutes.
4. Serve hot.

KINGSTON SPICY HASH BROWNS
This recipe is a favorite an a recommended recipe for any appetizer or breakfast.

INGREDIENTS
5 medium potatoes peeled and cooked,
1½ lb ham diced
½ cup onions chopped
4 green peppers chopped
1 scotch bonnet pepper chopped
½ cup butter
½ tbsp allspice
¼ tsp salt
¼ tsp black pepper
½ tsp paprika
¼ cup cheese shredded

PREPARATION
1. Sauté ham, onions and peppers in ¼ cup butter until tender.
2. Cool 10 minutes; add to potatoes. Add allspice and seasonings; mix well.
3. On a griddle, cook potatoes in remaining butter until browned; turn over and cook the second side until browned.
4. Place half of the potatoes on a platter; top with cheese and remaining potatoes.

JAMAICAN BAKED EGGS

Baking eggs has now become a popular recipe in Jamaica. This is a delicious recipe to savor.

INGREDIENTS

1 lg egg beaten
½ tbsp Worcestershire sauce
¼ cup escallions chopped
¼ cup onion chopped
¼ cup cheese shredded
¼ tsp allspice
¼ tsp black pepper
¼ tsp salt
2 sprigs parsley

PREPARATION

1. Break egg into a lightly greased individual baking dish.
2. Stir egg to break yolk then add Worcestershire sauce, escallions, onion and parsley.
3. Stir to mix thoroughly. Mix in half the cheese. Top with remaining cheese.
4. Place dish in a larger pan that has about 1 in. hot water. Bake at 350F for 10-15 minutes or until egg is firm.

JAMLET (JAMAICAN OMELET)

A special omlet with a Jamaican flavor.

INGREDIENTS

1 tbsp butter
4 eggs beaten
4 tbsp cows milk
3 slices of bacon cooked and crumbled
¼ cup escallions chopped
¼ cup onion chopped
¼ tsp allspice
¼ tsp black pepper
¼ tsp salt

PREPARATION

1. Beat eggs and milk and pour into a bowl and set aside.
2. Sauté escallions, onion, allspice, black pepper and salt then add egg and milk mixture.
3. Cook eggs for about 3 minutes then add cheese.
4. Serve with parsley.

SUNDAY MORNING SANDWICH
A popular Sunday morning breakfast recipe. This is served in many five-star Jamaican hotels.

INGREDIENTS
1 cup crescent rolls
1 tbsp onion chopped
4 cheese slices
½ cup milk
½ cup crumpled cooked bacon
2 lg eggs beaten

PREPARATION
1. Separate dough into 4 rectangles and place 2 rectangles in un-greased 8" square pan press over bottom and ½ up sides to form crust, sealing perforations.
2. Place cheese slices over dough. Sprinkle bacon and onions over evenly. Blend milk and eggs pour over bacon.
3. Separate remaining dough into triangles; arrange triangles over bacon-egg mix; do not seal. Bake for 30-35 minutes or until golden brown and filling is set.

COOLIE OMELETTE
This is a perfect curried omelet recipe made popular by chefs of Indian descent in Jamaica

INGREDIENTS
2 lg eggs beaten
¼ cup onion chopped
3 tbsp vegetable oil
1 tsp curry powder
1 stalk escallion chopped
¼ cup coconut milk
¼ tsp black pepper
½ tsp paprika
¼ tsp salt
½ tsp lime juice

PREPARATION
1. Beat eggs and coconut milk and pour into a bowl and set aside.
2. Sauté escallions, onion, allspice, paprika, black pepper, salt and curry powder then add egg and milk mixture.
3. Cook eggs for about 3 minutes then add a tip of lime juice.
4. Serve hot.

CHRISTMAS SORREL OMELET
A great Christmas breakfast with the sorrel leaves.

INGREDIENTS
3 sorrel leaves
3 tsp butter
3 eggs beaten
2 tbsp water
¼ tsp salt
¼ tsp black pepper
2 tbsp cream

PREPARATION
1. Cut sorrel leaves into strips and melt half the butter in a sauce pan and cook the leaves until they have wilted and turned a gray-green color.
2. Lightly beat the eggs with the water, season with salt and pepper, then stir in the sorrel.
3. Melt the remaining butter in the sauce pan and when it is hot, add the eggs.
4. As the edges cook, pull them into the middle of the pan with a fork, tilting the pan as you do so that uncooked eggs will flow into its place.
5. When the eggs are cooked fold the omelet in thirds and turn it out onto a plate.
6. Return the pan to the fire and add the cream.
7. Bring it to a boil and let it reduce enough just to thicken slightly.
8. Make a slice down the center of the omelet, pour in the cream and serve.

Cooking Tip

Sorrel is a strong Jamaican traditional recipe, however, when preparing this recipe take care **NOT** to leave any of the sorrel leaves in the omelet. Its always best to use the sorrel flavored melted butter only rather than use the sorrel leaves to add to the egg mixture. Also this is a very unique tasting Jamaican recipe, adding just a few sorrel leaves is advised.

OCHO RIOS SCRAMBLED EGGS
A great scrambled egg recipe with a slight difference due to ginger.

INGREDIENTS
1 small ginger grated, chopped
2 lg eggs beaten
3 tbsp vegetable oil
¼ cup onion chopped
3 tbsp vegetable oil
1 stalk escallion chopped
¼ tsp black pepper
½ tsp paprika
¼ tsp salt

PREPARATION
1. Place ginger in sauce pan with ¼ cup of water and bring to boil until only 1 teaspoon of water is left.
2. Sauté escallions, onion, allspice, paprika, black pepper and salt with vegetable oil then add liquefied ginger.
3. Beat eggs and pour into sauce pan with ginger mixture and scramble.
4. Remove and serve hot.

ROCKY POINT LOBSTER AND SCRAMBLED EGGS
A seafood breakfast recipe perfected by the chefs at Rocky Point fishing village.

INGREDIENTS
6 tbsp unsalted butter
½ sweet pepper chopped finely
1½ cup lobster meat cooked
2 tbsp onions chopped
6 lg eggs beaten
5 tbsp cream
¼ tsp salt
¼ tsp black pepper

PREPARATION
1. In a small skillet melt 2 tablespoons of the butter over medium heat.
2. Add the sweet pepper and onions and sauté.
3. Add the lobster and reheat until warmed through. Allow to cool then set aside.
4. In a medium heavy skillet melt 2 tablespoons more of the butter over low heat and swirl in the eggs and half the cream gently scrambling the eggs.
5. Add the remaining cream and 2 tablespoon butter to the eggs and continue stirring until the mixture is very thick and creamy.
6. Quickly fold in the warmed lobster mixture spooning with the scrambled eggs.
7. Season with salt and pepper.

JAMAICAN CHICKEN OMLET
Another splendid Jamaican breakfast recipe combining chicken and eggs.

INGREDIENTS
½ cup water
½ cup tomato chopped
1 tbsp vegetable oil
1 tsp allspice
1 tsp Jamaican Bouillon
1 cup chicken breast cubed cooked
5 lg eggs
¼ tsp salt
¼ tsp black pepper
4 tbsp margarine

PREPARATION
1. In a blender container, combine the ¼ cup of water, tomato, vegetable oil, allspice and bouillon.
2. Blend until very smooth then pour into a small saucepan.
3. Cook, stirring constantly, until thick, about 7 minutes. Stir in the chicken.
4. Season with a little salt and pepper and set aside.
5. With a fork, beat the eggs until well blended but not frothy.
6. In a sauce pan heat 2 tablespoons of the butter and add ½ cup of the egg mixture, leaving the heat on medium-high. Cook the omelet well.
7. As the egg sets spoon about ¼ cup of the chicken mixture down the center of the omelet.
8. Fold the sides of the omelet up over the chicken mixture.
9. Serve with parsley

JAMAICAN HONEY PANCAKES
A sweet honey pancake recipe with Jamaican herbs and spices

INGREDIENTS
¼ cup self-raising Flour
2 tbsp castor sugar
1 egg beaten
¼ cup milk
½ cup honey
3 banana pieces

PREPARATION
1. Sieve the flour into a large mixing bowl and stir in the caster sugar.
2. Make a well in the centre and stir in the beaten egg, milk and ¼ cup of honey to form a batter.
3. Heat the frying pan over a medium heat and place the batter in the shape of pancakes and cook for 2 to 3 minutes. Cook all pancakes.
4. Arrange the pancakes on a serving plate and drizzle the warmed left honey over the top.
5. Decorate with banana pieces

CHELSEA PORK OMLET
Chelsea is known for its jerk chicken and jerk pork now this recipe adds to the great taste.

NGREDIENTS
½ cup water
½ cup tomato chopped
1 tbsp vegetable oil
1 tsp allspice
1 tsp Jamaican Bouillon
1 cup chopped pork lean cooked
5 lg eggs
¼ tsp salt
¼ tsp black pepper
4 tbsp margarine

PREPARATION
1. In a blender container, combine the ¼ cup of water, tomato, vegetable oil, allspice and bouillon.
2. Blend until very smooth then pour into a small saucepan.
3. Cook, stirring constantly, until thick, about 7 minutes. Stir in the pork.
4. Season with a little salt and pepper and set aside.
5. With a fork, beat the eggs until well blended but not frothy.
6. In a sauce pan heat 2 tablespoons of the butter and add ½ cup of the egg mixture, leaving the heat on medium-high. Cook the omelet well.
7. As the egg sets spoon about ¼ cup of the pork mixture down the center of the omelet.
8. Fold the sides of the omelet up over the pork mixture.
9. Serve with parsley

AMAICAN OUP AND ROTH ECIPES

jamaican pumpkin
and carrot soup. ©

Jamaican Baked Potato Soup
This is a potato soup recipe handed down in 4 generations in St. Elizabeth

INGREDIENTS
4 lg baking potatoes
½ cup butter
½ cup flour
6 cups milk
1 pinch salt
1 pinch black pepper
4 stalks escallion chopped
10 slices bacon, cooked and crumbled
1¼ cups cheddar cheese shredded & divided
¼ cup sour cream

PREPARATION
1. Bake potatoes then allow them to cool.
2. Scoop out pulp and set aside. Discard skins.
3. Melt butter over low heat and add flour.
4. Add milk, until thick. Add potato pulp, salt, pepper, escallions, ½ cup of crumbled bacon and cup cheese.
5. Cook until thoroughly heated; stir in sour cream and heat through.

JAMAICAN VEGETABLE BROTH
A perfect blend of the most common Jamaican vegetables.

INGREDIENTS
½ cup cubed potatoes
½ cup cubed plantains
½ cup cubed green bananas
½ cup cubed chochos
½ cup cubed carrots
2 cup water, boiling
3 tbsp vegetable oil
½ cup escallions chopped
½ cup onions chopped
½ cup chopped tomatoes
½ tsp allspice

PREPARATION
1. While water is boiling stir ingredients together.
2. Simmer until vegetables are very soft.
3. Using the spoon mash the vegetables.
4. Continue to stir cooking under a low flame for another 15 minutes.
5. Strain broth and serve without any solids.

JAMAICAN VEGETABLE SOUP
This vegetable soup is a popular recipe especially when children are sick with the flu

INGREDIENTS
3 cups beef broth
2 cup water
1 cup tomato juice
2 potatoes
3 carrots
1 small onion
2 celery stalks
¼ cup diced green peppers
½ cup corn kernels
4 tbsp margarine
¼ tsp black pepper
½ tsp salt

PREPARATION
1. Melt 4 tablespoons margarine in skillet. Add the chopped green peppers, carrots, celery and onion.
2. Sauté on low heat until vegetables are softened and onion browned lightly.
3. Add this to the broth mixture which has been placed in a large, heavy pan with lid.
4. Add to this the potatoes and corn.
5. Cover and simmer for about 45 minutes or until all the vegetables are done.
6. Add the salt and pepper.
7. Remove about 2 cups of the mixture and put into blender.
8. Puree this mixture and return to pot with rest of soup.
9. Turn off heat and cover soup.

> **Cooking Tip**
> When preparing soup recipes, great care must be taken not to over-spice or over flavor the soup. This is because if the soup is meat, fruit or vegetable based each main ingredient carries its own flavor. If you utilize too much seasonings or spices it will drown the flavor of the base of the soup recipe. Likewise if meat is the base of the soup such as beef or pork, this can be cooked in a pressure cooker to reduce cooking time for the soup itself. The meat along with some of the gravy can be added to soup about ½ before serving.

JAMAICAN CHICKEN BROTH
A sweet chicken broth made by Jamaican cooks.

INGREDIENTS
2 cups cubed chicken breast
2 cup water, boiling
3 tbsp corn oil
1 tsp poultry seasoning
½ cup escallions chopped
½ cup onions chopped
1 tbsp vegetable broth
½ cup chopped tomatoes
½ tsp allspice
Onion salt to taste

PREPARATION
1. While water is boiling stir ingredients together then strain broth and serve without any solids.

JAMAICAN BEET SOUP
A perfect soup for the health conscious diner.

INGREDIENTS
4 ripe beets chopped
1 tbsp lemon juice
¼ tbsp salt and pepper mixed
1 lg onion, diced
4 carrots, sliced
1 tbsp vinegar
1 cup tomatoes chopped

PREPARATION
1. Put vegetables in a large pot with water to cover. Add remaining ingredients and mix thoroughly.
2. Simmer 2 to 2½ hours or until beets and carrots are tender.

DOWNTOWN BEEF SOUP
A favorite of cricket lovers. This hearty beef soup is quickly prepared and goes down easily.

INGREDIENTS
5 cups water
½ cup carrots sliced
½ cup potatoes
¼ cup escallion chopped
¼ tsp allspice
½ lb beef stew meat
1 onion chopped
¼ tsp salt
¼ tsp black pepper
5 cloves

PREPARATION
1. Cook beef and vegetables separately. Do not drain.
2. Mix all together with other ingredients and simmer until the flavors are mixed.

KINGSTON CHOWDER
A splendid chowder popular with Kingston chefs.

INGREDIENTS
½ cup bacon bits
1 carrot, thinly sliced
2 sticks celery, thinly sliced
1 onion, coarsely chopped
1 bay leaf
2 cloves of garlic
1 tsp pepper

PREPARATION
1. Fry the bacon in a large pot and remove. Add the carrot and celery and cook over medium heat for 2 minutes.
2. Add the onion, bay leaf and whole cloves of garlic. Stir and add the pepper.

NEGRIL BEEF AND CABBAGE SOUP
A blend of Jamaican beef and cabbage to make a delicious soup recipe

INGREDIENTS
1 lb ground beef
½ tsp garlic salt
¼ tsp garlic powder
¼ tsp black pepper
½ chopped head cabbage
½ cup chopped tomatoes *
4 beef bouillon cubes
Chopped parsley

PREPARATION
1. In a saucepan brown beef then add all remaining ingredients except parsley and bring to boil.
2. Reduce heat & simmer, covered for 1 hour.
3. Garnish with parsley.

JAMAICAN RED PEAS SOUP
A really popular Jamaican soup recipe, great tasting with added spices.

INGREDIENTS
1 cup red kidney beans
1 tbsp olive oil
1 lg onion chopped
1 clove garlic chopped
¼ cup escallion chopped
2 cups stewed tomatoes
4 cups condensed chicken broth
6 cups water
2½ cups lean ham
2 tbsp lemon juice
¼ tsp black pepper
¼ tsp chopped fresh parsley

PREPARATION
1. In large bowl, rinse and drain all beans. Cover with 8 cups fresh water and refrigerate.
2. Soak minimum of 4 hours, preferably overnight. In 8-quart pot, over medium-high heat, pour in olive oil.
3. When sizzling, cook onion, escallion and garlic 2-3 minutes, stirring frequently, until onion is translucent.
4. Drain beans and rinse under cold running water. Place beans in pot and add tomatoes, broth, and water.
5. Bring to boil, stirring occasionally. Reduce heat to medium-low. Cook soup, uncovered, 1 hour 50 minutes, or until beans are tender.
6. Stir occasionally. Stir in ham cubes, lemon juice and pepper. Cook 10-15 minutes, until ham is heated through. Serve garnished with parsley.

Cooking Tip
Vegetable based soups are usually best served with a side dish. A side dish such as garlic bread or toasted bread helps to add flavor to the soup recipe. It also helps in making the meal a bit more filling.

NEW KINGSTON BEEFY SPAGHETTI SOUP

A favorite for the businessman or woman on the go in Jamaica's business capital.

INGREDIENTS

½ lb ground beef, crumbled
½ cup onion chopped
1½ cup spaghetti
1 clove garlic minced
1 tsp parsley flakes
4 cups beef stock
¾ tsp salt
1 tsp olive oil
¼ tsp scotch bonnet pepper
1 bay leaf
½ cup tomato chopped

PREPARATION

1. In large frying pan combine ground beef, onion, garlic and oil.
2. Cook at high until meat is no longer pink stirring once during cooking.
3. Remove and place in soup pan and add other ingredients with at least ¾ cups of water.
4. Cover and allow to simmer under a low flame for at least 1 hour or until spaghetti is done.
5. Serve with garlic or cheese bread

SONNY'S OYSTER SOUP

Sonny is one of our featured chefs and this is his favorite Jamaican soup recipe.

INGREDIENTS

¼ cup escallions chopped
½ cup oyster liquor, drained from oysters
1 cup cream
½ tsp chopped onions
½ tsp chopped escallions
10 lg oysters, shucked
¼ tsp black pepper

PREPARATION

1. In a heavy bottomed pan over medium heat, cook the onions and escallions until evenly browned, about 10-15 minutes.
2. Remove to a bowl and crush with a spoon adding a few drops of oyster liquor and cream until a paste forms.
3. Heat the cream and oyster liquor together in a saucepan. Gradually stir in the onion and escallion paste, the add the oysters and continue to heat until oysters are just curled.
4. Season with black pepper.

JAMAICA'S ONION SOUP
A special soup treat for onion lovers

INGREDIENTS
½ cup onions sliced
¼ cup melted butter
2 tbsp corn oil
3 tbsp flour
½ cup Jamaican Chicken Broth
¼ cup Jamaican beef broth
4 slices Jamaican hard dough bread
¼ cup cheese shredded

PREPARATION
1. Sauté onions in butter and oil until onions are transparent but not well browned.
2. When tender, turn heat to lowest point and sprinkle with flour, stirring vigorously.
3. Pour into large pot and stir in broths and heat thoroughly and divide among 8 oven-proof bowls.
4. Float a slice of bread atop each serving.
5. Mix equal parts of cheese to smooth paste and spread over bread.

APPLETON V/X RUM SOUP
A Jamaican rum lovers dream, it gives the soup recipe a big jolt.

INGREDIENTS
2 cup onion, chopped
1 cup escallion chopped
6 sprigs parsley
2 tsp dried thyme
1 bay leaf
3 tbsp unsalted butter
1 lg ham hock
6 cup beef broth
¼ cup **Jamaican Appleton V/X rum**
½ tsp lemon juice
¼ tsp salt
¼ tsp black pepper

PREPARATION
1. In a sauce pan cook onion, parsley, thyme and bay leaf in the butter over mod-low heat, stirring, for 10 minutes.
2. Add ham hock, broth, 4 cups water, salt and pepper to taste. Bring the mixture to a boil, reduce heat, and simmer uncovered, adding more water if necessary.
3. Discard ham hock and bay leaf. Put the mixture through a medium disk of a food mill into a large bowl and then return it to the kettle.
4. Stir in rum, lemon juice, and salt and pepper to taste. Adjust the consistency with hot water and garnish for serving with the eggs, parsley and lemon slices.

JAMAICAN CHICKEN AND HAM SOUP
A perfect blend between chicken and ham.

INGREDIENTS
1 chicken breast fillet skinned and sliced thinly
1½ cup ham chopped
2 onions chopped
¾ cup Jamaican chicken stock
2 tsp light soy sauce
1 tsp corn flour

PREPARATION
1. Place chicken, ham, onions and stock in a pan. Bring to the boil.
2. Reduce heat and simmer uncovered for 5 minutes.
3. Blend soy sauce with the corn flour and add to the pan stirring constantly until the soup thickens.

CURRIED PUMPKIN SOUP
A popular soup recipe especially among the Indian population in Jamaica

INGREDIENTS
¼ cup melted butter
1 lg onion sliced
¼ tsp nutmeg
¾ cup sliced escallion
½ a medium sized pumpkin chopped
2 cups Jamaican chicken broth
1 bay leaf
½ tsp paprika
½ tsp sugar
¼ tsp curry powder
2 springs parsley
2 cups milk
¼ tsp salt
¼ tsp black pepper

PREPARATION
1. Melt butter in 4 to 6 quart saucepan over medium high heat.
2. Add onion and sauté until soft and golden brown. Stir in pumpkin, stock, bay leaf, sugar, curry powder, nutmeg and parsley.
3. Bring to simmer, then reduce heat and continue simmering uncovered for 15 minutes, stirring occasionally.
4. Transfer soup in batches to blender or food processor and puree.
5. Return to saucepan and add milk, and salt and pepper to taste.
6. Simmer 5 to 10 minutes, but do not allow to boil.
7. To serve hot, ladle into individual bowls. Float dollop of cream on each and sprinkle with paprika.
8. To serve cold, chill soup thoroughly then ladle into individual bowls.
9. Float tomato slice on top, cover with dollop of cream.

PORTLAND SOUP
From the rural hills of Portland, a popular soup recipe in those parts.

INGREDIENTS
1 tsp margarine
1 clove garlic, crushed
½ tsp curry powder
¼ cup mashed yam or sweet potato
1 cup Jamaican chicken broth
½ cup milk
¼ tsp salt
¼ tsp pepper
½ cup escallion chopped
3 sprigs parsley

PREPARATION
1. In small saucepan, melt butter. Add garlic and curry powder and sauté' until garlic is soft.
2. Add yam and broth bringing to boil, stirring constantly.
3. Stir in milk and heat without boiling. Adjust seasonings to taste.
4. Garnish with parsley.

JAMAICAN SOUP BOUILLON
A soup bouillon used by Jamaican cooks and Jamaican chefs.

INGREDIENTS
4 lb lean beef from shank
2 lb beef bone
2 cups cold water
½ cup diced onions
½ cup diced carrots
½ cup diced potatoes
½ cup diced onions
2 whole cloves
1 clove garlic crushed
¼ tsp salt
¼ tsp black pepper

PREPARED
1. Dice meat and crush bone. Add water and cloves. Heat slowly to boiling.
2. Cover and allow to simmer for 5 hours. Season to taste and add vegetables.
3. Simmer for another hour.
4. Cool and remove fat.

WESTMORELAND CARROT & GINGER SOUP
A great soup recipe loved by all in the western region.

INGREDIENTS
1 onion chopped
1 tbsp margarine
1½ lb carrots sliced
1 tsp grated ginger
¼ tsp black pepper
4½ cup light vegetable stock
1 lb otaheite apples chopped
1 tsp Jamaican Appleton V/X rum

PREPARATION
1. Sauté onion in margarine, covered, for 5 minutes without browning.
2. Add the carrots & ginger. Cover and cook a further 10 minutes. Stir occasionally.
3. Add the stock or water and bring to a boil, then simmer gently for 15 min, until the carrots are tender.
4. Puree the soup in a food processor then return soup to the rinsed-out pan.
5. Reheat gently and season to taste with pepper.

BLUE LAGOON FISH CHOWDER
A fish chowder prepared in the Blue Lagoon resort area which has now become a popular choice in the area.

INGREDIENTS
¼ lb small shrimp
½ lb fish filets
¼ lb clams
3 cup fish stock
1 cup orange juice
1 tbsp corn oil
3 cloves garlic, crushed
3 escallions diced
1 potato, peeled & diced
¼ cup stewed, chopped tomatoes
1 sweet pepper, diced
½ tsp basil
2 bay leaves
1 tsp paprika
¼ cup chopped onions
¼ cup chopped escallions
¼ tsp salt
¼ tsp pepper

PREPARATION
1. Heat the oil in a large soup pot. Sauté' the onion and garlic until the onions are translucent.
2. Add all of the other ingredients except the shrimp, clams and the fish.
3. Simmer for 1 hour or until the vegetables are tender.
4. Add the seafood and cook for 7 to 10 minutes at a low boil.

HEARTY CARROT SOUP
A great vegetable soup recipe that is a popular choice with vegetarians

INGREDIENTS
1 lb carrots peeled and sliced
3 cups chicken stock
3 tbsp butter
¼ cup onions chopped
¼ cup escallion chopped
¼ cup sweet pepper chopped
3 tbsp flour
2 cup milk
1½ cup cheese grated
¼ tsp black pepper
¼ tsp scotch bonnet pepper diced
¼ tsp salt to taste
4 sprigs parsley for garnish

PREPARATION
1. Cook carrots in stock until tender. Drain and mash carrots, reserving liquid.
2. Sauté onions and sweet pepper in butter until tender.
3. Add flour, stirring until smooth. Gradually add milk; cook stirring constantly, until slightly thickened.
4. Add enough water to carrot liquid to make 2 cups. Combine liquid, milk mixture, carrots, cheese and spices.
5. Stir constantly over moderate heat until soup is well heated and cheese is melted.
6. Garnish with parsley if desired.

JAMAICAN PAPAYA SOUP
A great mixture of the papaya and the chicken broth.

INGREDIENTS
½ cup chicken broth
½ cup fresh orange juice
1 egg white
1 papaya de-seeded and chopped
1 pinch salt
¼ tsp allspice
¼ tsp cinnamon
¼ cup coconut, grated

PREPARATION
1. Pour cold broth into a pot, sprinkle gelatin over top and set aside to soften for a few minutes.
2. Beat the egg white until frothy. Add egg white to soup mixture and bring to simmer, whisking constantly until soup is frothy.
3. Allow to cool down for about 10 minutes.
4. Mash the papaya and put into a food processor, adding the soup mixture and the orange juice and process to a puree.
5. Season to taste. Refrigerate few hours or better overnight.
6. Adjust seasonings before serving. Garnish with coconut.

KINGSTON CHEESE AND CHICKEN CHOWDER

A great tasting chowder which is an excellent starter or appetizer recipe.

INGREDIENTS

3 cups chicken broth
2 cups diced peeled potatoes
1 cup diced carrots
1 cup diced escallions
½ cup diced onion
1½ teaspoons salt
¼ teaspoon pepper
¼ cup butter`
¼ cup all-purpose flour
2 cup milk
2 cup shredded cheddar cheese
2 cup diced cooked chicken

PREPARATION

1. In a saucepan, bring chicken broth to a boil. Reduce heat; add potatoes, carrots, escallions, onion, salt and pepper.
2. Cover and simmer for 15 minutes or until vegetables are tender.
3. Meanwhile, melt butter in a medium saucepan; add flour and mix well.
4. Gradually stir in milk cook over low heat until slightly thickened.
5. Stir in cheese and cook until melted add to broth along with chicken.
6. Cook and stir over low heat until heated through.

Cooking Tip
Add flavor to Jamaican soup recipes by placing a small scotch bonnet pepper in the soup while simmering. However take great care to choose a green scotch bonnet pepper as the more ripened the pepper the more likely it is to burst open and make the soup inedible due to excessive pepper flavor.

OROCABESSA LEMON SOUP REIPE

A popular soup recipe on the North coast especially in the St. Mary region.

INGREDIENTS

1½ cups vegetable stock
½ cup brown rice
¼ tsp salt & black pepper
2 lemons, juiced, rind grated
2 tbsp escallions chopped
4 thin lemon slices to garnish

PREPARATION

1. Simmer the vegetable stock & rice in a covered pot with salt, pepper & lemon rind for 40 minutes.
2. Place in a blender and puree then return to the pot.
3. Mix in the lemon juice & simmer gently.
4. Cool & skim any fat, chill and serve with garnish.

JAMAICAN CHICKEN AND NOODLE SOUP WITH VEGETABLES
A Jamaican soup recipe which is prime stock for chefs in any restaurant.

INGREDIENTS
5 lb chicken
3 cups water
1 onion chopped
2 whole cloves
1 carrot diced
¼ tsp scotch bonnet pepper diced
½ pack egg noodles
1 cup escallions diced
6 sprigs parsley chopped
2 tbsp salt

PREPARATION
1. Place the whole chicken or the chicken pieces in a heavy 6-quart kettle with the water, onion, cloves, carrot, 1 tablespoon salt, and scotch bonnet pepper.
2. Bring to a boil and skim off any scum that forms on top. Reduce the heat and simmer for 2 hours.
3. Correct the seasoning. If you are using chicken parts, cook until they are tender 45 minutes to 1hour.
4. Remove the chicken, skim excess fat from the broth, and then remove the vegetables.
5. Add the noodles increase the amount if you like a very thick soup and peas, and boil for 5 to 9 minutes or until they are cooked.
6. Serve in heated soup plates or bowls and sprinkle with some chopped parsley.

JAMAICAN PEANUT SOUP RECIPE
The best peanut soup recipe this side of the hemisphere. A favorite among the traveling tourists.

INGREDIENTS
2 tbsp unsalted butter
1 onion, peeled and diced
2 carrots, peeled and diced
8 cup Jamaican Chicken broth
1 cup crunchy peanut butter
½ tsp allspice
½ tsp paprika
1 tomato, quartered
4 potatoes, peeled and cubed
1 green pepper, diced
3 tbsp minced fresh parsley
3 tbsp lemon juice

PREPARATION
1. Melt the butter in a large stockpot over medium heat.
2. When it is hot, add the onion and carrots and cook, stirring constantly, until the onion begins to turn translucent then mx 1 cup of the stock with the peanut butter in a medium-sized bowl until smooth.
3. Add the remaining 7 cups chicken stock to the vegetables. Stir and add the tomato, potatoes, roasted pepper, and 2 tablespoons of the parsley. Pour in the peanut butter mixture, and stir.
4. Cover and bring almost to a boil. Simmer, partially covered, until the potatoes are cooked through.
5. Add the lemon juice, stir, and season to taste with salt.
6. Ladle the peanut soup into warmed soup bowls, garnish with the remaining 1 tablespoon parsley, and serve immediately.

JAMAICAN CHICKEN FOOT SOUP
The chicken foot soup recipe which is the most popular soup recipe in the country.

INGREDIENTS
2 lb chicken feet
2 chicken breast, boned coarsely chopped
¼ cup Jamaican bouillon
2 cups water for boiling
1 small onion chopped
1 garlic cloves minced
2 escallion stalks chopped,
¼ tbsp flour
4 carrots peel and diced
Oil for sauté
Salt and pepper to taste

PREPARATIONS
1. sauté chicken feet in hot oil or butter for a few minutes.
2. Add vegetables and spices sauté a few minutes more.
3. Stir, make onions soft but not browned and cook over low heat for a few minutes do not cover skillet.
4. Boil water add bouillon and allow to dissolve. Throw in the whole mess from the skillet, all meat and vegetables toss in the feet bring to a boil and then simmer until the chicken is cooked and tender.

MANDEVILLE OKRA AND CHICKEN SOUP
Okra is a favorite Jamaican ingredients and loved when blended with chicken

INGREDIENTS
½ cup Jamaican chicken broth
1 lb okra
¼ cup onion chopped
¼ cup sweet pepper chopped
2 tbsp melted butter
2 tomatoes chopped
½ tsp salt and pepper mixed
1 tsp Worcestershire sauce
1 slice ham uncooked

PREPARATION
1. Remove the breast from a raw foul, and with the remaining chicken make a chicken broth.
2. Dice breast in small pieces. Put in vessel with a chopped onion and a chopped green pepper and a small amount of butter.
3. Simmer until the onion is soft, then add the chicken broth, 2 peeled tomatoes, salt and pepper to taste.
4. Boil slowly for ½ hour then add 1 pound of okra cut in pieces ¾ or an inch in length, and cook until the okra is soft.
5. Add 1 teaspoon Worcestershire sauce and slice of ham and serve with chopped parsley.

JAMAICAN COCONUT TOFU SOUP
A popular vegetarian soup recipe laced with Jamaican seasonings.

INGREDIENTS
½ lb tofu
2 cloves garlic, minced
2 tbsp vegetable oil
¼ cup coconut milk
1½ cup vegetable stock
1 tbsp light soy sauce
3 lime leaves
¼ cup grated ginger
1 pinch salt
1 pinch black pepper
1 scotch bonnet peppers stripped seedless

PREPARATION
1. Drain the tofu of extra water by placing a heavy weight over the tofu surrounded by 3 layers of paper towels.
2. Cut tofu into bite size pieces. Stir fry the garlic in the oil until golden, then stir fry the tofu until it is an even golden brown.
3. In a medium size sauce pan mix the coconut milk, stock and soy sauce. Add the tofu, lime leaves and ginger. Cook over low to medium heat for 15 minutes.
4. If the coconut taste is too strong add a little more of the lime leaves to reduce the sweetness of the coconut milk.
5. With the flat of a heavy knife pound one pepper until they are split in several places. Add to the soup, and let cook a couple minutes more.

ST. THOMAS JANGA (CRAWFISH) SOUP
A popular soup in the St. Thomas region.

INGREDIENTS
1 cup cooking oil
2 lg onions diced
4 stalks escallions
4 cloves garlic
2½ cup crawfish tails cooked and peeled
9 cup hot water
5 tsp salt
2 cup flour
¼ sweet pepper diced
5 sprigs of parsley
½ cup crawfish fat
2 tsp scotch bonnet pepper
¼ cup tomato chopped

PREPARATIONS
1. Grind onions, escallion, bell pepper, garlic and parsley. Make roux with oil and flour. Stir constantly until browned. Add ground seasonings.
2. Cook on low fire about. 30 min. Add tomato paste and crawfish fat.
3. Cook about 30 min more. Add hot water and let cook on low fire.
4. Add ground crawfish tails, add salt and pepper.
5. Cook on high fire about. 20 min. Add baked crawfish heads then cok on low fire about 1 hour.
6. More hot water may be added if too thick. Stir carefully.

JAMAICAN CORN CHOWDER
A great chowder using mainly Jamaican corn

INGREDIENTS
2 tbsp butter
3 tbsp chopped onion
2 lg potatoes peeled and diced
1 cup water
2 cups whole corn kernels
¾ cream
1 pinch salt
1 pinch black pepper

PREPARATION
1. Melt butter in soup kettle and sauté onion until limp. Add potatoes and water to kettle, season with salt and pepper, and bring to a boil.
2. Simmer over medium heat until potatoes are tender, about 30-40 minutes. Add corn and cream.
3. Heat, stirring frequently, for ten minutes.

NEGRIL CRAB BISQUE
A great crab bisque prepared by most Negril restaurants. Delicious with every taste.

INGREDIENTS
2 tbsp butter
1 tsp onion, finely chopped
1 tbsp parsley, finely chopped
1½ cup crabmeat, chopped
2 tbsp flour
2 cup Jamaican crab broth
2 cup cream, light
1 pinch black pepper and salt

PREPARATION
1. In a saucepan, melt the butter. Add the onion and cook slowly until golden.
2. Add the crabmeat and parsley and cook over low heat stirring constantly
3. Add the flour, stir to blend and cook for 3 minutes more.
4. Stir in the chicken broth and simmer gently for 20 minutes.
5. Add the cream and black pepper. Heat & add salt to taste.

Cooking Tip
Frozen crab meat can be kept for no longer than 4 months and canned crab should be used within 6 months. Cook raw crabs within 24 hours after the crab dies. Crabs are actually best cooked when they are alive, dead crabs are very toxic.

JAMAICAN CRAB AND LOBSTER GUMBO SOUP
A perfect mixture of crab and lobster meat with Jamaican spices

INGREDIENTS
1 lb crabmeat cooked
1 lb lobster meat cooked
1 onion; chopped
1 lg talk escallion chopped
1 clove garlic finely chopped
¼ cup margarine
6 tomatoes chopped
1 pack okra
1 bay leaf
2 tsp Salt
1 tsp Sugar
½ tsp Whole thyme
¼ tsp allspice
¼ tsp black pepper
3 cup cooked rice

PREPARATION
1. In a soup pot, cook onion, escallion and garlic in margarine until tender.
2. Add tomatoes, okra and seasonings. Cover and simmer for 1 hour or until okra is soft.
3. Add crabmeat and lobster meat and season with allspice, black pepper, thyme, sugar and heat through.

PORT ROYAL FISH TEA
This is one pf the most popular Jamaican soup recipes. Actually a fish broth but with loads of spices and fish meat.

INGREDIENTS
4 tbsp vegetable oil
1 chopped onion
3 cloves garlic, minced
¼ cup raw shrimp peeled and de-veined
4 cup peeled and chopped tomatoes
½ cup finely chopped carrots
¼ cup finely chopped escallion
1 tsp salt
½ tsp paprika
½ tsp diced scotch bonnet pepper
4 bay leaves
2 peeled green bananas chopped
2 ½ cups water
1 lb fillet fish

PREPARATION
1. Sauté onion, garlic, vegetable oil in heavy pan until golden.
2. Add shrimp, tomatoes, carrots, escallion, bananas, water and spices.
3. Simmer for about 1 hour. Add fish then let come to a boil till fish flakes with a fork.
4. Serve with buttered bread or garlic bread

JAMAICAN CUCUMBER SOUP
A great mixture of Jamaican cucumber and Jamaican spices.

INGREDIENTS
1 cucumber peeled and chopped
2 cup Jamaican chicken broth
1½ cup milk
1 tbsp lemon juice
½ tsp curry powder
¼ tsp salt
¼ tsp black pepper
1 carrot cut into sticks

PREPARATION
1. Dice cucumber. Put all ingredients in blender. Blend till smooth.
2. Store in refrigerator several hours or overnight.
3. Garnish each serving with cucumber slice and chopped chive.
4. Serve with carrot sticks.

KINGSTON DIET SOUP
A perfect diet recipe for many Jamaicans

INGREDIENTS
1 garlic cloves minced
1 onions chopped
3 stalks escallion
½ scotch bonnet pepper diced
5 tomatoes, stewed
½ cup Jamaican bouillon
1 tbsp garlic powder
1 tsp paprika
2 bay leaves
½ cup cheese grated

PREPARATION
1. Get a large stew pot and sauté garlic, onion, escallion and pepper.
2. Add remaining ingredients except cheese, bring to a boil, then reduce heat and simmer about 20 minutes.
3. Add about 1 tbsp of crumbled cheese to each serving.

ST. MARY CHICKEN POT SOUP
A great leftover chicken soup recipe perfect for a Monday dinner recipe.

INGREDIENTS
2 cups cubed chicken breast meat
½ cup mixed vegetables cooked
1 cup Jamaican baked potato soup
1 cup Jamaican chicken broth
2 cups milk
1 cup cubed potato

PREPARATION
1. In a medium saucepan, combine chicken, mixed vegetables, both soup recipes and milk.
2. Heat through, over medium high heat and serve with crumbled crackers on top.

SPANISH TOWN TOMATO SOUP

A great soup recipe served up by a top chef in Spanish town. The most delicious soup you will not find in the old capital.

INGREDIENTS

6 tomatoes chopped
1 onion chopped
3 stalks escallion chopped
2 cup Chicken broth
1 tbsp tomato paste or ketchup
½ tsp allspice
¼ tsp black pepper
¼ tsp diced scotch bonnet pepper
½ tsp salt
½ cup flavored yogurt

PREPARATION

1. Cut tomatoes into wedges and place in 1½ quart saucepan with all ingredients except yogurt.
2. Simmer uncovered 30 minutes. Strain to remove tomato skins and seeds.
3. Adjust seasonings.
4. Garnish with spoonfuls of yogurt.

KINGSTON COLD CHICKEN SOUP

Jamaicans love hot food but occasionally our chefs make a delicious cold chicken soup recipe

INGREDIENTS

2 lbs Chicken legs
2 lg onions, peeled
1 lg carrot, peeled
1 tsp black pepper
¼ tsp salt
1½ cup water
2 stalks escallion chopped
3 tbsp vegetable oil
5 cloves garlic, peeled

PREPARATION

1. Remove skin and fat from the chicken legs and place them in a saucepan with one of the onions, the carrot, the peppercorns and a salt.
2. Cover with the water, bring to the boil and simmer for 40-45 minutes.
3. Chop up the remaining onion and the escallion and put them to soften in the vegetable oil in a heavy, covered pan.
4. When they are soft and the chicken is cooked through, strain nearly all the stock from round the chicken over the onion and escallion and continue simmering for another 15-20 minutes.
5. Strip the chicken meat from the bones and cover it with one spoonful or so of stock to keep it moist.
6. Discard the bones and the carrot and the whole onion from the stock.
7. In a large mortar crush the garlic with a little salt. Pound in the chicken meat, which should be quite soft. Then bind in this mixture with the yoghurt, season it with pepper, liquidize the escallion soup and stir the chicken mixture in.

COLD PAPAYA SOUP
The pawpaw or papaya is a popular Jamaican fruit and though used in salads also makes a great soup recipe.

INGREDIENTS
1 ripe papaya, about 6" long
2 tbsp sugar, to taste
1 tbsp lime juice, to taste

PREPARATION
1. Peel the papaya & cut in half.
2. Spoon out the seeds & keep them in a small container in the refrigerator.
3. Cut the papaya into chunks & reduce to a liquid puree in the food processor.
4. Add the sugar & lime juice. If the puree is too thick, stir in a little water, but be very careful that you do not add too much water or you will lose the consistency.
5. Serve in fruit cups with a dab of the reserved seeds in the centre of each serving.

JAMAICAN COLD SWEET AND SOUR SOUP
A sweet and sour blended recipe to die for, carefully put together by Chinese cooks in Jamaica

INGREDIENTS
3 tbsp vegetable oil
1 large onion, chopped
1 large head cabbage, chopped
4 tomatoes chopped
1½ cup water
3¼ tbsp lemon juice
4 tbsp honey
3¼ tbsp orange juice
½ cup tofu balls

PREPARATIONS
1. Heat oil & sauté onions till translucent. Add cabbage & sauté 5 minutes more. Add tomatoes, water, lemon juice, honey & simmer for 15 to 20 minutes.
2. Season with salt & pepper & remove from heat. Pour soup into food processor & puree to a smooth consistency. Refrigerate for 6 to 8 hours then blend soup with orange juice.

ST. ELIZABETH COLD MELON SOUP
The watermelon is not known for its soup qualities but the St. Elizabeth chefs have made it a specialty

INGREDIENTS
3 cups chopped cantaloupe
3 cups chopped water melons
2 cups orange juice
3 tbsp honey
½ tsp Appleton V/X Rum
1 cup whipping cream

PREPARATION
1. Finely chop 1½ cups each of cantaloupe and melons.
2. Set aside and place remaining coarsely chopped melons in blender with orange juice, lime juice and honey and puree.
3. Pour into large bowl stir in V/X rum and reserved melon.
4. Cover and refrigerate until ready to serve.

JAMAICAN FRUIT SOUP II
A sweet blend of Jamaican fruits to a tasty cold soup recipe.

INGREDIENTS
10 garden cherries
2 cups Jamaican chicken broth
1¼ cup boiling water
½ cup pineapple juice
2 tbsp sugar
½ cup sour cream

PREPARATIONS
1. Pour cherries and juice into the container of a blender and blend until smooth.
2. In a large heat-resistant, non-metallic bowl, combine chicken bouillon, water, pineapple juice and sugar; stir until dissolved.
3. Chill several hours or overnight.
4. Serve garnished with a dollop of sour cream.

SPICY JAMAICAN TOMATO SOUP
A very spicy version to the rather mild Jamaican tomato soup recipe

INGREDIENTS
1½ cups ripe tomatoes chopped
1 garlic clove chopped
½ cup chicken or vegetable broth
½ tsp cinnamon
¼ tsp allspice
¼ tsp diced scotch bonnet pepper
¼ tsp salt
¼ tsp black pepper
2 tbsp lemon juice

PREPARATION
1. Fill a large pot with water and bring to a boil. Core each tomato and cut a small "x" in the skin on the opposite end.
2. Lower 2 or 3 tomatoes into the boiling water and let blanch for 15 to 20 seconds or until the skins start to peel. Immediately transfer the tomatoes to a large bowl of iced water.
3. Blanch the remaining tomatoes in the same manner. Peel each tomato by pulling the skins off with a paring knife. Cut each tomato in half crosswise and squeeze out the seeds. Coarsely chop the seeded tomatoes.
4. In a blender or food processor puree the garlic clove and the chopped tomatoes. Add the broth, cinnamon, salt, pepper, and 1 tablespoon lime juice, continuing to puree until smooth.
5. Pour the soup into a metal bowl, set the bowl in a bowl of iced water, and stir the soup occasionally until it is very cold. Serve

OCHO RIOS JUNE PLUM SOUP
The June plum is known mainly for juices but the Ocho Rios Chefs have made it into a great soup recipe.

INGREDIENTS
1 cup June plums
1 cup water
¼ cup sugar
1 tsp cinnamon
¼ tsp black pepper
1 pinch salt
1 cup sour cream
½ cup heavy cream
¼ cup Appleton V/X rum
1 tbsp cornstarch
2 tbsp lemon juice
1 tsp grated lemon rind
3 tbsp brandy

PREPARATION
1. Pit and chop plums, combine with water and sugar in a saucepan.
2. Add cinnamon, salt and pepper and bring to a boil, reduce heat, simmer 5 minutes stirring occasionally.
3. Mix wine and heavy cream with cornstarch, add to mixture and cook until thickened.
4. Stir in lemon juice, rind and rum and remove from heat.
5. Place ½ cup soup in small bowl, whisk in sour cream.
6. Add brandy and stir mix back into the soup pan until smooth.
7. Chill at least 4 hours.

BRACO MACARONI VEGETABLE SOUP
A hearty soup recipe prepared by the chefs from the stables of Braco.

INGREDIENTS
4 cups hot water
1½ cups tomato juice
1 head cauliflower
2 carrots
¾ cup macaroni elbows
1 cup Jamaican soup bullion
½ tsp. hot pepper sauce
1 cup cooked red peas
¼ cup grated cheese

PREPARATION
1. Put all ingredients except pepper sauce, red peas and cheese in a 4-5 quart saucepot over high heat.
2. Stir to blend, cover and bring to a slow boil. Uncover, reduce heat and simmer 8 minutes or until macaroni is tender.
3. Stir in pepper sauce and red peas; simmer 2 minutes until heated through.
4. If cheese is used, sprinkle on top of soup just before serving.
5. Serve with toasted whole wheat bread or cornmeal muffin.

MAY PEN EGG SOUP

This recipe was picked up from a young cook in a restaurant from May Pen, Clarendon.

INGREDIENTS

1 cup Jamaican chicken broth
¼ tsp salt
¼ tsp black pepper
1cup callaloo chopped
3 eggs beaten
¼ cup grated cheese

PREPARATION

1. Bring the chicken stock to a boil and season lightly with salt and pepper.
2. Stir in the callaloo and cook until wilted. Add the eggs with a bit more black pepper stirring constantly.
3. Beat in the grated cheese and continue to stir constantly.
4. Let simmer for at least 10—15 minutes more then serve.

EASTER DRIED BREAD SOUP

A favorite around Easter time served up by some good folks from Cave hill, Westmoreland.

INGREDIENTS

2 cups of hard dough bread **cut in chunks**
3 cups Jamaican soup bullion
¼ tsp salt
¼ tsp black pepper
2 tbsp. vegetable oil
¼ cup grated cheese

PREPARATION

1. Brown the bread chunks on a skillet or on a grill.
2. Heat the broth to an active simmer in a soup pot.
3. Stir in the grilled bread chunks.
4. Cook slowly and steadily, anywhere from 10 to 20 minutes, until the soup is thick and soft, but the bread chunks still have shape and integrity.
5. Turn the bread in the broth frequently and add vegetable oil to give flavor.
6. Sprinkle grated cheese and serve.

JAMAICAN CONCH BROTH

A sweet conch broth used by the fishermen of Portland where both the Bussu and Conch are staple diets.

INGREDIENTS

2 cups conch meat
2 cup water, boiling
3 tbsp vegetable oil
1 tsp fish seasoning
½ cup escallions chopped
½ cup onions chopped
1 tbsp vegetable broth
½ cup chopped tomatoes
½ tsp allspice
¼ tsp garlic powder

PREPARATION

1. While water is boiling stir ingredients together and strain broth and serve without any solids.

RED HILLS PAN MAN BEEFY VEGETABLE SOUP
We got this recipe from Chris, the famous jerk chicken chef in Kingston.

INGREDIENTS
2 tbsp vegetable oil
1½ cups minced beef
1 lg onion chopped
1 clove garlic minced
3 tomatoes chopped
2½ cups Jamaican beef broth
1 cup water
½ tsp salt
¼ tsp black pepper
½ cup cubed potatoes uncooked
¼ cup chopped escallion
½ cup noodles
¼ cup finely shredded cheese

PREPARATION
1. In large soup pot, heat oil. Add beef and cook over medium heat, stirring often to crumble the meat.
2. As meat browns, stir in onion; cook until onion is soft. Stir in garlic and escallions.
3. Add tomatoes and their liquid, beef broth, the water, salt, pepper and potatoes.
4. Bring to a boil, cover, reduce heat, and simmer for 45 minutes to an hour.
5. Add noodles and let simmer for 15 more minutes.
6. Serve garnished with shredded cheese.

JAMAICAN BEEF BROTH
A great beef broth recipe suitable as a base for any beef soup recipe.

INGREDIENTS
3 lb meaty beef bones
1½ cups carrot diced
¼ tsp garlic powder
½ cup onion chopped
2 stalks escallion chopped
1 cup tomatoes, crushed
1 cup water
¼ tsp salt (**optional**)

PREPARATION
1. Preheat oven to 450ºF and place bones in an open roasting pan in a single layer.
2. Place carrots atop bones and roast, uncovered, until meat and bones are browned.
3. Place bones and carrots in a soup pot and add water to roasting pan and stir to dissolve browned bits.
4. Add liquid from roasting pan to mixture in soup pot.
5. Add onions, escallions and tomatoes.
6. Add enough water to cover bones.
7. Bring to a boil, cover, reduce heat, and simmer for 5 hours.
8. Strain broth discarding **ALL** solids, and return to soup pot.
9. Boil gently, uncovered and allow to sit for at least an hour.
10. Remove any fat to the surface and serve.

JAMAICAN PORK BROTH
A great pork broth recipe suitable as a base for any pork soup recipe.

INGREDIENTS
3 lb meaty pork (**HAM**) bones
1½ cups carrot diced
½ cup onion chopped
¼ tsp garlic powder
2 stalks escallion chopped
1 cup tomatoes, crushed
1 cup water
¼ tsp salt (**optional**)

PREPARATION
1. Preheat oven to 450ºF and place bones in an open roasting pan in a single layer.
2. Place carrots atop bones and roast, uncovered, until meat and bones are browned.
3. Place bones and carrots in a soup pot and add water to roasting pan and stir to dissolve browned bits.
4. Add liquid from roasting pan to mixture in soup pot.
5. Add onions, escallions and tomatoes.
6. Add enough water to cover bones.
7. Bring to a boil, cover, reduce heat, and simmer for 5 hours.
8. Strain broth discarding **ALL** solids, and return to soup pot.
9. Boil gently, uncovered and allow to sit for at least an hour.
10. Remove any fat to the surface and serve.

> **Cooking Tip**
> Salt in soup is optional if you are using either salted beef or salted pork. However take care not to use the meat without boiling it to remove excess salt from the meat.

JAMAICAN CRAB BROTH
A sweet crab broth used by the fishermen of Negril Point.

INGREDIENTS
2 cups crab meat
2 cup water, boiling
3 tbsp vegetable oil
1 tsp fish seasoning
¼ tsp garlic powder
½ cup escallions chopped
½ cup onions chopped
1 tbsp vegetable broth
½ cup chopped tomatoes
½ tsp allspice
Onion salt to taste

PREPARATION
1. While water is boiling stir ingredients together.
2. Strain broth and serve without any solids.

JAMAICAN SHRIMP BROTH
A sweet shrimp broth used mainly in the parish of St. Elizabeth.

INGREDIENTS
2 cups shrimp peeled and de-veined
2 cup water, boiling
3 tbsp vegetable oil
1 tsp fish seasoning
½ cup escallions chopped
½ cup onions chopped
1 tbsp vegetable broth
½ cup chopped tomatoes
½ tsp allspice

PREPARATION
1. While water is boiling stir ingredients together.
2. Strain broth and serve without any solids.

JAMAICAN LOBSTER BROTH
Lobster broth is a must have for any lobster soup recipe, it give the recipe the required flavor.

INGREDIENTS
2 cups lobster meat
2 cup water, boiling
3 tbsp vegetable oil
1 tsp fish seasoning
½ cup escallions chopped
½ cup onions chopped
1 tbsp vegetable broth
½ cup chopped tomatoes
½ tsp allspice

PREPARATION
1. While water is boiling stir ingredients together.
2. Strain broth and serve without any solids.

Cooking Tip
Marinate the meat or seafood in your favorite marinade before serving it at the table. Plus when serving a combination of meat and vegetables or tofu, cook the meat first to flavor the broth more quickly.

jamaican chicken
soup.©

QUALITY SINCE 1922

Grace

LA QUALITÉ DEPUIS 1922

Cock

Soup Mix / Mélange à soupe de

Coq

SPICY
PIMENTÉ

CANADA
62

43 g

QUALITY SEAL
GRACE KENNEDY
SCEAU DE QUALITÉ

ST. ELIZABETH CREAM SOUP
A St. Bless classic soup recipe.

INGREDIENTS
1 cup red peas
5 cups water
2 cups soup meat cubed
1 cup salt beef cubed
2 cups cubed potatoes
2 slices of pumpkin
2 tbsp thyme leaves
3 stalks escallion chopped
1 scotch bonnet pepper diced
½ cup onion diced
1 cup Jamaican chicken broth
1 tbsp. butter
½ cup coconut milk
¼ tsp salt

PREPARATION
1. Soak salt beef overnight to remove excess salt.
2. Place soup meat, salt beef with peas in a pot with water and bring to the boil then skim off the scum.
3. Add one tablespoon of thyme, escallion, cubed potatoes and pumpkin then reduce to a simmer and cook for approximately 1½ hours
4. Strain the soup after peas and tubers are soft and discard all solids then return to soup pot.
5. Add coconut milk and remainder of seasoning and salt to taste.
6. Bring the soup to a simmer and if necessary adjust consistency.

ANCHOVY BREADFRUIT SOUP
This breadfruit soup is a popular in a little district outside Montego called Anchovy.

INGREDIENTS
1½ cups Jamaican beef broth
1½ cups Jamaican vegetable broth
2 cups roasted breadfruit in ¼ inch cubes.
¼ cup tomato juice
1½ carrots diced
1 onion diced
2 stalks escallion chopped
¼ cup diced green peppers
4 tbsp margarine
¼ tsp black pepper
½ tsp salt

PREPARATION
1. Melt 4 tablespoons margarine in skillet. Add the chopped green peppers, carrots, escallions and onion.
2. Sauté on low heat until vegetables are softened and onion browned lightly.
3. Mix the broth and add sauté vegetables in a large, soup pot with lid.
4. Add to this the breadfruit cubes and cover and simmer for about 45 minutes or until all the vegetables are done and mashed out and then add the salt and pepper.
5. Remove about 2 cups of the mixture and put into blender.
6. Puree this mixture and return to pot with rest of soup.
7. Turn off heat and cover soup.

TRELAWNY POTATO HAM SOUP
A favorite soup recipe in this parish, its one of the most loved recipes that you can think of in Jamaica

INGREDIENTS
1 cup potatoes, diced
¼ cup onion diced
½ cup escallion diced
¼ tsp black pepper
½ tsp salt
2 cups water
3 tbsp melted butter
1½ tbsp flour
2 cups milk
1 cup cooked ham diced

PREPARATION
1. Combine first six ingredients.
2. Simmer until vegetables are tender. Combine flour and melted butter.
3. Add butter, milk and diced ham to vegetables.
4. Heat just to boiling.
5. Set aside and allow flavors to blend.

PORT MARIA BANANA SOUP
Banana is almost the staple of St. Mary and Portland, their banana soup is excellent.

INGREDIENTS
1½ cups Jamaican chicken broth
1½ cups Jamaican vegetable broth
3 cups green bananas in ¼ inch cubes.
¼ cup tomato juice
1½ carrots diced
1 onion diced
2 stalks escallion chopped
¼ cup diced green peppers
4 tbsp margarine
¼ tsp black pepper
½ tsp salt

PREPARATION
1. Melt 4 tablespoons margarine in skillet. Add the chopped green peppers, carrots, escallions and onion.
2. Sauté on low heat until vegetables are softened and onion browned lightly.
3. Mix the broth and add sauté vegetables in a large, soup pot with lid.
4. Add to this the banana cubes.
5. Cover and simmer for about 45 minutes or until all the vegetables are done and mashed out.
6. Add the salt and pepper.
7. Remove about 2 cups of the mixture and put into blender.
8. Puree this mixture and return to pot with rest of soup.
9. Turn off heat and cover soup.

JAMAICAN ACKEE SOUP
A great ackee recipe that has found favor with many chefs and cooks.

INGREDIENTS
1½ cup boiled ackees or ½ can ackees
4 tomatoes chopped
½ cup chopped sweet pepper
1 cup Jamaican vegetable broth
½ tsp salt
¼ tsp black pepper
¼ cup onion diced
¼ cup escallion chopped

PREPARATIONS
1. Add seasonings and okra to vegetable stock and bring to boil and simmer until tender.
2. Season with salt and black pepper.
3. Serve hot.

RUNAWAY BAY PLANTAIN AND BEEF SOUP
We got this recipe from one of our top chefs in Runaway Bay, St. Ann.

INGREDIENTS
2 tbsp vegetable oil
1½ cups minced beef
1 lg onion chopped
1 clove garlic minced
3 tomatoes chopped
2½ cups Jamaican beef broth
1 cup water
½ tsp salt
¼ tsp black pepper
2 cups cubed ripe plantain uncooked
¼ cup chopped escallion
½ cup noodles
¼ cup finely shredded cheese

PREPARATION
1. In large soup pot, heat oil. Add beef and cook over medium heat, stirring often to crumble the meat.
2. As meat browns, stir in onion; cook until onion is soft. Stir in garlic and escallions.
3. Add tomatoes and their liquid, beef broth, the water, salt, pepper and ripe plantains.
4. Bring to a boil, cover, reduce heat, and simmer for 45 minutes to an hour.
5. Add noodles and let simmer for 15 more minutes.
6. Serve garnished with shredded cheese.

Cooking Tip
When bananas and plantain in soup recipes cook these separately then add them to the recipe when it is soon finished. This will prevent the bananas and the plantain from being mashed in the soup making it very thick.

JAMAICAN OKRA SOUP
The traditional Jamaican Okra soup.

INGREDIENTS
12 small okras chopped
4 tomatoes chopped
½ cup chopped sweet pepper
1 cup Jamaican vegetable broth
½ tsp salt
¼ tsp black pepper
¼ cup onion diced
¼ cup escallion chopped

PREPARATIONS
1. Add seasonings and okra to vegetable stock and bring to boil and simmer until tender.
2. Season with salt and black pepper.
3. Serve hot.

DARLISTON CHOCHO CREAM SOUP
A great cream soup recipe made from the chocho vegetable.

INGREDIENTS
5 cups water
1 tbsp vegetable oil
1 cup cooked chicken breast cubed
3 cups cubed chocho
½ slice of pumpkin
1 tbsp thyme leaves
3 stalks escallion chopped
1 scotch bonnet pepper diced
½ cup onion diced
½ cup Jamaican chicken broth
1 tbsp. butter
½ cup coconut milk
¼ tsp salt

PREPARATION
1. Place chicken breast and vegetable oil in a pot with water and bring to the boil.
2. Add thyme, escallion, cubed chocho and pumpkin then reduce to a simmer and cook for approximately 1½ hours.
3. Strain the soup vegetables are soft and discard all solids then return to soup pot.
4. Add coconut milk and remainder of seasoning and salt to taste.
5. Bring the soup to a simmer and if necessary adjust consistency.

Cooking Tip
Don't over cook other vegetables as this will make the soup very thick as the vegetables will mash out when stirring.

NEW KINGSTON CALLALOO SOUP
A great soup recipe made from the leafy vegetable the callaloo.

INGREDIENTS
1 small bunch callaloo chopped
8 cups water
1 slice salt pork
1 slice salt beef
¼ tsp black pepper
1 lg onion diced
1 stalk escallion diced
1 slice yam(**optional**)

PREPARATION
1. Soak both salt beef and salt pork in water overnight to remove excessive salty taste.
2. Bring 3 cups of water to boil and place chopped callaloo in.
3. Discard this water and bring other 5 cups of water to boil and place already boiled callaloo in.
4. Add salt beef and salt pork and allow to boil out.
5. Add yam and black pepper to taste.
6. Bring the soup to a simmer and if necessary adjust consistency.

MANCHESTER PUMPKIN AND SHRIMP SOUP
A pumpkin and shrimp soup that's popular in Manchester.

INGREDIENTS
1 cup cooking oil
2 lg onions diced
4 stalks escallions
4 cloves garlic
2½ cup shrimp peeled and de-veined
9 cup hot water
5 tsp salt
2 cup flour
¼ sweet pepper diced
5 sprigs of parsley
4 cups uncooked diced pumpkin
2 tsp scotch bonnet pepper
¼ cup tomato chopped

PREPARATIONS
1. Grind onions, escallion, bell pepper, garlic and parsley. Make roux with oil and flour. Stir constantly until browned. Add ground seasonings.
2. Cook on low fire about. 30 min. Add tomato paste and shrimp.
3. Cook about 30 min more. Add hot water and let cook on low fire.
4. Add pumpkin cubes salt and pepper.
5. Cook on high fire about. 20 min then simmer for about 1 hour.

JAMAICAN TURKEY SOUP
A popular recipe as a thanksgiving turkey leftover recipe.

INGREDIENTS
2 cups left over roasted turkey meat cut in cubes
1½ cup ham chopped
2 onions chopped
¾ cup Jamaican chicken stock
2 tsp light soy sauce
1 tsp corn flour

PREPARATION
1. Place turkey, ham, onions and stock in a pan. Bring to the boil.
2. Reduce heat and simmer uncovered for 5 minutes.
3. Blend soy sauce with the corn flour and add to the pan stirring constantly until the soup thickens

JAMAICAN GUNGO PEAS SOUP
Like the red peas the Jamaican gungo peas can be used not just as a side dish but as a soup recipe.

INGREDIENTS
1½ cups Jamaican vegetable broth
2 cups water
1 cup shelled gungo peas
1 cup cubed beef steak
¼ cup cubed salted beef
½ cup sweet potatoes cut in ¼ inch cubes.
½ cup yellow yam cut in ¼ inch cubes.
¼ cup tomato juice
1½ carrots diced
¼ tbsp dried thyme leaves
1 onion diced
2 stalks escallion chopped
¼ cup diced green peppers
4 tbsp margarine
¼ tsp black pepper
½ tsp salt

PREPARATION
1. Soak salt beef in water overnight to remove excessive.
2. Sauté on low heat until seasonings are browned lightly.
3. Mix the broth and add sauté vegetables in a large, soup pot with lid.
4. Add the meat, yams, sweet potatoes and gungo peas and cover and simmer for about 45 minutes or until all the meat and vegetables are cooked.
5. Add the salt and pepper.
6. Remove about 2 cups of the mixture and put into blender.
7. Puree this mixture and return to pot with rest of soup.
8. Turn off heat and cover soup.

YAM HILL SOFT YAM SOUP

Yams are a great tuber full of starch and absolutely delicious in this soup recipe from Yam Hill.

INGREDIENTS

1½ cups Jamaican vegetable broth
2 cups roasted soft yams cut in ¼ inch cubes.
¼ cup tomato juice
1½ carrots diced
1 onion diced
2 stalks escallion chopped
¼ cup diced green peppers
4 tbsp margarine
¼ tsp black pepper
½ tsp salt

PREPARATION

1. Melt 4 tablespoons margarine in skillet. Add the chopped green peppers, carrots, escallions and onion.
2. Sauté on low heat until vegetables are softened and onion browned lightly.
3. Mix the broth and add sauté vegetables in a large, soup pot with lid.
4. Add to this the soft yam cubes and cover and simmer for about 45 minutes or until all the vegetables are done and mashed out.
5. Add the salt and pepper.
6. Remove about 2 cups of the mixture and put into blender.
7. Puree this mixture and return to pot with rest of soup.
8. Turn off heat and cover soup.

JAMAICAN PEPPERPOT SOUP

Undoubtedly the most popular Jamaican soup recipe there is try it today.

INGREDIENTS

1½ cup callaloo chopped
6 okras chopped
1½ cup cooked chopped yam
½ cup boiled green bananas
5 cups water
1 scotch bonnet pepper diced
½ cup coconut milk
1 cup chopped salted beef
1 pigs tail chopped
½ cup shrimp peeled and de-veined
1 green pepper diced
1 clove garlic diced
2 stalks escallion diced

PREPARATION

1. Soak salted beef and pigs tail in water to remove excess salt.
2. Put beef and pigs tail in boiling water and cook for at least 2 hours.
3. Wash and cut up callaloo then add to cooked meats.
4. When callaloo is cooked remove and place in blender and puree and return to stock.
5. Add ochroes, yam, bananas, green pepper and garlic and simmer for 45 minutes.
6. Add escallions, scotch bonnet pepper, shrimp and coconut milk and cook for 15 more minutes.
7. Serve hot with garlic bread.

IRONSHORE DUCK SOUP
Duck is not a popular poultry in Jamaica but the chefs in Ironshore have come up with a sweet duck soup.

INGREDIENTS
1 cup duck breast skinned and sliced thinly
1½ cup ham chopped
2 onions chopped
¾ cup Jamaican chicken stock
2 tsp light soy sauce
¼ cup tomato juice
½ cup carrots diced
1 tbsp flour
2 stalks escallion chopped
¼ cup diced green peppers
¼ tsp black pepper
½ tsp salt

PREPARATION
1. Place chicken, ham, onions and stock in a pan. Bring to the boil.
2. Reduce heat and simmer uncovered for 5 minutes.
3. Puree all other ingredients in a blender and add to the pan stirring constantly until the soup thickens.

> **Cooking Tip**
> Duck meat takes a while to become tender cook it first then add it to the soup when it begins to become soft, some flavor might be lost but the flavor will be regained with the chicken stock.

HELLSHIRE LOBSTER BISQUE
Lobster is pretty expensive but if you can swim you can catch a few and make this great recipe.

INGREDIENTS
2 tbsp butter
1 tsp onion, finely chopped
1 tbsp parsley, finely chopped
1½ cup lobster meat, chopped
2 tbsp flour
2 cup Jamaican lobster broth
2 cup cream, light
1 pinch black pepper and salt

PREPARATION
1. In a saucepan, melt the butter. Add the onion and cook slowly until golden.
2. Add the lobster meat and parsley and cook over low heat stirring constantly
3. Add the flour, stir to blend and cook for 3 minutes more.
4. Stir in the lobster broth and simmer gently for 20 minutes.
5. Add the cream and black pepper. Heat & add salt to taste.

LINSTEAD GREEN PEAS SOUP

A Nestle worker in Linstead who cooks in his restaurant in his spare time contributed this tasty soup recipe.

INGREDIENTS

1½ cups Jamaican chicken broth
1 cup of green peas shelled
¼ cup tomato juice
1 onion diced
½ cup carrots diced
1 tbsp flour
2 stalks escallion chopped
¼ cup diced green peppers
4 tbsp margarine
¼ tsp black pepper
½ tsp salt

PREPARATION

1. Put all ingredients in blender and puree until smooth.
2. Heat in a soup pot until flour is cooked and vegetables are soft.

RASTAMAN TWO BEAN SOUP

The Rastafarian religion speaks to a vegetarian diet our Rasta recipe contributor gave us this great recipe.

INGREDIENTS

1½ cups Jamaican vegetable broth
2 cups water
½ cup shelled broad beans
1 cup shelled gungo peas
½ cup sweet potatoes cut in ¼ inch cubes.
½ cup yellow yam cut in ¼ inch cubes.
¼ cup tomato juice
1½ carrots diced
¼ tbsp dried thyme leaves
1 onion diced
2 stalks escallion chopped
¼ cup diced green peppers
4 tbsp margarine
¼ tsp black pepper

PREPARATION

1. Sauté on low heat until seasonings are browned lightly.
2. Mix the broth and add sauté vegetables in a large, soup pot with lid.
3. Add the yams, sweet potatoes, broad beans and gungo peas and cover and simmer for about 45 minutes or until all the vegetables are cooked.
4. Remove about 2 cups of the mixture and put into blender.
5. Puree this mixture and return to pot with rest of soup.
6. Simmer for another hour.

BLACK RIVER SHRIMP BISQUE
An earshot from Middle Quarters in St. Elizabeth, a great recipe using the abundant shrimp.

INGREDIENTS
2 tbsp butter
1 tsp onion, finely chopped
1 tbsp parsley, finely chopped
1½ cup shrimp meat, chopped
2 tbsp flour
2 cup Jamaican shrimp broth
2 cup cream, light
1 pinch black pepper and salt

PREPARATION
1. In a saucepan, melt the butter. Add the onion and cook slowly until golden.
2. Add the shrimp meat and parsley and cook over low heat stirring constantly
3. Add the flour, stir to blend and cook for 3 minutes more.
4. Stir in the shrimp broth and simmer gently for 20 minutes.
5. Add the cream and black pepper. Heat & add salt to taste.

PORTLAND CONCH SOUP
The conch and bussu are similar and are found in abundance in Portland and make a great soup recipe.

INGREDIENTS
1¼ lb small conch
½ lb fish fillets
2 cup Port Royal fish tea
1 tbsp vegetable oil
½ tsp scotch bonnet pepper diced
3 cloves garlic, crushed
¼ cup stewed, chopped tomatoes
1 sweet pepper, diced
¼ tsp allspice
1 tsp paprika
¼ cup chopped onions
¼ cup chopped escallions
¼ tsp salt
¼ tsp pepper

PREPARATION
1. Heat the oil in a large soup pot. Sauté the onion, garlic, escallions, fillet fish and conch until cooked.
2. Place all of the other ingredients in a blender and puree.
3. Add puree mixture to conch and seasonings and simmer for 1 hour.
4. Taste and serve.

JAMAICAN SECRET SOUP

Another popular soup recipe called the secret soup.

INGREDIENTS

2 tbsp butter
1 onion, finely chopped
1 tbsp parsley, finely chopped
2 tbsp flour
1½ cup Jamaican vegetable broth
2 cup cream, light
1 pinch black pepper and salt
1 cup crushed tomato
2 tbsp Appleton V/X Rum

PREPARATION

1. Place all ingredients in a blender and puree.
2. Remove and place over fire and bring to boil, then simmer for just an hour.
3. Serve with onion or garlic bread.

ITAL STEW SOUP

This is an ital stew soup recipe.

INGREDIENTS

2 tbsp butter
1 cup sweet potato chopped
1 onion, finely chopped
1 tbsp parsley, finely chopped
2 tbsp flour
1½ cup Jamaican vegetable broth
2 cup cream, light
1 pinch black pepper
1 cup crushed tomato
½ tsp dried thyme leaves

PREPARATION

1. Place all ingredients except sweet potato in a blender and puree.
2. Remove and place over fire and bring to boil add sweet potatoes then simmer for just an hour.
3. Serve with onion or garlic bread.

Jamaican
Chicken
And
Poultry
Recipes.

jamaican fried
chicken. ©

PLAIN JAMAICAN JERK CHICKEN
Great Jamaican jerk chicken recipe for home.

INGREDIENTS
4 Leg quarters chicken
1 broiler/fryer type
2 tbsp Jamaican hot pepper sauce
1 tsp salt and black pepper
½ tsp cinnamon
½ tsp allspice
¼ cup onion, minced
2 tbsp sugar
2 tbsp pepper, red, minced
2 tbsp Jamaican hot pepper jelly
¼ cup escallion chopped
1 cup rice, cooked

PREPARATION
1. In a shallow container, place the hot pepper sauce.
2. Add chicken, one piece at a time, turning to coat.
3. Sprinkle salt, cinnamon and allspice over the chicken.
4. Place the chicken, skin side up, in a single layer in a large shallow baking dish.
5. Bake at 400 F, basting twice with pan juices for 45 minutes or until the chicken is fork tender.
6. Arrange the rice and chicken on a serving platter.

OCHO RIOS STYLE BAKED CHICKEN
A common recipe in restaurants in this resort town.

INGREDIENTS
1 tbsp. brown sugar
1 tbsp. butter
6 tbsp. melted butter
¼ tsp allspice
¼ tsp garlic powder
¼ tsp onion powder
2 tsp. salt
¼ cup escallion chopped
1 tsp. black pepper
1 lg quartered chicken

PREPARATION
1. Remove giblets and sprinkle the quartered chicken with Jamaican pepper.
2. In a blender, puree the garlic powder, allspice, onion powder, escallion, salt and water to make marinate.
3. Pour marinate over the chicken and marinate, refrigerated for 2 hours (or overnight).
4. Preheat oven to 500'. Place quartered chicken in a large greased baking pan. Baste with the melted butter and bake for 15 minutes.
5. Turn the chicken and continue to bake another 15 minutes basting frequently. Lower temperature to 375', turn the chicken again and bake for 10 minutes.

OLD HARBOR BARBEQUE CHICKEN WINGS

A great barbeque recipe made popular by the cooks and chefs from Old Harbor.

INGREDIENTS
1 onion chopped
½ cup scallions chopped
2 garlic cloves
½ tsp thyme crumbled
1½ tsps salt
1½ tsps ground allspice (pimento)
¼ tsp nutmeg grated
½ tsp cinnamon
¼ cup scotch bonnet pepper minced
1 tsp black pepper
1 cup Jamaican barbeque sauce
2 tbsp soy sauce
¼ cup vegetable oil
15 chicken wings trimmed

PREPARATION
1. Pre pare the marinade by placing all the ingredients in a food processor or blender and puree.
2. In a large shallow dish arrange the wings in one layer and spoon the marinade over them, rubbing it in.
3. Let them marinate, covered & chilled, turning them once and leave them overnight.
4. Arrange the wings in one layer on an oiled rack set over a foil-lined roasting pan, spoon the marinade over them and bake in the upper third of a preheated 450F oven, 30-35 minutes or until they are cooked through.

KINGSTON BROILED CHICKEN

A sweet recipe for the health conscious that hate the oily foods.

INGREDIENTS
2 broiling chickens
1 tbsp allspice
¼ tsp salt
¼ tsp black pepper
½ cup vegetable oil
¼ cup chopped parsley
1 clove garlic finely chopped
¼ cup melted butter

PREPARATION
1. Split chickens down the back.
2. In a blender, puree the all ingredients except melted butter to make marinate.
3. Pour marinate over the chicken and marinate, refrigerate for 2 hours (or overnight).
4. Drain off marinade and discard. Preheat broiler.
5. Then place chickens in and broil for 50 minutes basting with the melted butter every 15 minutes.
6. Turn the chicken and continue to bake another 15 minutes basting frequently. Remove and serve hot.

> **Cooking Tip**
> Jerk chicken can be prepared in several ways. It does not actually require grilling, the chicken can be prepared by seasoning with a good jerk seasoning then while baking or broiling being basted with a good Jerk marinade. This is the essence of Jamaican jerk recipes by using seasonings to soak into the meat and by basting the blend of jerk ingredients is effectively captured in the meal.

LONG BAY FRICASSEED CHICKEN

A great tasting Jamaican recipe, the best tasting version of this recipe we found was all the way in Long Bay.

INGREDIENTS

4 quarters chicken chopped in serving portions
¼ cup flour
½ cup diced carrots
½ cup diced potatoes
¼ tsp salt
¼ tsp paprika
¼ cup vegetable oil
2 tbsp Jamaican hot pepper sauce
3 cups water
½ tsp allspice
¼ cup onion, minced
2 tbsp sugar
¼ cup soy sauce
¼ cup escallion chopped

PREPARATION

1. Dip chicken in flour and brown in vegetable oil.
2. Place all other ingredients except carrots and potatoes and puree in blender.
3. Add puree and carrots and potatoes to browned chicken and cook until vegetables are soft.
4. Ensure that sauce does not dry out.
5. Remove and serve hot.

> **Cooking Tip**
> Vegetables can be cooked and provided as a side dish rather than being cooked in the fricassee recipe.

ST. THOMAS PEANUT CHICKEN

A perfect blend between peanut and chicken perfected by the cooks in St. Thomas

INGREDIENTS

1 cup de-boned chicken breast cubed
3 sweet peppers chopped
¼ cup minced garlic
½ tbsp diced scotch bonnet pepper
1 cup raw peanuts crushed
½ cup onion chopped
¼ cup vegetable oil
¼ tsp salt
¼ tsp black pepper

PREPARATION

1. Debone the chicken breast. Slice the centre to make an opening.
2. Marinate with one sweet pepper, garlic, onion and scotch bonnet pepper.
3. Stuff chicken with crushed peanuts and tie.
4. Pre-heat grill then grill chicken breast.
5. Serve hot.

SPANISH TOWN BROWN STEW CHICKEN
A great brown stewed chicken recipe delicious with every bite.

INGREDIENTS
1 quartered chicken cut in serving portions
4 cups water
1 tbsp allspice
¼ tsp salt
¼ tsp black pepper
½ cup vegetable oil
½ cup carrots diced
½ cup potatoes diced
¼ cup chocho diced (**optional**)
¼ cup diced ripe plantains
¼ cup escallions chopped
¼ cup onions chopped
1 clove garlic finely chopped
¼ cup melted butter

PREPARATION
1. Place all ingredients except vegetables in a blender and puree until smooth.
2. Place in a sauce pan and bring to slight boil.
3. Add chicken and vegetables to mixture.
4. Stew until cooked and serve hot.

Cooking Tip
Brown stewed chicken and fricassee chicken recipes are similar however the major difference is that brown stewed involves less browning of the chicken and more stewing.

KINGSTON CHICKEN WITH CURRY POWDER
A popular Jamaican chicken recipe in Kingston blended with curry powder.

INGREDEIENTS
2 tbsps. vegetable oil
2 garlic cloves, finely chopped
1 tsp. curry powder
¾ cup chicken breast cubed,
¼ cup onion, chopped
½ cup potato diced
½ cup water
2 tbsps. Jamaican fish sauce
¼ cup grated ginger
¼ cup coconut milk

PREPARATION
1. In a frying pan, heat the oil and fry the garlic until golden brown.
2. Add the curry powder, stir to mix thoroughly, and cook for 1 minute.
3. Add the chicken and stir well to coat the meat in the curry mixture.
4. Add the onion, potato and a quarter-cup stock, and stir-fry over medium heat until the potato cooked.
5. Stir in the fish sauce, ginger and coconut milk, and simmer gently until the sauce thickens.
6. Turn into a bowl and serve.

JAMAICAN ORANGE CHICKEN DRUMETTES
A great chicken recipe which uses chicken wing drums blended with Jamaican orange.

INGREDIENTS
24 chicken drumettes
1 tsp. salt (optional)
1 tsp. black pepper
3 tbsps. brown sugar
1 tbsp. cornstarch
1 tsp. ground ginger
½ cup orange juice
¼ cup orange marmalade
1 tbsp. lemon juice
4 orange slices (optional)

PREPARATION
1. Remove and discard skin from drumettes; rinse wings with cold running water, pat dry.
2. Season with salt and pepper and place in a saucepan and combine remaining ingredients.
3. Simmer over medium heat until sugar dissolves and ingredients blend; remove from heat and allow to cool.
4. In large food-storage bag or large glass bowl, combine chicken and sauce; cover and marinate in refrigerator for at least 2 hours, turning occasionally.
5. Heat oven to 350ºF. Grease large baking pan; arrange drumettes in single layer.
6. Bake, basting with any leftover marinade, until cooked through and crisp, about 45 minutes.
7. Garnish with orange slices.

Cooking Tip
Chicken drumsticks refer to chicken legs while a chicken drumette is the short piece of the chicken wing that is really attached to the wing. Chicken drumettes are used mainly for Jamaican appetizer recipes such as Jerk Chicken wings or as a tasty morsel for a snack. The advantage is that chicken drumettes take a much shorter time to prepare.

SAV-LA-MAR SPECIAL SAUCED CHICKEN
A great recipe made with chicken marinated in a special sauce contributed by the cooks of Sav-la-mar.

INGREDIENTS
4 skinless, boneless chicken breast halves
½ cup Jamaican Wincarnis wine (or substitute)
1 tsp. dried thyme
1 cup Sav Special Sauce
1 cup shredded cheese

PREPARATION
1. Place chicken in a bowl and pour wine over chicken, add ½ cup Sav Special Sauce then sprinkle with thyme.
2. Cover dish and refrigerate to marinate for 2 hours.
3. Preheat oven to broil.
4. Remove chicken from dish or bowl, discarding remaining marinade, and broil until cooked through basting with remaining Sav Sauce.
5. Remove and sprinkle with cheese.
6. Serve hot.

MANDEVILLE CALYPSO CHICKEN
A great tasting recipe fully of spices an rum.

INGREDIENTS
2 tbsps. vegetable oil
2 garlic cloves, finely chopped
1 tsp. curry powder
¾ cup chicken breast cubed,
¼ cup onion, chopped
3 red sweet peppers chopped
3 cups water
½ cup chicken stock
1 cup white rice
1 tbsp Appleton V/X rum
¼ cup coconut milk

PREPARATION
1. In a frying pan, heat the oil and sauté the chicken until golden brown.
2. Remove chicken and add rice and stir in other ingredients.
3. Add chicken atop the rice cover and simmer.
4. When rice is cooked remove top and let simmer for a few more minutes.
5. Serve hot.

MAY PEN JERK-BUFFALO CHICKEN WINGS
A great Jamaican chicken wing recipe using both the traditional buffalo sauce and the jerk sauce.

INGREDIENTS
4 lb chicken wings
¼ tsp salt
¼ tsp black pepper
3 cups vegetable oil
4 tbs. butter
3 tbsp. Jamaican Jerk sauce
1 tbsp. cane vinegar
¼ cup cream cheese
4 stalks escallion chopped

PREPARATION
1. Season wings with salt and pepper.
2. Heat oil to 400 degrees in a deep fryer.
3. Add half of the chicken to the pan and cook until golden brown.
4. Then drain on paper towels. Repeat with the second half.
5. In a separate pan, melt the butter and add jerk sauce and vinegar.
6. Toss the wings in a bowl with the sauce.
7. Serve with a good bottled blue cheese dressing and celery sticks.

ST. THOMAS COCONUT CHICKEN
A great chicken in coconut shells with that special coconut blend.

INGREDIENTS
4 lb chicken de-boned
¼ tsp salt
¼ tsp black pepper
3 cups vegetable oil
4 tbs. butter
1 garlic clove chopped
½ cup sweet pepper diced
4 stalks escallion chopped
4 small coconuts

PREPARATION
1. Drain water from coconuts and open leaving meat inside.
2. Sauté chicken with seasonings until light brown.
3. Remove and place in coconut shells evenly and tie to cover
4. Place shells in 1 inch high water in basting pan and bake at 375 Degrees for 40 minutes
5. Remove allow to cool and serve.

NEGRIL STUFFED GRILLED CHICKEN
A great stuffed grill chicken recipe made popular by the cooks in Negril

INGREDIENTS
2 sweet peppers, roasted, seeded and peeled
6 boneless chicken breast halves with skin intact
2 tbsp vegetable oil
¼ cup garlic minced
¼ tsp salt
¼ lb smoked sausage chopped
½ cup vegetable oil for the grill
¼ cup lime juice

PREPARATION
1. Cut roasted sweet peppers into ½ inch strips.
2. Reserve and refrigerate peppers and any juices.
3. Marinate skin of chicken with vegetable oil and garlic.
4. Season chicken flesh with salt.
5. Cut each sausage in half and stuff the chicken with the sausages.
6. Spread roasted peppers over surface of chicken.
7. Tie the chicken with kitchen string and prepare grill for indirect-heat method of cooking.
8. Place chicken on lightly oiled grill rack directly over the coals searing on all sides
9. While grilling marinate with lime juice until prepared.
10. Serve hot.

SPANISH TOWN FRIED CHICKEN
A great fried chicken coated with seasoned bread crumbs. Delicious with every bite.

INGREDIENTS
6 de-boned chicken breasts
½ cup all-purpose flour
2 eggs, beaten
¾ cup dry breadcrumbs
1½ cup grated cheese
1 tbsp. vegetable oil
2 tbsps. butter
2 tbsps. all-purpose flour
1¼ cups milk
1 tsp. salt
¼ tsp. garlic powder
¼ tsp. onion powder
¼ tsp. allspice
¼ cup Jamaican tomato sauce

PREPARATION
1. Pat chicken dry and pound to flatten slightly.
2. Dust chicken lightly with flour and dip into egg.
3. Combine breadcrumbs with garlic powder, onion powder and allspice and ½ cup cheese.
4. After dipping in egg dip chicken in breadcrumb mixture.
5. Line a 9" x 13" baking dish with foil, brush with vegetable oil and arrange chicken in the dish in a single layer.
6. Bake in a preheated 400º F oven for 20 minutes.
7. In a saucepan, melt butter and whisk in 2 tbsps. Flour and cook without browning.
8. Add milk and bring to boil then add salt and pepper and tomato sauce.
9. Reduce heat. Cook for 5 minutes, stirring often.
10. Garnish each piece of chicken and sprinkle with grated cheese.
11. Bake for 15 minutes longer.

DOWN TOWN CHICKEN
A great chicken recipe served by a top restaurant in downtown Kingston.

INGREDIENTS
¼ cup vegetable oil
8 chicken thighs de-boned skin removed
¼ cup onion, chopped
2 cloves garlic minced
¼ tsp salt
¼ tsp black pepper
1 tbsp. Jamaican sweet chicken sauce
¼ tsp allspice
4 fresh basil leaves,
½ tbsp crushed scotch bonnet pepper
1 cup cooked white rice

PREPARATION
1. Heat oil in frying pan and add chicken and cook until browned.
2. Add onion and garlic and cook 2 minutes then add sweet chicken sauce, basil and pepper.
3. Heat to a boil and cover and cook over low heat until done.
4. Serve over rice.

SPICY TANGERINE CHICKEN

This is a stir-fried recipe that's loved by all who have tried it and one of our favorite recipes in this category.

INGREDIENTS

1 egg white
1 tbsp. Jamaican rice wine
1 tbsp. cornstarch
3 cups boneless skinned chicken breast, cut into 1/2-inch cubes
½ cup escallions
2 tbsps. minced ginger
2 tbsps. minced garlic
1 tbsp. grated tangerine
½ tsp. scotch bonnet pepper diced
½ cup chicken stock
2 tbsps. soy sauce
2 tbsps. cane vinegar
2 tbsps. sugar
3 tbsps. peanut oil
1 tbsp. cornstarch
¼ cup escallion chopped

PREPARATION

1. In a small bowl, combine egg white, rice wine and cornstarch and whisk until well mixed.
2. Pour marinade over chicken pieces and refrigerate at least 8 hours.
3. In a small bowl, combine escallion, ginger, garlic, tangerine and scotch bonnet pepper and set aside.
4. In another small bowl, combine stock, soy sauce, vinegar and sugar.
5. Stir to dissolve sugar and set aside.
6. 4. Preheat frying pan over high heat and when oil is hot add chicken and stir-fry until partially cooked.
7. Remove chicken clean frying pan and re-heat with oil.
8. Add onion-garlic-ginger mixture and stir-fry over medium-high heat until fragrant.
9. Add chicken-stock mixture and simmer, stirring frequently, until heated through.
10. Add chicken and cook until white and firm.
11. Reduce heat to low. Mix in cornstarch mixture and stir until sauce has a glossy finish.
12. Serve hot.

SPICY GINGER FLAVORED CHICKEN DRUMSTICKS
A great ginger flavored chicken recipe prepared to perfection.

INGREDIENTS
6 lg chicken drums
½ cup onion diced
2 onions sliced
1½ tsp. peeled and grated ginger
¼ tsp salt
½ cup egg white beaten
1 cup dried bread crumbs
¼ tsp black pepper
¼ tsp garlic powder
¼ tsp allspice
¼ cup minced escallion
4 cups cold water

PREPARATION
1. Combine the breadcrumbs with garlic powder and allspice and set aside.
2. Dip drumsticks in egg and in breadcrumbs and brown in frying pan.
3. Combine chicken, diced onion, ginger, salt, half the prunes and the water in a large pan.
4. Cover and simmer gently over low heat.
5. Turn the chicken periodically and stir occasionally.
6. Cook for 1 hour then arrange the sliced onions on top of the chicken pieces around the chicken.
7. Continue to cook uncovered on low heat for 30 minutes.
8. Add small amounts of water to make the sauce thick.
9. When the chicken is cooked, the prunes are soft and the stock is thick, adjust the seasoning. Serve hot.

PAPINE WHOLE GRILLED LEMON CHICKEN
This recipe was contributed by our own in-house chef made popular in the Papine area of Kingston

INGREDIENTS
1 whole chicken
½ cup lemon juice
1 tbsp minced garlic
½ cup diced lemon rind
¼ tbsp salt
¼ tbsp black pepper
3 tbsp vegetable oil
vegetable oil for grill
1 cup of cane vinegar

PREPARATION
1. Wash chicken thoroughly with cane vinegar and lemon juice and pat dry. Juice lemons.
2. Dice the lemon rind and make basting by combining half of the diced rind with garlic, salt and pepper, lemon juice and olive oil.
3. Rub into chicken inside and out reserve remainder.
4. Stuff chicken cavity with remaining diced rind.
5. Place chicken on oiled grill directly over heat source to sear on all sides
6. Move chicken over drip pan, breast side up. Close lid.
7. Cook 1 to 1½ hours, basting occasionally with reserved basting mixture.
8. Test chicken to see if ready remove and carve.

OCHO RIOS SAUTÉED CHICKEN BREAST SANDWICHES
A great sautéed chicken recipe made in seasoned chicken sandwiches

INGREDIENTS
3 skinless, boneless chicken breast halves pounded
¼ tsp black pepper
¼ tsp salt
1 tbsp. vegetable oil
6 slices Jamaican garlic bread
2 tbsp. mayonnaise
¼ cup creamed cheese
¼ cup chopped escallion
12 slices tomato
12 raw onion rings
½ cup Jamaican tomato sauce

PREPARATION
1. Sprinkle pepper and salt on one side of each chicken cutlet.
2. Heat oil in a large frying pan then add chicken, pepper-side-down.
3. Sauté chicken until cooked through and juices run clear.
4. In a small bowl combine the mayonnaise and cheese.
5. Mix together and spread mixture on garlic bread.
6. Place 1 chicken cutlet on each of these slices, then add onion rings and tomato slices and 1 tbsp tomato sauce.
7. Top each with another bread slice and hold with toothpick

BASIL'S CHICKEN RECIPE
A pundits dream this chicken recipe was contributed by Basil which uses a lot of basil seasonings.

INGREDIENTS
2 tbsp peanut oil
5 cloves garlic, chopped
10 de-boned chicken thighs cut into cubes
½ tbsp scotch bonnet pepper diced
¼ cup escallion chopped
1 tsp. sugar
1 tbsp. Jamaican sweet chicken sauce
2 tbsp. Jamaican chicken stock
1 cup basil leaves

PREPARATION
1. Pre-heat frying pan until hot then add oil.
2. Add garlic and cook until lightly browned then add chicken in small batches and stir-fry until it feels firm to the touch.
3. Add scotch bonnet pepper, escallions, sugar, sweet chicken sauce, and chicken stock.
4. Stir-fry until sauce thickens then add basil leaves and toss until leaves wilt.
5. Remove leaves and serve hot.

HIP STRIP ROAST CHICKEN
A great roast chicken recipe prepared by chefs on the Montego Bay hip strip.

INGREDIENTS
1 roasting chicken
1 tbsp vegetable oil
2 tsp. salt
1 tsp black pepper
1 tbsp thyme
½ tbsp allspice
¼ cup escallion diced
2 garlic cloves, lightly smashed
1 large lime
½ cup onion diced

PREPARATION
1. Sprinkle the chicken evenly inside and out with salt and pepper and allow to stand.
2. Preheat the oven to 350ºF and place a small piece of foil just large enough to cover the chicken's breast in a roasting pan coating it with oil and set aside.
3. Stuff the herbs and the garlic into the cavity of the chicken.
4. Prick the lemon about 25 times with a skewer and stuff it into the cavity.
5. Pin the neck and hind cavities closed and place the chicken breast down over the oiled piece of foil in the roasting pan.
6. Roast for 15 minutes and turn the bird breast up and carefully peel off the foil taking care not to rip the skin; discard.
7. Roast 20 minutes longer, then increase the oven temperature to 400 degrees.
8. Roast the chicken 20 to 25 minutes longer, until the skin is brown and crisp and the juices run clear when the leg is pricked with a kitchen fork.
9. Remove the toothpick from the hind end. Lift the chicken with two wooden spoons and tilt it slightly so the juices run out of the cavity into the pan and discard.
10. Place the chicken on a platter and keep warm.
11. Carve the chicken pour any juices that have collected on the plate.
12. Serve dry with any Jamaican sauce recipe of your choice.

CHICKEN CHOP SUEY JAMAICAN STYLE
A traditional Chinese recipe with Jamaican spices

INGREDIENTS
1 lb. deboned chicken breast
2 lbs. cabbage
1 lb. pak choy
1 lg carrot diced
1 medium onion chopped
1 Scotch Bonnet pepper diced
1 large sweet pepper diced
¼ tsp salt
¼ tsp black pepper
2 tbsps. soy sauce
2 tbsps. vegetable oil
¼ cup cane vinegar
1 stalk escallion diced

PREPARATION
1. Wash and cut chicken breast in small strips.
2. Season to taste with salt and pepper and let marinate.
3. Wash and cut vegetables
4. In large pot, add vegetable oil and cook chicken until tender.
5. Add vegetables, stir constantly for about three minutes.
6. Add soy sauce and simmer for two minutes.
7. Serve hot.

SPICY GARLIC CHICKEN STIR FRY
A special treat for garlic lovers with this great chicken recipe

INGREDIENTS
2 tbsp peanut oil
6 cloves garlic, minced
1 tsp. grated fresh ginger
¼ cup escallions chopped
1 tsp. salt
1 lb. de-boned chicken breasts, cut into strips
¼ cup minced onions
1 cup sliced cabbage
1 sweet pepper, thinly sliced
1 cup Jamaican chicken broth
2 tbsp. soy sauce
2 tbsp. white sugar
2 tbsp. corn starch

PREPARATION
1. Heat peanut oil in frying pan and quickly stir in 2 cloves minced garlic, ginger root, escallions and salt.
2. Stir fry until onion becomes translucent, about 2 minutes. Add chicken and stir until opaque.
3. Add remaining 4 cloves minced garlic and stir.
4. Add cabbage, sweet pepper and ½ cup of the broth and cover.
5. In a small bowl, mix the remaining ½ cup broth, soy sauce, sugar and cornstarch.
6. Add sauce mixture to frying pan and stir until chicken and vegetables are coated with the thickened sauce.
7. Serve hot.

JAMAICAN CORN STEWED CHICKEN
A special blend of Jamaican creamed style corn and spices.

INGREDIENTS
3 cups Jamaican chicken stock
1 can creamed corn
2 cups cubed chicken breast
3 tbsps vegetable oil
1 carrot diced
½ cup diced onions
1 stalk escallion diced
1 egg beaten
½ tsp. MSG (**optional**)
3 tbsps. water
1 tbsp flour
¼ tsp salt
¼ tsp black pepper
¼ tsp allspice
3 sprigs parsley

PREPARATION
1. Heat frying pan then add vegetable oil and fry cubed chicken breasts and set aside.
2. Bring chicken stock to a boil, add creamed corn, carrot, onions and escallions. And return to a boil to create a stew.
3. In a small bowl, blend water and flour. Slowly add flour mixture to stew, stirring constantly, until it reaches desired thickness then add cubed chicken breasts and egg.
4. Allow to simmer for 45 minutes.
5. Remove from heat and garnish with parsley.
6. Serve with white rice.

STARWBERRY HILLS GARLIC CHICKEN
A great chicken stock recipe with braised pak choy perfected with Jamaican spices

INGREDIENTS
½ cup dried thyme (**optional**)
¼ cup vegetable oil, for stir-frying
5 cloves garlic minced
½ cup diced carrot
1 tbsp. minced ginger
1 lb. pak choy
¼ cup escallions diced
¼ cup onions diced
1 cup chicken stock
1 tbsp. soy sauce

PREPARATION
1. Heat a frying pan and add a tablespoon of oil and stir-fry garlic and carrot until lightly browned.
2. Add ginger; stir-fry until fragrant then remove and reserve stir-fried ingredients.
3. Add a little more oil to the pot; stir-fry pak choy and escallions.
4. Add stock, soy sauce and thyme.
5. Reduce heat to medium-low, bring vegetables to a simmer
6. Cook, covered, 15 to 20 minutes, until carrots and garlic are tender.
7. Serve hot

MONTEGO BAY CHICKEN PIZZA
A great pizza recipe using Jamaican jerked chicken as a topping.

INGREDIENTS
1 cup Jamaican tomato sauce
1 tbsp. Jamaican hot pepper sauce
1 tbsp. cinnamon
1 tbsp. vegetable oil
2 cups Jamaican jerk chicken cubed
1 lg sweet pepper
½ lg onion sliced
1 tbsp. soy sauce
1 10-oz. package instant pizza dough
4 cups cheese, shredded

PREPARATION
1. Preheat oven to 425 degrees.
2. Spray 9 x 13" baking pan with vegetable cooking spray. Set aside.
3. In small bowl, stir together tomato sauce, pepper hot sauce. Set aside.
4. In large non-stick skillet over medium heat, heat oil just until it ripples, about 1 minute.
5. Add chicken, sweet pepper and onion to skillet and cook in hot oil, stirring frequently.
6. Add soy sauce to skillet and heat 1 minute longer. Remove from heat and set aside.
7. Press pizza dough into baking pan, covering bottom and about 1½ inch of the sides.
8. Spread tomato sauce mixture evenly over dough.
9. Distribute drained chicken/vegetable mixture over sauce.
10. Sprinkle shredded cheese evenly over pizza.
11. Bake 20 minutes or until crust is brown and cheese is melted.
12. Remove and slice into servings

Cooking Tip
Using thyme in Jamaican chicken recipes is best used when cooking down and not so much as a meat seasoning. The thyme should be placed as a whole stalk in the recipe and then removed before serving. This captures the entire thyme flavor.

REGGAE AND SOCA CHICKEN STEW
A great recipe that gets its name because of the spicy herbs used.

INGREDIENTS
1 lb. skinless, boneless chicken, cut into approximately 2½ inch strips
½ cup diced onion
½ cup vegetable oil
½ cup escallion minced
3 lg cloves garlic, minced
1½ cups milk
1 tbsp. cornstarch
1 cup Jamaican chicken broth
2 tbsp. allspice
¼ tsp. curry powder
2 tbsp sour cream

PREPARATION
1. Spray large frying pan with vegetable cooking spray and place over medium heat.
2. Add chicken, onion, escallions, and garlic to skillet and cook over medium heat until onions slightly brown.
3. Stir together milk and cornstarch. Add milk mixture, chicken broth, allspice and curry powder to skillet.
4. Increase heat to medium-high. Stir until sauce begins to thicken and chicken is no longer pink in centre.
5. Add sour cream product and heat
6. Serve over rice.

> **Cooking Tip**
> Prepare Jamaican pizza recipe as a normal pizza recipe you must add seasonings and jerk chicken when baking and not before. However to really catch the flavor some seasonings such as allspice can be used in the dough.

MANCHESTER ORATANIQUE CHICKEN
A popular recipe using the Ortanique to flavor the chicken.

INGREDIENTS
¼ cup Jamaican ortanique marmalade
2 tbsps soy sauce
1 (4-lb.) chicken rinsed and dried
1 tbsp salt
1 tbsp pepper

PREPARATION
1. Preheat the oven to 450 degrees. In a small bowl, mix the marmalade with the soy sauce.
2. Set the ortanique glaze aside.
3. Season the cavity of the chicken liberally with salt and pepper.
4. Carefully loosen the skin by running your fingers under the skin of the breast and legs, separating it gently from the meat underneath without tearing it.
5. Spoon half the ortanique glaze under the skin of the breast and legs.
6. Place the chicken, breast-side down, on a rack set above a rimmed sheet pan or baking dish and roast for 15 minutes.
7. Brush the outside of the chicken with some of the ortanique glaze and roast for 10 minutes longer.
8. Turn the chicken breast-side up. Roast for another 30 to 35 minutes basting with more of the ortanique glaze every 7 minutes
9. Remove and allow to stand before carving.

YHALLAS GRAPEFRUIT CHICKEN
A really authentic Jamaican chicken recipe.

INGREDIENTS
¼ cup Jamaican grapefruit marmalade
2 tbsps soy sauce
1 (4-lb.) chicken rinsed and dried
1 tbsp salt
1 tbsp pepper

PREPARATION
1. Preheat the oven to 450 degrees. In a small bowl, mix the marmalade with the soy sauce.
2. Set the grapefruit glaze aside.
3. Season the cavity of the chicken liberally with salt and pepper.
4. Carefully loosen the skin by running your fingers under the skin of the breast and legs, separating it gently from the meat underneath without tearing it.
5. Spoon half the grapefruit glaze under the skin of the breast and legs.
6. Place the chicken, breast-side down, on a rack set above a rimmed sheet pan or baking dish and roast for 15 minutes.
7. Brush the outside of the chicken with some of the grapefruit glaze and roast for 10 minutes longer.
8. Turn the chicken breast-side up. Roast for another 30 to 35 minutes basting with more of the grapefruit glaze every 7 minutes
9. Remove and allow to stand before carving.

DORREN'S SWEET CHICKEN
Doreen's 5 star chicken recipe we are sure you will ensure.

INGREDIENTS
1 lb. chicken breasts
3 tbsps. Soya sauce
2 cloves garlic, chopped
3 tbsps. corn oil
1 tsp. salt
1 onion, chopped
1 tsp. black pepper
1 cup tomato ketchup
1 cup red peas, cooked
1 tbsp. allspice
2 stalks escallion, chopped
1 tsp. sugar
½ tbsp scotch bonnet pepper diced

PREPARATION
1. Remove skin and bone from chicken breasts. Cut meat into strips.
2. Season with Soya sauce, garlic, salt and black pepper. Heat oil and stir-fry chicken breasts until done.
3. Add cooked red peas with liquid, tomato ketchup, onion, escallion, allspice, sugar and scotch bonnet pepper.
4. Simmer for 5 minutes.
5. Serve hot.

Cooking Tip
Citrus based chicken recipes are best prepared when using the juice of the citrus fruit in the cooking down of the chicken meat. Some of the fruit is self can be used but only as a garnish and not for flavoring. If you use the fruit it can mash out and confuse the guest as to exactly what they are eating. Remember a recipe is better when spices are tasted and not seen.

JAMAICAN CHICKEN IN OTAHEITE APPLE SAUCE
If you love sweet chicken recipes then this will tantalize your taste buds.

INGREDIENTS
2 chicken breasts, de-boned
1 tsp. garlic powder
1 tsp. chicken spice
¼ tsp salt
¼ tsp black pepper
¼ cup diced callaloo
1 egg white
1 cup otaheite apple, shredded
¼ cup vinegar
2 onions, chopped
½ cup sugar
3 tbsp. Jamaican wincarnis wine (**or substitute**)
2 tsp. cornstarch
1 tbsp. vegetable oil
1 cup chicken stock

PREPARATION
1. In a saucepan sauté chopped onion in oil. Remove and set aside.
2. Add remaining ingredients except cornstarch and wine and bring to a boil.
3. Dissolve cornstarch in wine and add to saucepan then stir until thicken, simmer for 5 minutes.
4. Stir in sauté onion and set aside.
5. Season chicken breast with garlic powder, chicken spice, salt and pepper and allow to marinate.
6. Bring water to a boil with salt to taste, blanch callaloo leaves and set aside.
7. Remove seasoned chicken breast from refrigerator, flatten with a mallet. Brush with egg white, place one callaloo leaf on each breast.
8. Roll breast to form a log. Rap tightly in plastic and marinate for hour.
9. Bring 3 cups of chicken stock to a boil. Remove chicken from refrigerator and poach in stock until cooked.
10. Remove slice and serve with apple sauce.

SANTA CRUZ GRILLED CHICKEN IN BRINE
Commonly called Santa chicken not because Santa Clause but for the chefs who contributed this recipe from Santa Cruz in St. Elizabeth.

INGREDIENTS
1 whole chicken
1 gallon ice cold water
¼ tbsp salt
¼ tbsp brown sugar
¼ cup lemon juice
¼ cup lime juice
1 tbsp minced garlic

PREPARATION
1. Add all ingredient together to make brine.
2. In a big pot, soak chicken in brine, breast side down.
3. Cover pot and leave overnight in a cool dark place.
4. Heat grill to 350F and place chicken on grill for an hour
5. Remove from grill when done, and let sit for a few minutes before carving.

JAMAICAN POACHED CHICKEN
Not a very popular Jamaican recipe but delicious nonetheless.

INGREDIENTS
1 whole chicken washed and trimmed
1 cup carrots, coarsely chopped
1 cup cubed potatoes
5 cups water
¼ cup escallion chopped
¼ cup onion chopped
¼ tsp salt
¼ tsp black pepper
1 cup Jamaican sweet sauce

PREPARATION
1. Place chicken in stockpot with vegetables and sweet sauce.
2. Add cold water to cover. With pot partially covered, bring slowly to a boil.
3. Reduce heat to medium-low and simmer gently, covered, until chicken is just tender.
4. Remove chicken from pot; set aside until cool enough to handle.
5. Strain broth and save for another use.
6. Remove meat in large pieces.
7. Serve hot.

PORT ANTONIO JELLY CHICKEN
Jelly chicken is a cold recipe that is expertly made by the cooks and chefs in Port Antonio.

INGREDIENTS
1 deboned chicken
2 cups water
½ cup powdered gelatin
1 tbsp. Worcestershire sauce
¼ tsp salt
¼ tsp black pepper
2 eggs boiled

PREPARATION
1. Cover chicken with cold water and bring to boil.
2. Simmer gently until tender and remove chicken, them boil quickly.
3. Stir in gelatin, sauce and salt and pepper to taste.
4. Strain and allow to cool.
5. Shred meat well and then add eggs to mixture.
6. Turn into a mould and chill.
7. Serve cold.

FALMOUTH CHICKEN BALLS IN HONEY SAUCE
A great honey and chicken recipe from our contributors from Falmouth, Trelawny

INGREDIENTS
1 cup chicken mince
1 egg white
1 tbsp very cold water
½ tsp salt
1 tbsp soy sauce
1 tsp black pepper
2 tsps vegetable oil
½ cup escallions finely chopped
1 tsp corn flour
1 tsp sugar
¼ cup garlic, finely chopped
½ cup honey
¼ cup water
2 scotch bonnet peppers diced

PREPARATION
1. Mixed the chicken in a blender or food processor for a few seconds.
2. Slowly add the add the egg white and cold water and mix until fully incorporated into the meat.
3. Add the other ingredients and mix until the meat mixture has become a light paste.
4. Form the mixture into balls.
5. Put the chicken balls on a rack in a frying pan with simmering hot water.
6. Cover and steam the chicken balls for about 15 minutes.
7. Heat the honey and water with the peppers bringing them to a boil.
8. Put the steamed chicken balls on a platter and pour the spicy honey sauce over them and serve.

FLAT BRIDGE CHICKEN WITH MANGO SAUCE RECIPE
A mouth watering Jamaican recipe special for Jamaican mango lovers.

INGREDIENTS
1 tbsp. brown sugar
1 tbsp. butter
¾ cup chopped fresh mango
1½ cups mango nectar juice
6 tbsp. melted butter
¼ cup water
2 tsp. salt
1 clove garlic chopped
1 tsp. black pepper
1 lg quartered chicken

PREPARATION
1. Remove giblets and sprinkle the quartered chicken with Jamaican pepper.
2. In a blender, puree the garlic, salt and water. Pour over the chicken and marinate, refrigerated for 2 hours.
3. To make mango sauce, puree the nectar and mangos and In a small frying pan melt butter, add mango puree and brown sugar and stir. When the mixture boils, remove from heat and set aside.
4. Preheat oven to 500'. Place quartered chicken in a large greased baking pan. Baste with the melted butter and bake for 15 minutes. Turn the chicken and continue to bake another 15 minutes basting frequently. Lower temperature to 375', turn the chicken again and bake for 10 minutes.
5. Remove from oven, drain juices from the pan and stir into the mango sauce. Baste the chicken with mango sauce and bake for another 5-7 minutes or until they are golden brown.

NEGRIL WEST-END PAPRIKA CHICKEN
A special treat for paprika lovers.

INGREDIENTS
2 tbsps. vegetable oil
½ tbsp flour
2 garlic cloves, finely chopped
¾ cup chicken breast cubed,
¼ cup escallion chopped
¼ cup onion, chopped
3 red sweet peppers chopped
½ cup Jamaican sweet sauce
3 tbsps paprika
¼ cup sour cream

PREPARATION
1. Sprinkle chicken with salt.
2. Sauté onions in vegetable oil until browned and then add all other ingredients.
3. Add chicken and sauce and cover
4. Remove chicken and add rice and stir in other ingredients.
5. Stir in flour and sour cream and cook well.
6. Remove and serve hot

ANNATTO BAY CHICKEN WITH PINEAPPLE SAUCE RECIPE
A thrill for pineapple lovers a perfect blend of pineapple juice and chicken spices.

INGREDIENTS
1 tbsp. brown sugar
1 tbsp. butter
¾ cup chopped fresh pineapple
1½ cups pineapple juice
6 tbsp. melted butter
¼ cup water
2 tsp. salt
1 clove garlic chopped
1 tsp. black pepper
1 lg quartered chicken

PREPARATION
1. Remove giblets and sprinkle the quartered chicken with Jamaican pepper.
2. In a blender, puree the garlic, salt and water. Pour over the chicken and marinate, refrigerated for 2 hours.
3. To make pineapple sauce, puree the pineapple juice and pineapples.
4. In a small frying pan melt butter, add pineapple puree and brown sugar and stir.
5. When the mixture boils, remove from heat and set aside.
6. Preheat oven to 500'. Place quartered chicken in a large greased baking pan. Baste with the melted butter and bake for 15 minutes.
7. Turn the chicken and continue to bake another 15 minutes basting frequently. Lower temperature to 375', turn the chicken again and bake for 10 minutes.
8. Remove from oven, drain juices from the pan and stir into the pineapple sauce.
9. Baste the chicken with pineapple sauce and bake for another 5-7 minutes or until they are golden brown.

BROWNS TOWN RALLY BACK CHICKEN
A great recipe from Rally Back a local Browns Town chef.

INGREDIENTS
1 lb. chicken breasts
3 tbsps. Soya sauce
2 cloves garlic, chopped
3 tbsps. vegetable oil
1 tsp. salt
1 onion, chopped
1 tsp. black pepper
1 cup Rally Backs Secret Sauce
1 tbsp. allspice
2 stalks escallion, chopped
1 tsp. sugar
½ tbsp scotch bonnet pepper diced

PREPARATION
1. Remove skin and bone from chicken breasts. Cut meat into strips and marinate with ½ sauce and seasonings.
2. Remove chicken heat oil and stir-fry chicken breasts until done.
3. Place sauce, soy sauce and water in pot bring to boil and add chicken
4. Simmer for 25 minutes the remove.
5. Serve hot.

BLUE MOUNTAIN SPIT ROASTED CHICKEN
We got this recipe while on a trip in the Blue Mountain area a great tasting recipe we are sure you will enjoy.

INGREDEIENTS
1 roasting fowl
2½ tbsp butter
1 tbsp lime juice
¼ tsp salt
¼ tsp pepper

PREPARATION
1. Wipe chicken clean inside and out.
2. Mix ingredients and season inside the bird.
3. Impale the bird on a stick.
4. Cook slowly over a wood fire.
5. Use butter to continuously baste the chicken.
6. When bird is cooked and crisp carve and serve with a sauce of your choice.
7. Serve hot.

Cooking Tip
Pineapple is a very good complement for Jamaican chicken recipes and when used should not be used with a lot of spices.

JAMAICAN CHICKEN KABOBS IN MANGO SAUCE RECIPE
For all the kabob lovers this is a great tasting recipe with a blend of mango sauce

INGREDIENTS
1 tbsp. curry powder
½ cup salad dressing
¼ cup honey
12 bamboo skewers
2 cups mango chunks
3 cups cooked chicken chunks
3 cups June plum chunks

PREPARATION
1. Marinate chicken in Jamaican salad dressing, Jamaican curry and Jamaican honey at least 3 hours.
2. Thread on bamboo skewers alternately with Jamaican mango & June plum. Brush with marinade.
3. Broil or barbecue, basting until done.

COOLIE TOWN CURRIED CHICKEN IN MANGO SALAD RECIPE
A perfect blend of curried chicken and mango salad a great recipe.

INGREDIENTS
1½ tsp. curry powder
1 tsp. Jamaican mango chutney recipe
½ tsp. allspice
¼ cup low fat mayonnaise
¼ cup plain nonfat yogurt
2 mangos, peeled and chopped
2 tbsp cashews, chopped
2 tbsp lime juice
2 tsp scotch bonnet pepper, diced
4 cups cooked chicken breast halves, diced
4 escallions, sliced thin
1 head lettuce
½ tbsp salt and pepper mixed

PREPARATION
1. In a large bowl, combine chicken, Jamaican lime juice, Jamaican mangoes, Jamaican scotch bonnet pepper, and Jamaican scallions.
2. In a small bowl, whisk together the yogurt, mayonnaise, Jamaican mango chutney, Jamaican curry powder, allspice and salt and pepper to taste.
3. Add to chicken mixture; toss. Arrange a mound of chicken on top of lettuce.

SPICED JAMAICAN CHICKEN WITH SWEET POTATOES AND CINNAMON
A great Jamaican recipe using chicken cooked with cinnamon, brown sugar, apples, and sweet potatoes.

INGREDIENTS
3 to 4 pounds chicken pieces
¼ cup vegetable oil
½ cup dry vermouth
1½ tsp salt
¼ tsp scotch bonnet pepper diced
¼ tsp cinnamon
1 tbsp brown sugar
2 otaheite apples, cored, cut in wedges
3 sweet potatoes, cooked and sliced

PREPARATION
1. Brown chicken pieces in a heavy skillet in hot vegetable oil.
2. Drain off all but 1 tablespoon of the oil.
3. Combine dry vermouth with salt, pepper, cinnamon, and brown sugar.
4. Add vermouth mixture to chicken in skillet along with the apple wedges the baste chicken.
5. Cover skillet and cook over low heat for 25 minutes.
6. Add the cooked sliced sweet potatoes and baste again with cooking liquid.
7. Cover and simmer until heated

RED STRIPE BEER CHICKEN
A treat for all Red Stripe Beer lovers, chicken marinated in the Jamaican beer and cooked with spicy herbs.

INGREDIENTS
4 quartered chicken
½ cup Jamaican sweet sauce
1 tbsp seasoning salt
1 tsp garlic powder
1 tsp onion powder
½ tbsp salt and pepper mixed
½ cup Red Stripe beer

PREPARATION
1. Wash and blot chicken dry. Combine the dry rub ingredients and season chicken inside and out.
2. Inject ½ Jamaican sweet chicken sauce into breast, legs and thighs.
3. In a mixing bowl pour beer and remaining sauce make marinade.
4. Place chicken on grill and while grilling baste the chicken with beer marinade.
5. Remove from grill and serve hot

jamaican stuffed
chicken breast ©

MONTEGO BAY TERIYAKI CHICKEN
A special recipe used for preparing chicken actually Chinese in origin but now with Jamaican spices and herbs.

INGREDIENTS
2½ lb chicken cut into quarters and split pieces
¼ cup soy sauce
¼ cup sugar
¼ cup Jamaican rice wine
¼ tsp salt
¼ tsp Monosodium glutamate MSG (**optional**)
1 tbsp vegetable oil
1 tsp ginger root

PREPARATION
1. In a large bowl combine all ingredients and marinate chicken for 4 hours.
2. Pre-heat oven at 375 Degrees and place chicken on baking tin basting with marinate.
3. Bake for 50 minutes basting every 15 minutes.
4. Remove and serve hot.

CRAB STUFFED CHICKEN BREAST
A perfect blend between crabmeat, chicken breast and Jamaican herbs and spices.

INGREDIENTS
6 chicken breast halves
3 slices boiled ham
3 tbsp mayonnaise
1 tbsp flour
1 tsp salt
¼ tsp black pepper
½ cup bread crumbs
¼ tsp Jamaican seafood seasoning
1 tbsp parsley, chopped
1 cup crabmeat
2 tbsp vegetable oil

PREPARATION
1. Preheat the oven to 400 degrees and pound the chicken breasts between 2 sheets of waxed paper until very thin.
2. Mix the mayonnaise, seasonings and crabmeat then mound the crabmeat on the end of each chicken breast.
3. Roll each breast up around the filling and prick each breast to seal. Roll the breasts in flour and mix the parsley with the bread crumbs.
4. Roll the breasts in the bread crumbs and heat the oil in a skillet. Brown the breasts all over.
5. Arrange the breasts on a lightly greased cookie sheet and bake for 15 minutes.
6. Serve hot.

LILIPUT CRISPY CHICKEN DRUMSTICKS
A popular fried chicken recipe contributed by our chef from Lilliput, St. James

INGREDIENTS
8 chicken drumsticks, skinned
1½ cup breadcrumbs
¼ cup grated cheese
2 tbsp minced fresh parsley
¼ tsp garlic powder
¼ tsp black pepper
¼ cup milk

PREPARATION
1. Rinse chicken with cold water, and pat dry. Combine bread crumbs and other ingredients stirring well.
2. Dip drumsticks in milk. Dredge in breadcrumb mixture, coating well.
3. Place drumsticks in a 10x6x2" baking dish.
4. Bake at 350 deg F for 1 hour until tender.
5. Serve hot.

ISLINGTON CHICKEN IN COCONUT MILK
A great chicken recipe that offers a blend between coconut milk and other spices and herbs.

INGREDIENTS
3 lb chicken fryer, cut into serving portions
¼ cup garlic clove, minced
2¼ cup coconut milk
1 tbsp parsley
½ tsp thyme
¼ cup onion, finely chopped
½ tbsp salt and black pepper mixed
1 scotch bonnet pepper diced

PREPARATION
1. Towel dry the chicken. In a large, heavy skillet heat the oil.
2. Add chicken pieces and fry until lightly browned.
3. Remove from the skillet a aside in the same skillet, sauté the onion and garlic.
4. Return the chicken to the skillet and add the coconut milk a and pepper to taste.
5. Tie the parsley, hot pepper and thyme in a cheese pouch to form a bouquet garni and add to the skillet.
6. Cover and simmer the chicken is tender, about 1¼ hours.
7. Serve hot.

JAMAICAN STYLE CHICKEN KIEV
A popular Jamaican recipe in the South Coast Hotel Resorts

INGREDIENTS
4 lb chicken breasts
2 eggs, beaten
2 tbsp water
2 tbsp parsley, snipped
½ cup flour
1 tsp allspice
¼ cup chopped escallions
½ cup bread crumbs
½ cup melted butter

PREPARATION
1. Remove bones and skin from chicken breasts and pound out to ¼ inch hick.
2. Cut Butter into quarters and lay one in center of each chicken piece.
3. Evenly divide onions and parsley between breasts.
4. Roll each chicken piece into a log and secure with a toothpick.
5. Mix eggs and water. Roll a chicken log in flour, then dip in egg and cover with bread crumbs.
6. Wrap n plastic wrap and refrigerate for at least 1 hour or overnight.
7. Deep fry until brown, then bake at 375 degrees for 10 minutes.
8. Serve hot

FESTIVAL TIME CHICKEN
The most popular Jamaican chicken recipe during the Jamaican Independence celebration.

INGREDIENTS
8 bacon strips
4 chicken breasts halves
1 cup soy sauce
½ cup sugar
4 garlic cloves minced
3 tsp grated ginger
¼ tsp paprika
½ tbsp hot pepper sauce

PREPARATION
1. Wrap two bacon strips around each chicken breast; place in a shallow glass baking dish and set aside.
2. In a small mixing bowl, combine soy sauce and sugar, add remaining ingredients.
3. Pour over chicken, turning to coat evenly. Cover with plastic wrap and refrigerate for several hours or overnight.
4. Drain and reserve marinade then bake at 325~F. for 50-60 minutes or until chicken tests done, basting occasionally with marinade.

Cooking Tip
Curry chicken means giving the flavor of curry to the chicken. By dredging the chicken in the flour and curry allows the curry to be burned into the chicken.

JAMAICAN CHICKEN SATAY RECIPE
A delicious chicken recipe

INGREDIENTS
½ cup chicken stock
¼ tsp black pepper
½ cup creamed cheese
½ tsp black pepper
¼ cup chopped unsalted peanuts
1 lb Skinless, de-boned chicken breast, cut into long thin strips
¼ cup smooth peanut butter
2 tsp allspice
¼ cup chopped escallions
1 tbsp soy sauce
1 tbsp minced garlic
¼ cup minced onion
½ tsp salt

PREPARATION
1. In a medium saucepan over high heat, combine seasoning ingredients except allspice. Bring to a boil, reduce heat, & simmer, stirring, for 3 minutes.
2. Remove from heat. On metal skewers, thread chicken the long way dividing it equally among skewers.
3. Sprinkle allspice over meat, and pat seasoning into meat. Heat a large skillet over high heat, and sear chicken till brown on each side.
4. Spoon a generous amount of sauce onto each individual plate, arrange skewers on top and sprinkle with green onions.
5. Serve hot.

KINGSTON CURRIED CHICKEN
Curried chicken is one of the most popular recipes in Jamaican especially when prepared with peppers.

INGREDIENTS
3 chicken breasts, halved
3 tbsp flour
1½ cup onion chopped
1 tbsp Water
¼ tsp curry powder
¼ tsp grated ginger
¼ tsp allspice
½ tsp salt
¼ tsp black pepper
1 cup Jamaican chicken broth
1 tbsp scotch bonnet pepper diced

PREPARATION
1. Preheat oven to 350F. Rinse chicken, pat dry; dredge in flour and curry powder.
2. Spray a large non stick skillet with vegetable spray; heat over medium high.
3. Add chicken and cook just until brown; turn and brown other side.
4. Put chicken in a medium size shallow casserole. In skillet over low heat, cook onion in 1 tbsp water 5 minutes.
5. Spoon over chicken and sprinkle with spices
6. Pour broth over all and cook, covered, 55 min or until tender.

GINGER HONEY ROAST CHICKEN

Honey basted with grated ginger and used to marinate the chicken is what gives this recipe its special flavor.

INGREDIENTS
1 whole chicken quartered
¼ tsp salt
¼ tsp black pepper
¼ cup ginger root grated
¼ cup soy sauce
¼ cup honey
¼ cup vegetable oil
½ tbsp scotch bonnet pepper

PREPARATION
1. Rub chicken with salt and pepper and stuff with chopped ginger root.
2. Place in oven on baking tray and bake.
3. Prepare baste by combining oil, soy, honey, chilies, and ground ginger.
4. Stir vigorously and baste chicken when it is 80% done.
5. Baste frequently, during the final stages of cooking to ensure that the honey does not burn.
6. Serve hot.

JAMAICAN JAMBALAYA

A blaster Jamaican chicken recipe.

INGREDIENTS
½ cup sweet peppers chopped
½ cup onion diced
½ cup garlic chopped
½ tsp thyme
3 cups Jamaican tomato sauce
2 lb boneless chicken cut into cubes
1 bay leaf
1 tbsp allspice
¼ tsp salt
1 cup hot steamed rice

PREPARATION
1. Puree peppers, onions, garlic and herbs (except the bay leaf) in a food processor.
2. Transfer to a large pot add the tomato sauce the chicken, bay leaves and allspice.
3. Cover and bring to a boil.
4. Reduce heat to medium an cook for about 35 minutes.
5. Remove and serve hot.

JAMAICAN KENTUCKY FRIED CHICKEN

A popular recipe that was heavily requested in our Second Edition©.

INGREDIENTS

2 tbsp salt
2 cups flour
2 tbsp black pepper
4 tbsp paprika
1 tsp garlic salt
1 tbsp mustard
1 tbsp thyme
1 tsp oregano
1 tbsp ginger grated
9 chicken pieces
4 tbsp vegetable oil

PREPARATION

1. Mix all spices and flour together.
2. Take pieces of cut-up chicken and dip in raw egg.
3. Roll in spices. Fry chicken in oil.
4. Bake in 350 F oven for 45 minutes in foil.

BICKERSTETH OVEN-FRIED HERB CHICKEN

A great recipe from the little community of Bickesteth in St. James

INGREDIENTS

½ cup solid butter
1½ cup seasoned stuffing mix
2 tbsp parsley flakes
2 tsp allspice
½ tsp garlic powder
2½ lb chicken cut into 8 pieces

PREPARATION

1. Heat oven to 350. In 13x 8 inch baking pan melt butter in over (5minutes).
2. Meanwhile, in 9 inch pie pan combine stuffing mix, parsley, sage, and garlic powder; mix well.
3. Dip chicken pieces into melted butter, then roll in seasoned crumb mixture to coat.
4. Place skin-side up, in prepared pan. Sprinkle with remaining crumbs.
5. Bake for 70 to 80 minutes or until chicken is no longer pink.
6. Serve hot

JAMAICAN PIMENTO CHICKEN
A perfect blend of other spices and the age old famous pimento or allspice.

INGREDIENTS
1 cup Jamaican chicken broth
¼ cup pimento cheese
3 hard cooked eggs sliced
¼ tsp salt
¼ tsp black pepper
2 tbsp melted butter
1 tbsp juice
2 cups cooked chicken, diced
3 tbsp creamed cheese

PREPARATION
1. Blend soup and cheese and heat add eggs salt, pepper and butter.
2. Then add mushrooms with juice and chicken. Do not boil.
3. Add cream shortly before serving. Serve over Chinese noodles, in pastry shells or anything you prefer.

NEGRIL SHRIMP AND CHICKEN IN TOMATO SAUCE
A sweet blend between shrimp and chicken in Jamaica's sweet tomato sauce, a top chicken recipe.

INGREDIENTS
1 tbsp vegetable oil
½ cup onion diced
¼ cup escallion chopped
¼ cup carrot diced
¼ cup minced garlic
½ tsp garlic powder
2 cup tomatoes crushed
½ tbsp salt and black pepper mixed
4 de-boned chicken breast
2 tbsp melted butter
1 cup shrimp, peeled and de-veined
2 tbsp Appleton V/X rum

PREPARATION
1. Heat the oil in a saucepan and add the onion, carrot, escallion and the minced garlic.
2. Cook, stirring, until the onion is wilted.
3. Add the tomatoes, rum, salt and pepper to taste. Bring to a boil and let simmer about 15 minutes.
4. Meanwhile, cut away all membranes and fat attached to the chicken breast cut the chicken into ½ inch wide shreds.
5. Melt the butter in a skillet and, when it is quite hot but not brown, add the chicken.
6. Sprinkle with salt and pepper to taste. Cook, stirring to separate the pieces, about 45 seconds.
7. Add the shrimp and stir. Cook, stirring occasionally.
8. Stir in the tomato sauce and bring to a boil then serve.

LYME CAYE SPICY ISLAND CHICKEN

Though Lyme Caye chefs specialize mainly in fish recipes we found this recipe too good not to put in the Third Edition.

INGREDIENTS

1 cup chicken breast, cooked cubed
2¼ cup water
1 tsp garlic powder
½ tsp curry powder
2 tsp lime juice
1 pack chicken-flavor noodles/sauce
¼ cup green beans, frozen
1 tbsp coconut, flaked

PREPARATIONS

1. Shred chicken. Stir together water, garlic, curry, and lime juice. Bring to boil, then stir in noodles and green beans.
2. Continue boiling over medium heat, stirring occasionally, 7 minutes or until noodles are tender.
3. Stir in chicken and coconut heat through.
4. Serve hot.

NORMA CHIN'S SWEET 'N' SOUR CHICKEN

Ms. Norma is a popular chef in Kingston who contributed her secret sweet and sour chicken recipe.

INGREDIENTS

1½ cup carrots
1 lg green pepper sliced
1 lg onion
2 tbsp tapioca—quick-cooking
3 lb chicken pieces
8 oz pineapple chunks
¼ cup brown sugar
¼ cup red wine vinegar (or substitute)
1 tbsp soy sauce
½ tsp chicken bouillon granules
¼ tsp garlic powder
¼ tsp ginger grated
Hot cooked rice

PREPARATION

1. In crock-pot, combine carrots, green pepper, and onion. Sprinkle tapioca over vegetables. Place frozen chicken pieces atop vegetables.
2. For sauce, in a small bowl combine un-drained pineapple, brown sugar, vinegar, soy sauce, bouillon, garlic powder, and ginger.
3. Pour sauce over chicken pieces.
4. Cover; cook on low-heat setting for 10-12 hours or on high-heat setting for 5-6 hours.
5. Serve over rice.

> **Cooking Tip**
> Most stewed poultry recipes are prepared differently because some poultry takes a longer time to prepared because of the texture of the meat.

JAMAICAN JERK TURKEY
A special treat for turkey lovers. Its usually prepared during thanks giving but we have found it to be a delicious year round recipes.

INGREDIENTS
2 Leg quarters chicken chopped in serving portions
2 tbsp Jamaican hot pepper sauce
1 tsp salt and black pepper
½ tsp cinnamon
½ tsp allspice
¼ cup onion, minced
2 tbsp sugar
2 tbsp pepper, red, minced
2 tbsp hot pepper jelly
¼ cup escallion chopped
1 cup rice, cooked

PREPARATION
1. In a shallow container, place the hot pepper sauce.
2. Add turkey, one piece at a time, turning to coat.
3. Sprinkle salt, cinnamon and allspice over the turkey.
4. Place the turkey, skin side up, in a single layer in a large shallow baking dish.
5. Bake at 400 F, basting twice with pan juices for 45 minutes or until the turkey is fork tender.
6. Arrange the rice and turkey on a serving platter.

DOWN TOWN STEW TURKEY NECK
Turkey neck is a popular meat used by many cooks and chefs in Jamaica and the stewed turkey neck has become a popular choice.

INGREDIENTS
2 lbs chopped turkey neck
4 cups water
1 tbsp allspice
¼ tsp salt
¼ tsp black pepper
½ cup vegetable oil
½ cup carrots diced
½ cup potatoes diced
¼ cup chocho diced (**optional**)
¼ cup diced ripe plantains
¼ cup escallions chopped
¼ cup onions chopped
1 clove garlic finely chopped
¼ cup melted butter

PREPARATION
1. Place all ingredients except chicken and vegetables in a blender and puree until smooth.
2. Place in a sauce pan and bring to slight boil.
3. Add chicken and vegetables to mixture.
4. Stew until cooked and serve hot.

THANKSGIVING TURKEY JAMAICAN STYLE

This recipe was contributed by one of our chefs living in the Tri-State area, who is of Jamaican descent but was born in the USA. This recipe is now used by many of the major resort hotels island wide.

INGREDIENTS

1 large roasting turkey
2 cups Jamaican turkey stuffing
1 tbsp allspice
2 tbsp salt
1 tbsp black pepper
1 cup melted butter
1 cup Jamaican Turkey marinade

PREPARATION

1. Clean the turkey well with lime juice and cane vinegar and pat dry.
2. Rub in salt and black pepper on the bird then stuff with turkey stuffing.
3. Fasten all openings with skewers and place the bird on roasting pan breast up.
4. Preheat oven at 300 Degrees then put bird in.
5. Allow 25 minutes per pound for birds over 12 pounds and 20 minutes for smaller birds.
6. Baste with melted butter and turkey marinade constantly to prevent burning.
7. Remove from oven and remove stuffing from chicken
8. Remove and carve into serving portions.

JAMAICAN FRICASSEED LEFTOVER TURKEY RECIPE

A sweet recipe as the flavors of the leftover turkey give the sauce a unique flavor.

INGREDIENTS

3 cups leftover roasted turkey chopped in serving portions
¼ cup flour
½ cup diced carrots
½ cup diced potatoes
¼ tsp salt
¼ tsp paprika
¼ cup vegetable oil
2 tbsp Jamaican hot pepper sauce
3 cups water
½ tsp allspice
¼ cup onion, minced
2 tbsp sugar
¼ cup soy sauce
¼ cup escallion chopped

PREPARATION

1. Place turkey in flour and brown in vegetable oil.
2. Place all other ingredients except carrots and potatoes and puree in blender.
3. Add puree and carrots and potatoes to browned turkey and cook until vegetables are soft.
4. Ensure that sauce does not dry out.
5. Remove and serve hot.

SHORT MAN'S FAMOUS ROAST TURKEY
A few NFL lovers commission there favorite Jerk Chicken man to come up with a great Thanksgiving recipe for the 2005-2006 NFL Thanksgiving game they weren't disappointed and we know you will love this recipe.

INGREDIENTS
1 small roasting turkey
1½ cups Jamaican turkey stuffing
1 tbsp vegetable oil
2 tsp. salt
1 tsp black pepper
1 tbsp thyme
½ tbsp allspice
¼ cup escallion diced
2 garlic cloves, lightly smashed
1 large lime
½ cup onion diced

PREPARATION
1. Sprinkle the turkey evenly inside and out with salt and pepper and allow to stand.
2. Preheat the oven to 350ºF and place a small piece of foil just large enough to cover the turkey's breast in a roasting pan coating it with oil and set aside.
3. Stuff the herbs and the garlic into the cavity of the turkey.
4. Prick the lemon about 25 times with a skewer and stuff it into the cavity.
5. Pin the neck and hind cavities closed and place the turkey breast down over the oiled piece of foil in the roasting pan.
6. Roast for 15 minutes and turn the bird breast up and carefully peel off the foil taking care not to rip the skin; discard.
7. Roast 20 minutes longer, then increase the oven temperature to 400 degrees.
8. Roast the turkey 20 to 25 minutes longer, until the skin is brown and crisp and the juices run clear when the leg is pricked with a kitchen fork.
9. Remove the toothpick from the hind end. Lift the turkey with two wooden spoons and tilt it slightly so the juices run out of the cavity into the pan and discard.
10. Place the turkey on a platter and keep warm.
11. Carve the turkey pour any juices that have collected on the plate.
12. Serve dry with any Jamaican sauce recipe of your choice.

JAMAICAN SPICY TURKEY FINGERS
A super sweet turkey recipe complemented by the Jerk-BQ Sauce

INGREDIENTS
2 cups leftover turkey breast cut in strip
½ cup dried breadcrumbs
1 egg beaten
¼ cup Jerk Sauce
½ cup milk
1 cup cornmeal
½ cup Jerk-BQ Sauce

PREPARATION
1. Dip turkey strips in egg and in bread crumbs. Fry until golden brown.
2. Add Jerk sauce and milk to cover.
3. Remove and dip again in bread crumbs then fry in oil again.
4. When crisp remove from frying pan.
5. Serve with Jamaican Jerk-BQ Sauce.

JAMAICAN COCONUT TURKEY
The sweet coconut blend with the Jamaican turkey leftovers absolutely delicious.

INGREDIENTS
2 cups sweetened coconut flakes
¼ cup flour
2 eggs
2 cups cubed leftover turkey breast
½ cup vegetable oil
3 tbsp honey
3 tbsp orange marmalade
1 tbsp soy sauce

PREPARATION
1. Place coconut in medium sized bowl, place flour in a second bowl and lightly beat eggs in a third bowl.
2. Dip turkey pieces in flour, then egg, and then roll in coconut flakes.
3. Place on a baking sheet. Pour enough oil into skillet to reach a depth of ½ inch.
4. Heat over medium heat. When hot add turkey with slotted spoon, 6 pieces at a time.
5. Cook 4-6 minutes until cooked through and light golden, turning once.
6. Adjust heat as needed to prevent over browning. Drain on paper towel.
7. To prepare sauce, combine all ingredients in small bowl.

JAMAICAN CURRIED TURKEY
Now a unique taste, this recipe gives a great flavor to leftover turkey and if using our Roasting recipe the spices will resonate throughout the sauce.

INGREDIENTS
4 cups leftover roasted turkey cut in serving portions
2 garlic cloves, finely chopped
1 tsp. curry powder
¼ cup onion, chopped
½ cup potato diced
½ cup water
2 tbsps. Jamaican hot pepper sauce
¼ cup grated ginger
¼ cup coconut milk

PREPARATION
1. In a frying pan, heat the oil and fry the garlic until golden brown.
2. Add the curry powder, stir to mix thoroughly, and cook for 1 minute.
3. Add the turkey and stir well to coat the meat in the curry mixture.
4. Add the onion, potato and a quarter-cup stock, and stir-fry over medium heat until the potato is just cooked.
5. Stir in the hot pepper sauce, ginger and coconut milk, and simmer gently until the sauce thickens.
6. Turn into a bowl and serve.

Cooking Tip
Turkey is a very versatile meat. It has a delicious taste whether served hot or served cold, which makes turkey a great poultry for left over recipes which are very popular in Jamaican cuisine.

JAMAICAN TURKEY PUFFS
Used as an appetizer of a snack recipe made from leftover roasted turkey.

INGREDIENTS
4 tbsps butter
½ cup boiling water
½ cup flour
2 eggs
½ cup cheese grated
2 cups turkey cubes cooked
¼ cup onions diced
¼ cup garlic diced
¼ tbsp allspice (pimento)

PREPARATION
1. Melt butter in boiling water then add flour; stir vigorously.
2. Cook and stir until mixture forms a ball that doesn't separate and forms a dough.
3. Remove from heat and cool slightly. Preheat oven to 400 Degrees.
4. Add egg; beat vigorously until smooth. Stir in cheese.
5. Drop dough onto greased baking sheet, using 1 level tsp dough for each puff.
6. Bake for 20 minutes. Remove from oven; cool and split.
7. Finely chop cooked turkey, pimiento, garlic and onions.
8. Combine with remaining ingredients. Fill each puff with 2 tsps.
9. Serve warm.

JAMAICAN BROILED TURKEY
A savory turkey recipe chosen by some who prefer not to go through the arduous task of roasting their turkey.

INGREDIENTS
2 small broiling turkeys
1 tbsp allspice
¼ tsp salt
¼ tsp black pepper
½ cup vegetable oil
¼ cup chopped parsley
1 clove garlic finely chopped
¼ cup melted butter

PREPARATION
1. Split turkeys down the back.
2. In a blender, puree the all ingredients except melted butter to make marinate.
3. Pour marinate over the turkey and marinate, refrigerate for 2 hours (or overnight).
4. Drain off marinade and discard.
5. Preheat broiler and place turkeys in and broil for 50 minutes basting with the melted butter every 15 minutes.
6. Turn the turkey and continue to bake another 15 minutes basting frequently.
7. Remove and serve hot.

jamaican fried chicken
with mash potatoes

©

MOUNT ROUSSEAU CHICKEN FINGERS
A great recipe we found in a little restaurant while going over Mount Rousseau.

INGREDIENTS
2 lbs boneless chicken breast cut into strips
¼ cup orange juice
¼ cup lime juice
3 tbsp sugar
2 tbsp onion powder
2 tbsp crushed thyme
1 tbsp ground red pepper
1 tbsp black pepper
1½ tbsp allspice
1 tbsp salt
1½ tsp nutmeg
1 tsp ground cloves

PREPARATION
1. Lay strips in baking dish and pour juice over top. Cover and refrigerate 1 hour.
2. In small bowl, combine remaining ingredients. Sprinkle generously over chicken strips.
3. Marinate for 1 hour.
4. Grill should be medium hot and grate set on highest level.
5. Lay out chicken and grill on both sides 1 hour or until done.

BRACO'S SPECIAL ROAST DUCK
The secret to this recipe is that it has been flavored with the Jamaican grapefruit.

INGREDIENTS
¼ cup Jamaican grapefruit marmalade
2 tbsps soy sauce
1 small duck rinsed and dried
1 tbsp salt
1 tbsp pepper

PREPARATION
1. Preheat the oven to 450 degrees. In a small bowl, mix the marmalade with the soy sauce.
2. Set the grapefruit glaze aside.
3. Season the cavity of the duck meat liberally with salt and pepper.
4. Carefully loosen the skin by running your fingers under the skin of the breast and legs, separating it gently from the meat underneath without tearing it.
5. Spoon half the grapefruit glaze under the skin of the breast and legs.
6. Place the duck meat, breast-side down, on a rack set above a rimmed sheet pan or baking dish and roast for 15 minutes.
7. Brush the outside of the duck meat with some of the grapefruit glaze and roast for 10 minutes longer.
8. Turn the duck meat breast-side up. Roast for another 30 to 35 minutes basting with more of the grapefruit glaze every 7 minutes
9. Remove and allow to stand before carving.

JAMAICAN FRIED TURKEY

This recipe isn't actually a fried turkey recipe as it uses leftover turkey but is still delicious nonetheless.

INGREDIENTS

4 cups cubed turkey breast
½ cup all-purpose flour
2 eggs, beaten
¾ cup dry breadcrumbs
1½ cup grated cheese
1 tbsp. vegetable oil
2 tbsps. butter
2 tbsps. all-purpose flour
1¼ cups milk
1 tsp. salt
¼ tsp. garlic powder
¼ tsp. onion powder
¼ tsp. allspice
¼ cup Jamaican tomato sauce

PREPARATION

1. Pat turkey dry and pound to flatten slightly.
2. Dust turkey lightly with flour and dip into egg.
3. Combine breadcrumbs with garlic powder, onion powder and allspice and ½ cup cheese.
4. After dipping in egg dip turkey in breadcrumb mixture.
5. Line a 9" x 13" baking dish with foil, brush with vegetable oil and arrange turkey in the dish in a single layer.
6. Bake in a preheated 400° F oven for 20 minutes.
7. In a saucepan, melt butter and whisk in 2 tbsps. Flour and cook without browning.
8. Add milk and bring to boil then add salt and pepper and tomato sauce.
9. Reduce heat. Cook for 5 minutes, stirring often.
10. Garnish each piece of turkey and sprinkle with grated cheese. Bake for 15 minutes longer.

JAMAICAN ROAST DUCK IN JUNE PLUM SAUCE
A sweet recipe with a new blend of sauce the June plum sauce is absolutely delicious.

INGREDIENTS
2 duck quarters chopped in serving portions
1 tsp. garlic powder
1 tsp. allspice
¼ tsp salt
¼ tsp black pepper
¼ cup diced callaloo
1 egg white
1 cup otaheite apple, shredded
¼ cup vinegar
2 onions, chopped
½ cup sugar
2 tsp. cornstarch
1 tbsp. vegetable oil
1 cup June Plum Sauce
1 cup vegetable stock

PREPARATION
1. In a saucepan sauté chopped onion in oil. Remove and set aside.
2. Add remaining ingredients except cornstarch and bring to a boil.
3. Dissolve cornstarch and add to saucepan then stir until thicken, simmer for 5 minutes.
4. Stir in sauté onion and set aside.
5. Season duck meat with garlic powder, allspice, salt and pepper and allow to marinate.
6. Bring water to a boil with salt to taste, blanch callaloo leaves and set aside.
7. Remove seasoned duck meat from refrigerator, flatten with a mallet. Brush with egg white, place one callaloo leaf on each portion.
8. Roll meat to form a log. Rap tightly in plastic and marinate for hour.
9. Bring 3 cups of duck stock to a boil. Remove duck meat from refrigerator and poach in vegetable stock until cooked.
10. Remove slice and serve with June plum sauce.

Maggi ®

LET's EAT!

JAMAICAN BEEF, MEAT AND VEAL RECIPES.

jamaican corner shop branded with Maggi Brand. ©

One of our top chefs has contributed his secret ingredients for his Cow Foot and Bean recipe, not to mention the ingredients he uses in his Tripe and Beans recipe. But we must make you aware that as good as these recipes are they are only good because **FRESH INGREDIENTS** are used. Spoilt ingredients do not only lead to a poor tasting recipe but can have serious repercussions to the health of all those consuming the meal. Some of these recipes are best served with aged wines of your choice. We invite you to try at least one of these recipes each week for the year and we guarantee that you will never be disappointed. **DINE AND ENJOY!**

JAMAICAN SWEET BEEF SUPPER
This is a great Jamaican beef recipe that we picked up in Portland. Its absolutely delicious.

INGREDIENTS
3 cups pasta shells
¼ cup vegetable oil
¼ cup onion, thinly sliced
¼ cup escallion diced
2 cloves garlic, minced
1 lb. lean beef
1½ cup pumpkin, chopped
1 lg sweet pepper cut into thin strips
1 cup whole kernel sweet corn
1 cup Jamaican sweet sauce
1½ tsp allspice
½ tsp scotch bonnet pepper diced
½ tbsp salt and black pepper mixed
1 cup grated cheese

PREPARATION
1. Cook pasta according to package directions.
2. Meanwhile, heat oil and sauté onion, escallion, garlic and ground beef until beef is browned.
3. Stir in pumpkin and peppers and sauté until softened.
4. Stir in remaining ingredients including cooked pasta, but not cheese. Spoon into shallow baking dish.
5. 3. Sprinkle with cheese and bake at 350ºF for 20 to 25 minutes or until bubbly.

NEGRIL BAKED MEATBALLS
These are to die for a new and exciting way to make your beef balls.

INGREDIENTS
1 lb. ground beef
½ cup dry bread crumbs
¼ cup milk
¾ tsp. salt
½ tsp. Worcestershire sauce
¼ tsp. pepper
¼ cup onion, chopped
1 egg

PREPARATION
1. Mix all ingredients, shape into twenty 1½ inch meatballs.
2. Place in un-greased rectangular pan and bake uncovered in 400ºF oven until done and light brown.
3. Serve with sauce of your choice.

MS. NORMA'S SPAGHETTI WITH MEATBALLS
A great recipe that is best served with boiled ripe plantain on the side, absolutely delicious.

INGREDIENTS
¾ lb. ground beef
½ cup breadcrumbs
1 egg
½ cup milk
1 tsp. salt
¼ tsp. pepper
2 tbsp. vegetable oil
1 onion, chopped
3 cloves garlic, finely chopped
¼ tsp pepper flakes
2 tbsp. flour
1 cup milk
1 cup tomatoes crushed
1 cup Jamaican tomato sauce
½ tbsp salt and black pepper mixed
¾ lb. spaghetti
2 tbsp. chopped parsley
½ cup grated cheese

PREPARATION
1. To make meatballs combine ground beef with breadcrumbs, egg, milk, salt and pepper and shape into mini meatballs and set aside.
2. For the sauce heat oil in a Dutch oven or large saucepan. Add onions, garlic and pepper flakes and cook until lightly browned.
3. Add flour and continue to cook for 2 minutes then whisk in the milk and bring to a boil.
4. Add tomatoes and tomato paste, breaking tomatoes up with a spoon and bring to a boil.
5. Reduce the heat.
6. Simmer, uncovered, stirring occasionally every 10 minutes.
7. Add meatballs to sauce and continue to cook under low heat while season with salt and pepper.
8. Cook spaghetti in a large pot of boiling, salted water and drain spaghetti well.
9. Top with sauce, parsley and cheese. Toss well and serve.

Cooking Tip
When preparing beef ensure that you identify the type of meat, whether salted beef, steak, sirloin steak, veal or otherwise. This is important in determining just how you prepare the mean, whether roasting, baking or stewing. It also determines cooking time and which ingredients to add and which ingredients not to add.

KINGSTON BEEF IN BREADFRUIT
If you have ever tasted breadfruit you will know that it can be served with almost any meat, but with beef it has a very special taste.

INGREDIENTS
1 cup ground beef
1 tbsp allspice
1 small onion, chopped
salt and black pepper to taste
2 tbsps. cooking oil
2 tbsps. tomato paste
¼ cup water
1 breadfruit

PREPARATION
1. Scoop out heart of breadfruit.
2. Cook ground beef with seasonings, onion and tomato paste.
3. Drain off excess oil.
4. Stuff breadfruit with mixture, replace stem and roast in hot oven 425 Degrees °F for ½ hour, then reduce heat to 350 Degrees°F for another half hour.
5. Test to see if the breadfruit is tender with fork or skewer.

ST. ANN STEWED BEEF
This is not a popular stewed beef recipe however is quickly gaining approval in the larger hotels and resorts. We think its absolutely delicious.

INGREDIENTS
½ cup corn starch
2 tsps. salt
¼ tsp black pepper
½ tsp paprika
3½ cups stewing beef cut in ½ inch cubes
3 tbsps. vegetable oil
1½ cups carrots diced
3 cups potatoes diced
½ cup onions, diced
¼ cup escallion diced
¼ cup Jamaica's onion soup
1 tbsp. Worcestershire sauce
¼ cup Jamaican sweet sauce
1¾ cups milk

PREPARATION
1. Combine corn starch, salt, pepper and paprika. Dust meat cubes lightly with corn starch mixture; reserve excess corn starch mixture.
2. Toss meat cubes with oil in 4-litre oven-proof bowl or deep casserole.
3. Bake, uncovered, in preheated 450°F (230°C) oven 30 minutes; stir once.
4. Add carrots, potatoes, onions and escallions to meat.
5. Combine reserved corn starch mixture with onion soup, Worcestershire sauce and sweet beef sauce and gradually stir in milk.
6. Pour over meat and vegetables in pan and reduce oven temperature to 350 degree F.
7. Bake, covered, 1 hour then remove cover and stir to combine meat, vegetables and sauce.
8. Return to oven; bake, covered, 45 minutes or until meat and vegetables are tender.

APPLETON RUM BEEF

One of our 'rum companions' from the Appleton Estate contributed this sweet recipe to our archives.

INGREDIENTS

1 pot roast
¼ cup vegetable oil
½ cup garlic chopped
½ cup onion chopped
½ tsp allspice
¼ tsp ginger powder
¼ tsp nutmeg
¼ tsp cinnamon powder
¼ tsp salt
¼ tsp black pepper
½ tsp Jamaican jerk seasoning powder
½ cup Pepsi or coke
3 tbsp. Appleton white rum
¼ cup Jamaican sweet sauce
2 tsp. sugar
1 tsp. tomato paste.

PREPARATION

1. Wash and drain pot roast.
2. Stuff pot roast with onion, garlic and allspice
3. Marinate overnight in Pepsi and white rum.
4. Remove from liquid and cover with powdered seasoning, salt and pepper.
5. Brown pot roast in hot vegetable oil for 2 minutes on each side.
6. Remove from frying pan and place in pre-heated oven for 45 minutes until thoroughly cooked.
7. Serve with sauce and fluffy white rice with steamed vegetables.

MANDEVILLE CALLALOO AND BEEF STEW

If you want to taste a great recipe try on this for size we were left in awe in an Mandeville Restaurant.

INGREDIENTS

1 bunch callaloo chopped
¼ tsp salt
¼ cup vegetable oil
3 lb boneless top round, trimmed of fat and cubed
½ cup onion finely chopped
¼ cup garlic minced
1 cup tomatoes peeled and chopped
1 tbsp Jamaican tomato sauce
¼ tsp nutmeg
¼ tsp black pepper
¼ cup red wine
¼ cup chopped parsley

PREPARATION

1. Steam callaloo and set aside.
2. In a large frying pan, heat the oil and brown beef cubes on all sides. Add onion and garlic and cook until onion is soft.
3. Add tomatoes, tomato paste, salt, nutmeg, pepper and wine and bring to a boil, cover, and immediately reduce heat to low.
4. Simmer slowly until beef is very tender.
5. Add reserved callaloo stirring in gently. Cover and cook until beef is fully tender.
6. Sprinkle with chopped parsley before serving.

JAMAICAN CORNED BEEF CASSEROLE

Jamaican love corned beef and there term for it is Bulli beef, this is a tasty treat for corned beef lovers.

INGREDIENTS
1 tin corned beef
1 cup cheese, shredded
½ cup onion finely chopped
¼ cup escallion finely chopped
1 tsp allspice
½ cup sweet pepper, diced
½ tsp scotch bonnet pepper diced
½ cup carrots, diced
½ cup whole kernel corn
¼ cup garlic finely chopped

PREPARATION
1. Mash the corned beef and in a medium-sized bowl combine all ingredients except cheese.
2. In a medium-sized lightly greased casserole dish, arrange alternate layers of corned beef mixture and cheese, leaving enough cheese to cover the top.
3. 3. Bake in a pre-heated oven at 300 degrees for 15 minutes or until cheese melts.

SPANISH TOWN CORNED BEEF & RICE COOKUP—FIRE ENGINE

The fire engine is a hearty recipe which mixes corned beef and white long grain rice. TASTY!

INGREDIENTS
1 tin corned beef
¼ cup escallion chopped
½ tbsp thyme leaves
¼ cup coconut milk
¼ tsp black pepper
¼ tsp salt
1 cup white long grain rice

PREPARATION
1. In a Dutch pot or any medium-sized pot, put corned beef and escallion.
2. Cook for a few minutes then add rice to the pot and enough water to cook rice.
3. Add Coconut milk, thyme, black pepper and salt and let simmer until rice is cooked.
4. Remove and serve hot.

DOWN TOWN CORNED BEEF AND BEANS
Another great Jamaican corned beef recipe a favorite during the Hurricane Gilbert era.

INGREDIENTS
1 tin corned beef
¼ cup onion chopped
¼ cup escallion chopped
¼ cup tomatoes chopped
¼ cup tinned baked beans
½ tsp. allspice
¼ tsp black pepper
¼ tsp salt

PREPARATION
1. Over a medium flame, sauté onion, escallion, and tomatoes with a bit of the fat from the corned beef.
2. Add all the corned beef and cook for several minutes.
3. Add the tin of beans, including liquid, and the seasoning.
4. Turn down the heat and let simmer until some of the liquid is gone.
5. Serve hot.

ST. BESS CORNBEEF AND CABBAGE MIX UP
We stopped on our way to Westmoreland and picked up this recipe in a small restaurant just outside Lacovia.

INGREDIENTS
2 tins of corned beef
½ cup carrots cut up
¼ cup escallion chopped
¼ cup garlic chopped
2 cups cabbage sliced
¼ cup onion, diced
2 cups potatoes cubed

PREPARATION
1. Sauté onion and garlic in Dutch pot for a few minutes.
2. Add carrots, celery, cabbage and enough water to cover.
3. Cook for about 20 minutes then add potatoes and corned beef.
4. Cook until potatoes are tender.
5. Serve hot.

STRAWBERRY HILL BARBECUE BEEF RIBS
This is an exquisite recipe from the Hills just below the Blue Mountains.

INGREDIENTS
5 lb Beef short ribs
3 cup Jamaican Jerk-BQ Sauce

PREPARATION
1. Place ribs in a flat pan or dish. Pour sauce over ribs, turning so as to coat both sides; pierce meat with a large fork.
2. Marinate 8 hrs. turning once. Remove ribs from marinade and brush off excess sauce.
3. Cook over coals for 10 minutes.
4. Brush with marinade and cook 4-5 minutes. more.
Heat remaining sauce and serve with ribs.

FALMOUTH OATS BEEF BALLS
On our round trip we picked up this sweet recipe in Falmouth, Trelawny

INGREDIENTS
2 cups ground beef minced
¾ cup oats
2 tbsp all purpose soy sauce
1 tsp. garlic minced
½ tsp. black pepper
½ cup tomatoes, chopped
½ cup onion chopped
1 tbsp. dark sugar
¼ cup escallion chopped
½ cup tomato ketchup
¼ cup water

PREPARATION
1. Combine thoroughly, beef, oats, soy sauce, garlic and black pepper.
2. Shape into balls and place into a skillet.
3. Add all ingredients except escallion and bring to a boil.
4. Then reduce to a simmer and allow to cook for a 10 minutes, stirring occasionally.
5. Continue to simmer until balls are no longer pink.
6. Serve hot.

ST. MARY CORNED BEEF RICE CAKES
The good people of St. Mary contributed this rice cake recipe.

INGREDIENTS
¼ cup vegetable oil
½ cup onion chopped
¼ cup garlic chopped
½ cup sweet pepper chopped
2 cups long grain rice, cooked
2 eggs beaten
1 cup corned beef
2 tbsp flour
1 tsp curry
¼ tsp salt
¼ tsp black pepper
3 tbsp. breadcrumbs

PREPARATION
1. In a saucepan, heat 1 tbsp. oil, sauté onion, garlic and sweet pepper.
2. In a bowl mix with onion, garlic and sweet pepper with rice, eggs, corned beef, flour and seasoning.
3. With dampened hands, shape into cakes. Dredge with breadcrumbs.
4. Over moderate heat, heat remaining oil in pan. Fry cakes for 10 minutes on each side and serve hot.

MAROON TOWN BEEF KEBABS

We got these recipes from two maroons in Accompong, a Maroon town more than 200 years old.

INGREDIENTS

¼ cup garlic chopped
2 large onions
6 large sweet peppers, 3 red and 3 green
3 cups beef cubed
1 tsp. curry powder
¼ cup escallion chopped
1 tbsp thyme leaves
½ tbsp scotch bonnet pepper diced
¼ tsp salt
¼ tsp black pepper
1tbsp. vegetable oil

PREPARATION

1. Clean beef and trim excessive fat.
2. Cut into portions and marinate with vegetable oil, chopped escallion, garlic, pepper, thyme, onion and salt and pepper.
3. Slice red and green peppers and stick on each skewer.
4. Allow to set for at least 10 minutes then heat the grill with one teaspoon vegetable oil.

ST. MARY COW TONGUE

Not a very appealing sound but a delicious taste enjoyed by many Jamaicans.

INGREDIENTS

1 large cow tongue
½ tbsp onion powder
½ tbsp escallion chopped
¼ tbsp garlic powder
¼ tsp salt
¼ tsp black pepper
¼ tsp allspice
½ tbsp thyme leaves
¼ cup vegetable oil

PREPARATION

1. Mix all ingredients together until a brine is made.
2. Leave tongue in brine for 3-4 days.
3. To cook use brine with seasonings and boil.
4. Strip the tongue while it is hot.
5. Roll the tongue and place in a basin.
6. When cooled slice and serve cold

KINGSTON'S OXTAIL AND BEANS RECIPE
One of the most delicious Jamaican recipes there are, try this recipe today.

INGREDIENTS
3 cups oxtail chopped
½ cup onions minced
½ cup escallion minced
¼ cup garlic minced
1 tbsp soy sauce
¼ tsp salt
¼ tsp black pepper
¼ tsp allspice
½ tbsp thyme leaves
1 cup broad beans
¼ cup vegetable oil
½ cup carrots chopped

PREPARATION
1. Season oxtail with seasoning and allow to marinate for at least 1 hour.
2. In a large frying pan (or substitute in pressure cooker) cook broad beans in water until they are somewhat soft, then add soy sauce, carrots and oxtail and cook until meat and carrots are tender.
3. Serve hot.

MAY PEN'S BREADED OXTAIL
A breaded version of the Jamaican oxtail recipe.

INGREDIENTS
2 cups oxtail chopped
½ tbsp onion powder
½ tbsp escallion chopped
¼ tbsp garlic powder
1 tbsp soy sauce
¼ tsp salt
¼ tsp black pepper
¼ tsp allspice
½ tbsp thyme leaves
¼ cup vegetable oil
1 egg beaten
1 cup bread crumbs

PREPARATION
1. Cook the oxtail in a pressure cooker or in boiling water until soft.
2. Remove and season oxtail with seasoning and allow to marinate for at least ½ hour.
3. Dip in egg and then in bread crumbs.
4. In a large frying pan sauté escallions and add breaded oxtails.
5. Fry until brown.
6. Serve hot.

JAMAICAN POT ROAST BEEF
This is a great Jamaican beef recipe that we know that you will love.

INGREDIENTS
4 lb boneless cut beef
½ tbsp onion powder
½ tbsp escallion chopped
¼ tbsp garlic powder
¼ tsp salt
¼ tsp black pepper
¼ tsp allspice
½ tbsp thyme leaves
¼ cup vegetable oil
¼ cup Jamaican sweet sauce

PREPARATION
1. Season beef with dry seasonings and coat with beef sauce.
2. Heat large pot and add vegetable oil. Then brown on all sides.
3. Add water and sweet beef sauce and cover pot.
4. When the meat is fully cooked garnish with grapefruit and orange slices.
5. Slice and serve hot.

JAMAICAN COW FOOT RECIPE
Sweet cow foot though not loved by all loved by most beef lovers.

INGREDIENTS
2 lb cow foot
½ cup onion chopped
½ cup escallion chopped
¼ cup garlic chopped
¼ tsp salt
¼ tsp black pepper
¼ tsp allspice
½ tbsp thyme leaves
¼ cup vegetable oil
1 cup chopped ripe plantain
1 cup chopped potatoes
1 cup chopped pumpkins

PREPARATION
1. Cook the calves feet in water in a sauce pan or in a pressure cooker until meat is soft.
2. Add seasonings and vegetables and cook until the vegetables are soft and a stew is made.
3. Serve with cooked white rice and hot.

JAMAICAN STEWED PEAS WITH BEEF
A great tasting stew peas recipe.

INGREDIENTS
1 pt. red peas
1 cup salted pigs tail chopped
2 cups salted beef cubed
2 cups stew beef cubed
¼ cup escallion chopped
¼ cup onion chopped
¼ cup garlic chopped
½ tsp thyme
½ tsp salt and pepper mixed
½ tsp scotch bonnet pepper diced
2 cups coconut milk

PREPARATION
1. Soak peas in water to soften and pig tail a meat to remove salty taste.
2. Place meat and peas together in a large saucepan with coconut milk and enough water to cover meat and cook until soft.
3. Add seasonings and cook for a further 30 minutes until sauce is thick.
4. Serve with plain rice.

ST. THOMAS BAKED BEEF
In St. Thomas baked beef is commonplace in the finest restaurants. We got this great recipe from a top chef in the parish.

INGREDIENTS
1½ lb ground beef
1 cup bread crumbs
1 cup milk
½ cup chopped onion
¼ cup peanuts chopped
1 tbsp lemon juice
2 tsp curry powder
1½ tsp salt
¼ tsp pepper
2 eggs—beaten
1 cup milk
¼ tbsp paprika

PREPARATION
1. Mix beef, bread crumbs, 1 cup milk, 1 egg, the onion, peanuts, lemon juice, curry powder, salt and pepper.
2. Spread mixture in un-greased 2-quart casserole.
3. Cook uncovered in 325 degree oven 45 minutes; drain excess fat.
4. Mix beaten eggs and 1 cup milk; pour over beef mixture.
5. Sprinkle with paprika.
6. Place casserole in oblong pan, 13 x 9 x 2 inches, on oven rack.
7. Pour very hot water into pan.
8. Cook uncovered until beef is done.
9. Garnish with lemon slices and pimiento if desired.
10. Cut into wedges to serve

LIME HALL STEWED TRIPE AND BEAN
A wowser Jamaican recipe of stewed tripe and beans a Jamaican favorite. We got this recipe from Ms. Effie in Lime Hall, St. Ann.

INGREDIENTS
1 lb chopped tripe
1 cup broad beans
2 tbsp tomato ketchup
¼ cup lime juice
2 cups potatoes cubed
½ tbsp onion powder
½ cup escallion chopped
¼ tbsp garlic powder
¼ tsp salt
¼ tsp black pepper
¼ tsp allspice
½ tbsp thyme leaves
¼ cup vegetable oil

PREPARATION
1. Cook tripe into small pieces and clean thoroughly with lime juice and water.
2. Heat oil in frying pan and lightly brown the tripe.
3. Using a pressure cooker pressure the tripe and beans with salt added.
4. When tripe is soft add all seasonings and stew for at 45 minutes.
5. Serve hot.

> **Cooking Tip**
> Always clean the tripe meat thoroughly before preparing. Use either cane vinegar or lime juice and rinse the meat and then pat dry.

JAMAICAN MEAT LOAF
A popular recipe in Jamaica served in almost every Jamaican patty store you can think of.

INGREDIENTS
1 ½ lb Lean Ground Beef
½ cup ketchup
3 bread slices
1 egg large
1 cup milk
¼ cup onion chopped
1 tsp Salt
¼ tsp black pepper
¼ tsp garlic powder
¼ cup Jamaican sweet sauce
1 tbsp Worcestershire Sauce

PREPARATION
1. Heat the oven to 350 degrees F then mx all the ingredients except the ketchup together.
2. Spread the meat mixture into an un-greased loaf pan.
3. Spoon ketchup onto the loaf and bake, uncovered, for 1 to 1 ¼ hours or until done.
4. Drain off the excess fat and serve sliced on a heated platter.

OCHO RIOS LEMON STEAK
A great tasting steak recipe served up by the top chefs from this Jamaican resort city.

INGREDIENTS
2 lb round steak
2 lemons sliced
3 tbsp vegetable oil
4 lemon slices
½ cup onions minced
¼ cup garlic
½ cup flour
1 cup Jamaican beef broth
1 tbsp brown sugar
¼ cup parsley flakes
2 tsp thyme
¼ tsp salt
¼ tsp black pepper
2 cup rice cooked
½ cup sweet pepper chopped
½ cup chopped tomatoes

PREPARATION
1. Cut steak into serving size pieces.
2. Brown on both sides in 3 tablespoons oil and add lemon slices.
3. Remove steak to baking pan.
4. Layer onions and garlic over meat.
5. Sprinkle flour over top, then combine beef broth, beer, sugar, parsley flakes, thyme, salt and pepper.
6. Pour over steak and bake uncovered in 325 degree oven for 3 hours.
7. Serve over cooked broad noodles or cooked rice.
8. Garnish with green pepper slices, fresh parsley and tomatoes.

MONTEGO BAY BARBECUED STEAKS

INGREDIENTS
3 lb round steak
2 tbsp lemon juice
1 cup Jamaican Jerk-BQ Sauce

PREPARATION
1. Pound steak on both sides with a wooden mallet or the edge of a heavy plate.
2. Combine lemon juice and sauce and spread over both sides of steak.
3. Allow to stand 4-5 hours at room temperature.
4. Broil steaks about 4 inches above glowing coals on barbecue grill for 4-5 minutes on each side

JAMAICAN BEEF IN HOT PEPPER SAUCE

INGREDIENTS
1½ lb boneless beef sirloin cut into strips
1 cup sweet peppers chopped
½ tbsp scotch bonnet pepper minced
¼ cup garlic chopped
¼ cup white wine (**optional**)
¾ tbsp ginger minced
½ tsp salt
½ tsp black pepper
½ tsp allspice
¼ tsp cinnamon powder
½ tsp Jamaican hot pepper sauce
1 tbsp margarine
1 tbsp vegetable oil
½ cup onion chopped
1 cup cooked rice

PREPARATION
1. Place the chopped sweet pepper, scotch bonnet pepper, garlic, wine, ginger, salt, pepper, allspice, cinnamon, and hot pepper sauce in a blender on medium-high speed until smoothly blended.
2. Heat the margarine and the oil in a frying pan over medium-high heat until hot.
3. Add the beef and cook until meat is browned on all sides.
4. Remove the beef set aside and keep warm.
5. Add the onion and more sweet pepper strips to the skillet and cook until brown.
6. Return the beef to the skillet and add the blender mixture.
7. Heat to boiling, then reduce the heat and simmer uncovered until the beef is hot and the sauce is slightly thickened.
8. Serve over rice.

NEGRIL JERK-BQ MEAT LOAF
A popular version to the Jamaican meat loaf recipe absolutely exquisite.

INGREDIENTS
1 ½ lb Lean Ground Beef
½ cup ketchup
3 bread slices
1 egg large
1 cup milk
¼ cup onion chopped
1 tsp Salt
¼ tsp black pepper
¼ tsp garlic powder
¼ cup Jamaican jerk-barbeque sauce
1 tbsp Worcestershire Sauce

PREPARATION
1. Pre-heat the oven to 350 degrees F and mx all the ingredients except the ketchup together.
2. Spread the meat mixture into an un-greased loaf pan.
3. Mix ½ cup of jerk-bq sauce and 2 tbsp of water in a skillet.
4. Place the slices of meatloaf in the skillet, turning to coat all sides with the jerk-bq sauce.
5. Cover and cook over low heat, brushing the sauce on the slices occasionally, until the meat is hot.

ST. ANN POTATOES AND MEAT LOAF
A popular version to the Jamaican meat loaf recipe absolutely exquisite.

INGREDIENTS
1 ½ lb Lean Ground Beef
½ cup ketchup
3 bread slices
1 egg large
1 cup milk
¼ cup onion chopped
1 tsp Salt
¼ tsp black pepper
¼ tsp garlic powder
1 cup mashed potatoes
¼ cup Jamaican sweet sauce
1 tbsp Worcestershire Sauce
½ cup shredded cheese

PREPARATION
1. Heat the oven to 550 degrees F.
2. Mix all the ingredients except the ketchup together.
3. Spread the meat mixture into an un-greased loaf pan.
4. Mix ½ cup of jerk-bq sauce and 2 tbsp of water in a skillet.
5. Place the slices of meatloaf in the skillet, turning to coat all sides with the sauce.
6. Cover and cook over low heat, brushing the sauce on the slices occasionally, until the meat is hot.
7. Spread the potatoes on the slices and sprinkle with shredded cheese.
8. Broil until the cheese is melted and serve hot.

> **Cooking Tip**
> Beef takes a while to prepare some times cutting the beef in bite size chunks or using a pressure cooker speeds up the process.

ST. BESS BEEF AND RED STRIPE BEER
A great treat for Jamaican red stripe Beer lovers, this is one of our five star recipes.

INGREDIENTS
4 lb boneless chuck
¼ tsp salt
¼ tsp black pepper
¼ tsp garlic powder
1 cup Red Stripe Beer
½ cup onions thinly sliced
½ tbsp scotch bonnet pepper diced
1½ tbsp Jamaican sweet sauce
½ cup sweet peppers sliced

PREPARATION
1. Season meat with salt, pepper and garlic.
2. Brown lightly in heavy skillet then add onions, scotch bonnet pepper and sweet peppers and brown lightly and then pur Red Stripe Beer over all, stir in sauce.
3. Cover tightly and simmer slowly for 2 to 2 ½ hours or until meat is tender.

HELLSHIRE SURF AND TURF

The best beef and seafood recipe from the St. Catherine area.

INGREDIENTS

½ cup Jamaican salad dressing
¼ cup Jamaican sweet sauce
¼ cup red wine (**optional**)
1 tsp Worcestershire sauce
Salt—to taste
Pepper—to taste
1½ lb round steak
12 shrimp, raw and shelled
¼ cup bacon cut in squares
½ cup sweet pepper sliced
½ cup onion sliced

PREPARATION

1. Make a marinade by combining salad dressing, sauce, wine, Worcestershire sauce, salt and pepper.
2. Cut steak into 1-1/2 inch cubes. Put steak cubes and raw shrimp in marinade and let stand in refrigerator 3 hours.
3. Remove beef and shrimp from marinade; alternate 8 beef cubes and 8 shrimp on 6 skewers, using squares of bacon, slices of pepper and onion, and mushrooms between meats.
4. Place skewers 4 to 6 inches above medium heat on grill.
5. Cook 8 to 10 minutes on each side, brushing with marinade occasionally.

JAMAICAN BRAISED BEEF

The best braised beef recipe that we found across our travels in the country.

INGREDIENTS

¼ cup escallion chopped
¼ cup gingerroot chopped finely
½ tsp allspice
¼ cup dry wine
2½ tbsp vegetable oil
1 tsp brown sugar
2 lb beef chuck
¼ cup garlic, minced
½ cup soy sauce
½ tsp salt
¼ tsp black pepper
2 cup chicken stock

PREPARATION

1. Combine all ingredients except meat, oil and chicken stock in bowl and set aside.
2. Heat oil in heavy skillet and brown meat quickly on all sides.
3. Add mixture from bowl and cook, stirring to heat and blend.
4. Heat stock in saucepan and add to beef. Simmer covered 90 minutes to 2 hours or until meat is tender.
5. Slice meat and serve hot or cold.
6. Reserve gravy for master sauce.

WEST KINGSTON STYLE BAKED BEEF TENDERLOIN
We got this tenderloin from two cooks from the West Kingston area, an absolute peach of a recipe.

INGREDIENTS
6 tbsps melted butter
½ cup onions sliced
¼ cup garlic minced
½ tsp allspice
½ tsp scotch bonnet pepper diced
¼ lb ground beef
4 lb beef tenderloin
2 tbsps Jamaican sweet sauce
½ tsp Jamaican hot pepper sauce
½ tsp Worcestershire sauce
¼ cup red wine (**optional**)
¼ cup beef bouillon
1 tbsp flour
4 bacon slices cooked

PREPARATION
1. Make marinade by melting butter, sauté onions, garlic and pepper.
2. Add ground beef, beef sauce, seasonings, wine and beef bullion then set aside.
3. Sprinkle meat with salt and pepper to taste dust with flour.
4. Place 2 strips of bacon on meat. Broil 7 minutes.
5. Turn, cover with other bacon strips and broil 7 minutes more.
6. Place meat in glass dish covered with marinade overnight.
7. Bake in marinade at 450 degrees about 20 minutes.
8. Serve hot.

UPTOWN PLAZA BEEF TERIYAKI
A sweet recipe we garnered from a Chinese chef cooking in a Jamaican restaurant.

INGREDIENTS
1½ lb sirloin steak
½ cup soy sauce
½ cup white wine (**optional**)
¼ cup garlic, minced
1 tsp ginger minced
1 tbsp cornstarch
1 tbsp brown sugar

PREPARATION
1. Slice beef into ½ inch strips and arrange in shallow casserole.
2. Combine soy sauce, wine, garlic, and ginger then pour over meat, cover and refrigerate. Marinate 2 hours.
3. Broil beef 1½ minutes on each side. Pour marinade into saucepan.
4. Add cornstarch and cook over medium heat, until sauce thickens.
5. Remove from heat, stir in sugar. Serve sauce over meat.

> **Cooking Tip**
> When using grated ginger in a marinade or a sauce always be sure to strain the sauce or marinade in order to prevent chunks of ginger in the sauce. This is very annoying to guests.

JAMAICAN CURRIED BEEF
A Jamaican curry recipe to die for. All curry lover should try this great recipe.

INGREDIENTS
¾ pound boneless beef top round steak
½ cup chopped sweet pepper
¾ cup chopped onion
1 cup cooked cubed potatoes
1 cup cooked sweet potatoes
1 tsp vegetable oil
2 tsp curry powder
¾ cup tomato crushed
1 tsp Jamaican sweet sauce
½ cup cold water
1 tbsp cornstarch

PREPARATION
1. Trim fat from meat and thinly slice across the grain into bite-size strips.
2. Preheat a coated non-stick skillet over medium-high heat.
3. Add pepper and onion and stir-fry for 2 minutes remove vegetables and set aside.
4. Add cooking oil to skillet. Add beef and stir-fry over high heat for till nearly done.
5. Add curry powder stir-fry for 1 minute more.
6. Carefully stir in tomato, cooked vegetables and beef sauce.
7. Stir together cold water and cornstarch and stir into meat mixture.
8. Cook and stir until thickened and bubbly then cook and stir.
9. Serve over hot rice.

Cooking Tip
You can make curry sauce by adding butter and curry powder in a saucepan and frying. Spread on uncooked meat to soak to give the meat the added curry flavor.

JAMAICAN JERK-BQ HAMBURGHER
A Jamaican burgher recipe that is leaps and bounds over popular burgher recipes used by fast food joints.

INGREDIENTS
1 lb ground beef
½ cup chopped sweet pepper
¼ cup chopped onion
¼ cup escallion chopped finely
¼ cup garlic chopped finely
1 tsp vegetable oil
¼ cup bread crumbs
1 tsp Jamaican jerk-bq sauce

PREPARATION
1. Combine all ingredients and form into round patties.
2. Brown the patties in the vegetable oil each side and then add the jerk-bq sauce.
3. Cook until done and then remove.
4. Serve over hamburger rolls.

PORT MARIA BACON AND STEAK
We tried this great tasting recipe from Port Maria in St. Mary. A delicious tasting recipe.

INGREDIENTS
4 strips bacon
1½ lb ground beef
½ pound ground pork
¼ cup chopped onions
½ cup chopped green pepper
¼ tsp salt
¼ tsp black pepper
½ tbsp scotch bonnet pepper diced
¼ cup chopped parsley
¼ cup vegetable oil

PREPARATION
1. Combine all ingredients and form into round patties.
2. Brown the patties in the vegetable oil each side.
3. Broil at 375 Degrees turning over on each side.
4. Serve hot.

DRAGON BAY SAVORY MEAT LOAF
A great tasting recipe from this world renowned tourist resort in Portland.

INGREDIENTS
2 lb ground beef
1 egg beaten
¼ cup onion minced
½ tsp salt
¼ tsp black pepper
½ cup Jamaican vegetable broth
½ cup Jamaican sweet sauce

PREPARATION
1. Combine all ingredients and shape into a loaf.
2. Place in greased baking tin and Bake at 350 Degrees F.
3. Continue to baste with sweet beef sauce until done.
4. Remove and serve hot.

PORUS BAKED CORN BEEF
Traveling through the south coast we picked up this tasty treat in the community of Porus.

INGREDIENTS
1 cup corned beef
1 cup brown sugar
1 whole clove
¼ cup onion chopped
¼ cup escallion chopped
1 tsp Jamaican sweet sauce

PREPARATION
1. Cover corned beef with water and then bring to a boil and skim the drain well. In a baking dish add all ingredients except sweet sauce. Place in oven and bake at 325 Degree F basting with sauce. Remove and served hot.

MONTEGO BAY STUFFED STEAK

Oh My! Was all we could say about this recipe its absolutely moth watering.

INGREDIENTS

4 steaks
¼ tsp salt
¼ tsp black pepper
2 tbsp flour
1 cup bread crumbs
¼ cup onion minced
¼ cup escallion minced
¼ cup garlic minced
2 tbsp butter melted
2 tbsp water
1 cup crushed tomatoes

PREPARATION

1. Season steak with salt and black pepper.
2. Mix all other ingredients together in a bowl to make stuffing.
3. Pour on steaks and roll together holding with a skewer.
4. Place in a greased baking dish and bake at 350 Degrees F until steaks are tender
5. Remove and slice into ½ inch servings.
6. Serve hot.

COOLIE TOWN CURRIED BEEF

A little variation of curried beef due to more pepper being used and no vegetables.

INGREDIENTS

¾ pound boneless beef top round steak
½ cup chopped sweet pepper
½ tbsp scotch bonnet pepper diced
¾ cup chopped onion
1 tsp vegetable oil
2 tsp curry powder
¾ cup tomato crushed
1 tsp Jamaican sweet sauce
½ cup cold water
1 tbsp cornstarch

PREPARATION

1. Trim fat from meat and thinly slice across the grain into bite-size strips.
2. Preheat a coated non-stick skillet over medium-high heat.
3. Add pepper and onion and stir-fry for 2 minutes remove vegetables and set aside.
4. Add cooking oil to skillet. Add beef and stir-fry over high heat for till nearly done.
5. Add curry powder stir-fry for 1 minute more.
6. Carefully stir in tomato, scotch bonnet pepper and beef sauce.
7. Stir together cold water and cornstarch and stir into meat mixture.
8. Cook and stir until thickened and bubbly then cook and stir.
9. Serve over hot rice.

Cooking Tip

When baking a steak ensure that the steak is well seasoned and that you continuously baste the steak in regular intervals. Be careful not to over-bake the beef because it will become very hardened and difficult to chew.

DOREENS BEEF DUMPLINGS
Doreen literally hit the nail on the head with this recipe a great dish that can be used as a side dish.

INGREDIENTS
2 cups dumpling dough
1 cup ground beef cooked
½ cup minced onions
1 cup shredded cheese
½ cup vegetable oil
½ cup melted butter
1 cup Jamaican sweet sauce

PREPARATION
1. Roll out dough and form into 1 inch cubes and baste with melted butter.
2. Place beef, onions and shredded cheese evenly on each cube.
3. Close cubes and form into balls.
4. In a large skillet slightly brown each dumpling then place on baking tin and bake at 450 Degrees F for NO LONGER than 10 minutes.
5. Baste continuously with sauce
6. Remove and serve hot.

JAMAICAN JELLIED MEAT LOAF
A perfect blend of Jamaican herbs and spices, beef and gelatin.

INGREDIENTS
1 tbsp gelatin
¼ cup cold water
¾ cup boiling water
¼ cup vinegar
¼ tsp salt
2 cups diced cooked beef
¼ cup diced escallion
½ tbsp allspice
½ cup sweet pepper chopped
¼ cup minced onion
2 hard cooked eggs (**optional**)

PREPARATION
1. Soften gelatin in cold water and then dissolve in boiling water.
2. Add vinegar and salt and wait until mixture begins to cool.
3. Add all other ingredients and wait until cold.
4. Arrange egg slices on mold.
5. Refrigerate and serve cold.

DOREENS SCRAMBLE BEEF
Another one of Doreen's delicious beef recipes.

INGREDIENTS
1 cup diced cooked steak
¼ cup onion chopped
½ cup green pepper diced
2 tbsp vegetable oil
½ cup whole kernel sweet corn
½ cup Jamaican tomato sauce
½ tbsp allspice
¼ tsp salt

PREPARATION
1. Sauté meat, onions and green pepper in vegetable oil until brown.
2. Add tomato juice, allspice and corn and simmer until cooked.
3. Serve hot.

JAMAICAN SWEET AND SOUR BEEF
A Jamaican version to the great Chinese recipe.

INGREDIENTS
1½ lb sirloin steak cut in cubes
½ cup vegetable oil
2 eggs beaten
¼ cup garlic minced
1 tbsp flour
½ cup chopped pineapple slices
1 cup water
¼ cup vinegar
2 tbsp sugar
¼ tsp salt
½ cup sweet pepper chopped
½ cup tomatoes chopped

PREPARATION
1. Whisk eggs and beat in garlic, dip steak cubes in mixture and then into flour.
2. Brown steak cubes in oil and drain on absorbent paper.
3. Drain pineapple and reserve chunks, stir in pineapple juice in egg dip along with water, vinegar, sugar, and salt.
4. Turn mixture into already hot pan and cook slowly, adding beef, pineapple, green peppers and tomatoes.
5. When cooked pour out into a bowl.
6. Serve hot

PLAIN OL' JAMAICAN HAMBURGHER
This is a plain old Jamaican hamburger recipe, that everyone should know.

INGREDIENTS
1 lb ground beef
½ cup chopped sweet pepper
¼ cup chopped onion
¼ cup escallion chopped finely
¼ cup garlic chopped finely
1 tsp vegetable oil
½ cup melted butter

PREPARATION
1. Combine all ingredients and form into round patties.
2. Brown the patties in the vegetable oil each side and then add the jerk-bq sauce.
3. Broil turning on each side until done basting with melted butter.
4. Serve over hamburger rolls.

JAMAICAN JERK BEEF
More jerking recipes with beef that are absolutely spicy and delicious.

INGREDIENTS
3 large beef steaks
2 tbsp Jamaican hot pepper sauce
1 tsp salt and black pepper
½ tsp cinnamon
½ tsp allspice
¼ cup onion, minced
2 tbsp sugar
2 tbsp pepper, red, minced
2 tbsp hot pepper jelly
¼ cup escallion chopped
1 cup rice, cooked

PREPARATION
1. In a shallow container, place the hot pepper sauce.
2. Add beef steak, one piece at a time, turning to coat.
3. Sprinkle salt, cinnamon and allspice over the beef steak chops.
4. Place the beef steak chops in a single layer in a large shallow baking dish.
5. Bake at 400 F, basting twice with pan juices for 45 minutes or until the beef steak is fork tender.
6. Serve hot.

CHANTELLE'S FAMOUS BEEF STEW
A great tasting recipe from one of the staff at the Jamaican Pegasus Hotel

INGREDIENTS
¼ cup escallion chopped
¼ cup gingerroot chopped finely
½ cup onions minced
½ tsp allspice
¼ cup dry wine
2½ tbsp vegetable oil
1 tsp brown sugar
2 lb beef chuck
¼ cup garlic, minced
½ cup soy sauce
½ tsp salt
¼ tsp black pepper
2 cup chicken stock

PREPARATION
1. Combine all ingredients except meat, oil and chicken stock in bowl and set aside.
2. Heat oil in heavy skillet and brown meat quickly on all sides.
3. Add mixture from bowl and cook, stirring to heat and blend.
4. Heat stock in saucepan and add to beef. Simmer covered 90 minutes to 2 hours or until meat is tender.
5. Slice meat and serve hot or cold.
6. Reserve gravy for master sauce.

HIP STRIP JERK-BURGHER
The best Jamaican burgher recipe around. Great beef laced with the famous get Jamaica sauce

INGREDIENTS
1 lb ground beef
½ cup chopped sweet pepper
¼ cup chopped onion
¼ cup escallion chopped finely
¼ cup garlic chopped finely
1 tsp vegetable oil
¼ cup bread crumbs
1 tsp Get Jamaica Jerk Sauce©

PREPARATION
1. Combine all ingredients and form into round patties.
2. Brown the patties in the vegetable oil each side and then add the jerk sauce.
3. Cook until done and then remove.
4. Serve over hamburger rolls.

Cooking Tip
Jamaican hamburgers must be complemented by fresh vegetables and fresh bread or rolls. No matter how good the meat tastes whether, beef, chicken, fish and even pork if the other ingredients are not fresh it takes away from the taste of the recipe. Also allow your guests to actually prepare there own burgher as you wont know how much condiments they would desire on the recipe. Always substitute margarine with low fat butter, this recipe is a bit high on the cholesterol side and low fat ingredients are advisable.

KINGSTON ROAST LEG OF LAMB
A great recipe from two chefs at the Hilton Hotel in Kingston.

INGREDIENTS
1 leg of lamb
¼ tsp salt
¼ tsp paprika
½ tsp allspice
¼ cup onion, minced
2 tbsp sugar
½ cup flour
¼ cup minced ginger
¼ cup minced garlic
¼ cup escallion chopped

PREPARATION
1. Make gashes to the lamb leg and season with seasonings.
2. Season well with seasonings then dredge with flour.
3. Place in roaster fat side up and roast, uncovered in slow oven until tender.
4. When completed brush off all visible seasonings.
5. Remove cut in serving portions and serve hot.

JAMAICAN BEEF STEAK IN OTAHEITE APPLE SAUCE
This apple recipe is to die for. Beef and the otaheite apple are a perfect blend.

INGREDIENTS
2 cups cubed steak in ½ inch cubes
1 tsp garlic powder
1 tsp allspice
¼ tsp salt
¼ tsp black pepper
1 egg white
1 cup Jamaican otaheite apple sauce
¼ cup vinegar
2 onions, chopped
½ cup sugar
3 tbsp Jamaican wincarnis wine (**or substitute**)
2 tsp cornstarch
1 tbsp vegetable oil
1 cup Jamaican beef broth

PREPARATION
1. In a saucepan sauté chopped onion in oil. Remove and set aside.
2. Add remaining ingredients except cornstarch and wine and bring to a boil.
3. Dissolve cornstarch in wine and add to saucepan then stir until thicken, simmer for 5 minutes.
4. Stir in sauté onion and set aside.
5. Season beef steak with garlic powder, allspice, salt and pepper and allow to marinate.
6. Remove seasoned beef steak from refrigerator and brush with egg white then return to refrigerator and allow to marinate for 1 hour.
7. Bring 3 cups of beef stock to a boil. Remove beef from refrigerator and cook in stock until done.
8. Remove slice and serve with apple sauce.

ROSE HALL POT ROASTED BEEF
A great pot roasted recipe from the White which of rose hall!.

INGREDIENTS
1 pot roast
½ cup whole cloves
¼ cup vegetable oil
½ cup garlic chopped
½ cup onion chopped
½ tsp allspice
¼ tsp ginger powder
¼ tsp nutmeg
¼ tsp cinnamon powder
¼ tsp salt
¼ tsp black pepper
¼ cup Jamaican sweet sauce
2 tsp. sugar
1 tsp. tomato paste.

PREPARATION
1. Wash and drain pot roast.
2. Stuff pot roast with onion, garlic and allspice
3. Marinate overnight in sweet beef sauce.
4. Remove from liquid and cover with powdered seasoning, salt and pepper.
5. Brown pot roast in hot vegetable oil for 2 minutes on each side.
6. When browned stuff whole cloves into the pot roast.
7. Remove from frying pan and place in pre-heated oven for 45 minutes until thoroughly cooked.
8. Serve with sauce and fluffy white rice with steamed vegetables.

BUFF BAY STEW MUTTON
A sweet blend of mutton and spices we picked up in a restaurant on the outskirts of Buff bay, Portland.

INGREDIENTS
¼ tsp salt
¼ cup vegetable oil
3 lb boneless mutton cubed
½ cup onion finely chopped
¼ cup garlic minced
1 cup tomatoes peeled and chopped
1 tbsp Jamaican tomato sauce
¼ tsp nutmeg
¼ tsp black pepper
¼ cup red wine
¼ cup chopped parsley

PREPARATION
1. In a large frying pan, heat the oil and brown mutton cubes on all sides. Add onion and garlic and cook until onion is soft.
2. Add tomatoes, tomato paste, salt, nutmeg, pepper and wine and bring to a boil, cover, and immediately reduce heat to low.
3. Simmer slowly until mutton is very tender.
4. Add reserved callaloo stirring in gently. Cover and cook until mutton is fully tender.
5. Sprinkle with chopped parsley before serving.

JAMAICAN MUTTON KEBABS
A great kebab recipe even more delicious than the beef kebab recipe.

INGREDIENTS
¼ cup garlic chopped
2 large onions
6 large sweet peppers, 3 red and 3 green
3 cups mutton cubed
1 tsp. curry powder
¼ cup escallion chopped
1 tbsp thyme leaves
½ tbsp scotch bonnet pepper diced
¼ tsp salt
¼ tsp black pepper
1tbsp. vegetable oil

PREPARATION
1. Clean mutton and trim excessive fat.
2. Cut into portions and marinate with vegetable oil, chopped escallion, garlic, pepper, thyme, onion and salt and pepper.
3. Slice red and green peppers and stick on each skewer.
4. Allow to set for at least 10 minutes then heat the grill with one teaspoon vegetable oil.

OLD HARBOR BRAISED MUTTON
Braising mutton is a tricky technique but a great tasting recipe.

INGREDIENTS
¼ cup escallion chopped
¼ cup gingerroot chopped finely
½ tsp allspice
¼ cup dry wine
2½ tbsp vegetable oil
1 tsp brown sugar
2 lb mutton chopped into serving portions
¼ cup garlic, minced
½ cup soy sauce
½ tsp salt
¼ tsp black pepper
2 cup chicken stock

PREPARATION
1. Combine all ingredients except meat, oil and chicken stock in bowl and set aside.
2. Heat oil in heavy skillet and brown meat quickly on all sides.
3. Add mixture from bowl and cook, stirring to heat and blend.
4. Heat stock in saucepan and add to mutton. Simmer covered 90 minutes to 2 hours or until meat is tender.
5. Slice meat and serve hot or cold.
6. Reserve gravy for master sauce.

Cooking Tip
To sauté meat actually means to brown the meat in a small amount of oil. This means swirling the meat around in the pot ensuring the meat does not burn.

BALACLAVA BAKED MUTTON
St. Bess is renowned for its goat recipes and this baked mutton recipe is another flower in its hat.

INGREDIENTS
1½ lb finely chopped mutton
1 cup bread crumbs
1 cup milk
½ cup chopped onion
¼ cup peanuts chopped
1 tbsp lemon juice
2 tsp curry powder
1½ tsp salt
¼ tsp pepper
2 eggs beaten
1 cup milk
¼ tbsp paprika

PREPARATION
1. Mix mutton, bread crumbs, 1 cup milk, 1 egg, the onion, peanuts, lemon juice, curry powder, salt and pepper. Spread mixture in un-greased 2-quart casserole.
2. Cook uncovered in 325 degree oven 45 minutes; drain excess fat.
3. Mix beaten eggs and 1 cup milk and pour over mutton mixture.
4. Sprinkle with paprika. Place casserole in oblong pan, 13 x 9 x 2 inches, on oven rack.
5. Pour very hot water into pan. Cook uncovered until mutton is done.
6. Garnish with lemon slices and pimento if desired. Cut into wedges to serve

BROWNS TOWN BROILED MUTTON
Not a popular recipe but we found it tasty enough to add.

INGREDIENTS
2 lbs mutton
1 tbsp allspice
¼ tsp salt
¼ tsp black pepper
½ cup vegetable oil
¼ cup chopped parsley
1 clove garlic finely chopped
¼ cup melted butter

PREPARATION
1. In a blender, puree the all ingredients except melted butter to make marinate.
2. Pour marinate over the mutton and marinate, refrigerate for 2 hours (or overnight).
3. Drain off marinade and discard.
4. Preheat broiler and place mutton in and broil for 50 minutes basting with the melted butter every 15 minutes, then Turn the mutton and continue to bake another 15 minutes basting frequently.
5. Remove and serve hot.

Cooking Tip
Mutton can take a while to prepare, it is advisable to soften the meat in a pressure cooker then prepare with seasonings in a saucepan. This ensure that the mutton is nice and soft when eating. Also the seasonings are also easily absorbed.

FERN GULLY'S CURRIED MUTTON
One of the sweetest if the not the most sweet curry recipes in this cookbook.

INGREDIENTS
1½ tsp. curry powder
½ tsp. allspice
¼ cup vegetable oil
½ cup onion diced
¼ cup garlic diced
1 tbsp sugar
2 tbsp lime juice
½ cup **Get Jamaica Curry Sauce**
2 tsp scotch bonnet pepper, diced
5 cups chopped mutton boneless cooked
4 escallions, sliced thin
½ tbsp salt and pepper mixed

PREPARATION
1. In a large bowl, combine mutton and all seasonings and allow to marinate.
2. Place in a skillet and brown, then reduce heat and add Get Jamaica Curry Sauce.
3. Allow to simmer until cooked.
4. Serve with potatoes and white rice.

> **Cooking Tip**
> Mutton like beef does take a while to cook and if not careful will become hardened and distasteful. Ensure to cover the saucepan when cooking to keep in as much steam to soften the meat.

MORANT BAY CURRY MUTTON WITH VEGETABLES
Morant Bay has an exquisite scenery and this recipe has kept the exquisite trend.

INGREDEIENTS
2 tbsps. vegetable oil
2 garlic cloves, finely chopped
1 tsp. curry powder
3 cups boneless mutton cubed,
¼ cup onion, chopped
½ cup potato diced
½ cup water
2 tbsps. **Get Jamaica Curry Sauce©**
¼ cup grated ginger
¼ cup coconut milk

PREPARATION
1. In a frying pan, heat the oil and fry the garlic until golden brown.
2. Add the curry powder, stir to mix thoroughly, and cook for 1 minute.
3. Add the mutton and stir well to coat the meat in the curry mixture.
4. Add the onion, potato and a quarter-cup stock, and stir-fry over medium heat until the potato is just cooked.
5. Stir in the curry sauce, ginger and coconut milk, and simmer gently until the sauce thickens and the mutton is cooked.
6. Turn into a bowl and serve.

WALKERSWOOD COCONUT MUTTON
A mutton recipe where the taste has been heightened by the coconut.

INGREDIENTS
5 cups boneless mutton cooked
¼ tsp salt
¼ tsp black pepper
3 cups vegetable oil
4 tbs. butter
1 garlic clove chopped
½ cup sweet pepper diced
4 stalks escallion chopped
4 small coconuts

PREPARATION
1. Drain water from coconuts and open leaving meat inside.
2. Sauté mutton with seasonings until light brown.
3. Remove and place in coconut shells evenly and tie to cover
4. Place shells in 1 inch high water in basting pan and bake at 375 Degrees for 40 minutes
5. Remove allow to cool and serve.

LUCEA'S BREADFRUIT AND CURRY MUTTON
An absolute masterpiece of a recipe. We had to go to the least popular of all parishes to get.

INGREDIENTS
1 roasted yellow heart breadfruit
5 cups boneless mutton cooked
¼ tsp salt
¼ tsp black pepper
3 cups vegetable oil
4 tbs. butter
1 garlic clove chopped
½ cup sweet pepper diced
4 stalks escallion chopped
½ cup melted butter
½ cup **Get Jamaica Curry Sauce**©

PREPARATION
1. Peel the breadfruit and cut down the middle and remove center, then baste with a generous amount of melted butter.
2. Sauté mutton with seasonings until seasonings brown.
3. Remove and place in center of breadfruit, cut away to create more space if needed.
4. Place breadfruit in 1 inch high water in basting pan and cover mutton with foil and bake at 375 Degrees for 20 minutes.
5. Baste the breadfruit halves every 6 minutes with curry sauce.
6. Remove allow to cool and serve.

Cooking Tip
Baking the breadfruit is easily done, cover the breadfruit with the foil and place in a baking pan in water, then bake at no more than 375 degrees and check on progress every 15 minutes until soft.

MOUNT CAREY FRICASSEED MUTTON
Just simply delicious, you cant get better spicy mutton recipes than this.

INGREDIENTS
5 cups boneless mutton chopped
¼ cup flour
½ cup diced carrots
½ cup diced potatoes
¼ tsp salt
¼ tsp paprika
¼ cup vegetable oil
2 tbsp Jamaican hot pepper sauce
3 cups water
½ tsp allspice
¼ cup onion, minced
2 tbsp sugar
¼ cup soy sauce
¼ cup escallion chopped

PREPARATION
1. Place mutton in flour and brown in vegetable oil.
2. Place all other ingredients except carrots and potatoes and puree in blender.
3. Add puree and carrots and potatoes to browned mutton and cook until mutton and vegetables are soft.
4. Ensure that sauce does not dry out.
5. Remove and serve hot.

> **Cooking Tip**
> There are two ways to curry meat recipes. The first and more preferred method is to 'burn' the curry meaning that the curry powder is placed in a pot and sautéed with other seasonings then the meat is added and cooked. The second is to season the meat with the curry powder then add to the pot to cook. The first method is usually preferred as this does not leave an unwanted effect after eating. As curry powder is reputed to be a strong laxative if not burnt or cooked down well.

RUNAWAY BAY BARBEQUE LAMB
A great recipe we found in Runaway Bay similar to the Jerk-Bq just a different sauce and less spice.

INGREDIENTS
3 cups cooked lamb cubed
¼ cup vegetable oil
¼ tsp salt
½ tsp allspice
¼ cup onion, minced
¼ cup minced garlic
¼ cup escallion chopped
2 cups Jamaican Bar-BQ Sauce

PREPARATION
1. Brown lamb and seasonings in vegetable oil slightly.
2. Add sauce and cook through for 10 minutes.
3. Remove and serve hot.

MONTEGO BAY JERK-BQ LAMB
Montego Bay has a winner recipe, we got this one from one of the top restaurants on the Hip Strip.

INGREDIENTS
3 cups cooked lamb cubed
¼ cup vegetable oil
1 cup potatoes cooked diced
¼ tsp salt
¼ tsp paprika
½ tsp allspice
¼ cup onion, minced
2 tbsp sugar
¼ cup minced garlic
¼ cup escallion chopped
2 cups Jamaican Jerk-BQ Sauce

PREPARATION
1. Brown lamb and seasonings in vegetable oil slightly.
2. Add sauce and potatoes and cook through for 10 minutes.
3. Remove and serve hot.

JAMAICAN GLAZED LAMB ROAST
A great tasting recipe even though not a popular meat in Jamaica, lamb is popular in North Coast Hotels.

INGREDIENTS
4 lb de-boned shoulder of lamb rolled and tied
¼ tsp salt
¼ tsp paprika
¼ cup vegetable oil
1 tbsp Worcestershire sauce
½ tsp allspice
¼ cup onion, minced
2 tbsp sugar
¼ cup soy sauce
¼ cup escallion chopped

PREPARATION
1. Place in a blender and blend all ingredients together except oil and lamb.
2. Use ¾ to marinate in lamb meat and then discard.
3. Place lamb on rack in roasting pan and roast at 325 Degree F for 90 minutes basting with remaining marinate every 15 minutes.
4. Remove cut in serving portions and serve hot.

Cooking Tip
It is best when serving to cut the lamb meat in to bite size chunks and to serve with a side dish such as mashed potatoes. The fact is that lamb meat should be differentiated from baby lamb meat, as the latter is softer and easy to prepare. Much like goat meat, lamb meat should be placed in a pressure cooker and cooked down to soften then seasoned and cooked down further to soften.

HONEYWELL LAMB CHOPS IN OTAHEITE APPLE SAUCE
A bombshell of a recipe in the native Jamaican apple sauced up.

INGREDIENTS
6 lamb chops
¼ tsp salt
½ tsp allspice
¼ cup onion, minced
¼ cup minced garlic
¼ cup escallion chopped
1 cup potatoes mashed
2 cups Jamaican Otaheite Apple Sauce

PREPARATION
1. Broil lamb chops on both sides in preheated oven at 350 Degrees F
2. Season with seasonings and place mashed potatoes in center of chop and close with skewer.
3. Return to broiler and cook until chops are tender.
4. Remove and cover with sauce then return to broiler for 5 minutes.
5. Remove and cut in serving portions and serve hot.

DRAX HALL SPICY LAMB SHANKS IN FRUIT SAUCE
Drax hall the home of the Jamaican kite, served up a great tasting lamb recipe.

INGREDIENTS
4 lamb shanks
¼ tsp salt
¼ tsp black pepper
½ tsp allspice
¼ cup onion, minced
¼ cup minced garlic
¼ cup escallion chopped
3 whole clove
½ tsp cinnamon
1 cup potatoes mashed
1 cup Jamaican Fruit Sauce

PREPARATION
1. Season meat with salt and pepper, dredge with flour and place in greased baking dish.
2. Cover and bake in moderate oven until meat is tender.
3. Combine with remaining ingredients heat to boiling and allow to simmer
4. Drain fat from cooked shanks add fruit sauce and cover and bake for 30 minutes at 400 Degrees F.
5. Remove and serve hot.

ROUND HILL LAMB STEW
The premier recipe from the Round Hill area, extremely sweet.

INGREDIENTS
¼ tsp salt
¼ tsp black pepper
¼ cup vegetable oil
4 cups lamb shanks
½ cup onion finely chopped
¼ cup garlic minced
½ cup flour
1 cup tomatoes peeled and chopped
1 cup water
¼ tsp nutmeg
1 cup cooked potatoes cubed
1 cup cooked carrots diced

PREPARATION
1. Dredge lamb in the flour and brown in skillet.
2. Season with salt and pepper cover with water and simmer until nearly tender.
3. Add all vegetable and other ingredients and continue to cook.
4. Add a little flour to thicken sauce.
5. Remove and serve with cooked rice hot.

JAMAICAN BRAISED LAMB RIBLETS
Close to beef ribs, lamb riblets are as delicious when prepared in this manner.

INGREDIENTS
¼ tsp salt
¼ tsp black pepper
¼ cup vegetable oil
4 lbs lamb riblets
½ cup onion finely chopped
¼ cup garlic minced
½ cup flour
1 cup tomatoes peeled and chopped
1 cup water
¼ tsp nutmeg
1 cup cooked potatoes cubed
1 cup cooked carrots diced

PREPARATION
1. Cut riblets into serving portions rub with garlic, salt, pepper and flour.
2. Brown riblets in a skillet add water cover closely and simmer.
3. Add all vegetable and other ingredients and continue to cook.
4. Add a little flour to thicken sauce.
5. Remove and serve with cooked rice hot.

JAMAICAN JERK LAMB
Great Jamaican jerk lamb recipe for home.

INGREDIENTS
3 lamb chops
2 tbsp Jamaican hot pepper sauce
1 tsp salt and black pepper
½ tsp cinnamon
½ tsp allspice
¼ cup onion, minced
2 tbsp sugar
2 tbsp pepper, red, minced
2 tbsp hot pepper jelly
¼ cup escallion chopped
1 cup rice, cooked

PREPARATION
1. In a shallow container, place the hot pepper sauce.
2. Add lamb, one piece at a time, turning to coat.
3. Sprinkle salt, cinnamon and allspice over the lamb chops.
4. Place the lamb chops in a single layer in a large shallow baking dish.
5. Bake at 400 F, basting twice with pan juices for 45 minutes or until the lamb is fork tender.
6. Serve hot.

CLAREMONTS BROILED LAMB CHOPS
We visited a farm in Claremont and got this great recipe from Mr. Bloomfield the farm owner.

INGREDIENTS
8 lamb chops
¼ tsp salt
¼ tsp black pepper

PREPARATION
1. Broil chops on one side for a few minutes.
2. Season with salt and pepper on one side then broil on the other.
3. Once broiled serve hot

JAMAICAN SHEPERED PIE
A great lamb recipe made into a delicious pie.

INGREDIENTS
3 cups mashed potatoes
2 cups diced lamb cooked
½ cup gravy from lamb stew

PREPARATION
1. Arrange half potatoes in greased baking dish.
2. Add lamb and gravy.
3. Cover with remaining potatoes.
4. Bake in moderate oven at 325 Degrees F for 20 minutes.

SALEM'S STEWED PEAS WITH VEAL

This recipe is the North Coast version of Jamaican stewed peas recipe with beef but just as tasty.

INGREDIENTS

1 pt. red peas
1 cup salted pigs tail chopped
2 cups veal cubed
¼ cup escallion chopped
¼ cup onion chopped
¼ cup garlic chopped
½ tsp thyme
½ tsp salt and pepper mixed
½ tsp scotch bonnet pepper diced
2 cups coconut milk

PREPARATION

1. Soak peas in water to soften and pig tail a meat to remove salty taste.
2. Place meat and peas together in a large saucepan with coconut milk and enough water to cover meat and cook until soft.
3. Add seasonings and cook for a further 30 minutes until sauce is thick.
4. Serve with plain rice.

CLARKS TOWN JERK VEAL KEBABS

Clarks Town is a little town with great tasting recipes such as this veal recipe.

INGREDIENTS

3 cups veal cut in 1 inch cubes
1 tsp salt
½ tbsp allspice (pimento)
1 small lemon juiced
6 tbsps plain yogurt
½ stalk ginger peeled and grated
3 cloves garlic crushed
2 stalks escallion chopped finely
2 large sweet peppers
½ cup unsalted melted butter
1 sliced cucumber for garnish

PREPARATION

1. Lay the veal cubes in a single layer on a platter.
2. Sprinkle the salt and the juice from the lemon over them and rub into the veal. Set aside for 20 minutes.
3. Put the yogurt in a small bowl. Beat it with a fork or whisk until it is smooth and creamy.
4. Add the ½ ginger, ½ garlic and 1 escallion stalk. Stir into mix.
5. Make a paste out of the left ginger, garlic and escallion and ¼ cup of water in a food processor.
6. Add the paste to the yogurt mixture.
7. After the veal has sat around for 20 minutes, hold a sieve over the veal pieces and pour the yogurt mixture into the sieve and push through as much as you can with a rubber spatula.
8. Mix well with the veal pieces and refrigerate for 6-24 hours, in an airtight container.
9. Preheat over to maximum temperature .
10. Thread the veal pieces on skewers.
11. Brush the veal with half the melted butter and put in the over for about 7 minutes.
12. Take out the baking tray and skewers. Turn the veal pieces over and brush with the rest of the butter.
13. Bake for another 8-10 minutes. Serve with thick slices of cucumbers.

PETERSFIELD VEAL CHEESE BALLS

A sweet blend of tender veal and cheese, absolutely delicious.

INGREDIENTS

½ cup cream cheese
1 small tin minced veal
1 small onion diced
2 tbsp melted butter

PREPARATION

1. Sauté minced veal and onions in 2 tablespoons butter.
2. Combine beef with creamed cheese.
3. Roll into ball, then roll in remaining minced veal.

DUNCANS BAR-BQ VEAL LOAF

A great recipe we found on our way to Montego Bay absolutely sublime.

INGREDIENTS

1½ lb minced veal
½ cup ketchup
3 bread slices
1 egg large
1 cup milk
¼ cup onion chopped
1 tsp Salt
¼ tsp black pepper
¼ tsp garlic powder
¼ cup Jamaican bar-bq sauce
1 tbsp Worcestershire Sauce

PREPARATION

1. Preheat the oven to 350 degrees F.
2. Mix all the ingredients except the ketchup together.
3. Spread the veal mixture into an un-greased loaf pan.
4. Mix ½ cup of bar-bq sauce and 2 tbsp of water in a skillet.
5. Place the slices of veal loaf in the skillet, turning to coat all sides with the bar-bq sauce.
6. Cover and cook over low heat, brushing the sauce on the slices occasionally, until the veal is hot.

JAMAICAN SPIT ROASTED VEAL

Sweet and savory with the right sauce and tender comparing to none.

INGREDEIENTS

1 large roasting veal
2½ tbsp butter
1 tbsp lime juice
¼ tsp salt
¼ tsp pepper

PREPARATION

1. Pat dry veal . Mix ingredients and season the veal. Impale the veal on a stick.
2. Cook slowly over a wood fire. Use butter to continuously baste the veal.
3. When veal is cooked and crisp carve and serve with a sauce of your choice. Serve hot.

jamaican beef with white rice, okra and steamed potatoes.

jamaican stew beef ©

KINGSTON CURRIED VEAL IN MANGO CHUTNEY
Another masterpiece from the archives of the Second Edition.

INGREDIENTS
1½ tsp. curry powder
1 tsp. Jamaican mango chutney recipe
½ tsp. allspice
¼ cup low fat mayonnaise
¼ cup plain nonfat yogurt
2 mangos, peeled and chopped
2 tbsp cashews, chopped
2 tbsp lime juice
2 tsp scotch bonnet pepper, diced
4 cups cooked diced veal
4 escallions, sliced thin
1 head lettuce
½ tbsp salt and pepper mixed

PREPARATION
1. In a large bowl, combine veal, lime juice, mangoes, scotch bonnet pepper and escallions.
2. In a small bowl, whisk together the yogurt, mayonnaise, mango chutney, curry powder, allspice and salt and pepper to taste.
3. Add to veal mixture; toss. Arrange a mound of veal on top of lettuce.

HOT POT PORK AND VEAL LOAF
A hot pot pork recipe a wicked combination sure to tantalize you.

INGREDIENTS
1 lb ground veal
¼ lb ground pork fat
3 salted crackers crushed
1 tbsp milk
2 tsp lemon juice
¼ tsp black pepper
¼ tsp salt
¼ cup minced onion
1 lb ground fresh pork
½ lb minced ham
2 eggs beaten
½ cup bread crumbs
½ cup tomato juice

PREPARATION
1. Combine veal, pork fat, crackers, milk, lemon juice, black pepper, salt and onion and pack into greased loaf pan.
2. In a bowl mix other ingredients and pour atop of veal mixture.
3. Bake in at 350 Degrees F for 2 hours.

Cooking Tip
Veal recipes are excellent and the meat should not be over cooked or it will mash out as veal meat is very soft when cooked. Veal meat also has some interesting facts, as we here in Jamaica find that braising veal works best. It retains the natural beef juices and adds to the flavor of the dish

---

SAV-LA-MAR QUICK VEAL STEW
A sweet veal stew ready in minutes with leftover veal.

INGREDIENTS
2 cups diced cooked veal
2 tbsp vegetable oil
2 tbsp flour
1 cup Jamaican beef broth

PREPARATION
1. In a small bowl combine all powdered seasonings.
2. Dip cutlets in egg and then in powder mixture.
3. Heat vegetable oil in a skillet and place breaded cutlets in and sauté slowly until cooked.
4. Remove and serve hot.

DOWNTOWN FRIED VEAL
Veal can be bought at most meat shops and coated with bread crumbs and fried they are delicious.

INGREDIENTS
4 cups veal cutlets
¼ tsp salt
¼ tsp black pepper
¼ tsp allspice
¼ tsp onion powder
¼ tsp garlic powder
½ cup vegetable oil
2 eggs beaten
1 cup bread crumbs

PREPARATION
1. In a small bowl combine all powdered seasonings.
2. Dip cutlets in egg and then in powder mixture.
3. Heat vegetable oil in a skillet and place breaded cutlets in and sauté slowly until cooked.
4. Remove and serve hot.

HOLLAND BAMBOO VEAL AND APPLETON WHITE RUM
Rum combined with veal has a wily effect and is a real treat with rum in every bite.

INGREDIENTS
1 lb veal steak
1 tbsp vegetable oil
¼ tsp salt
¼ tsp black pepper
1 cup Jamaican sweet sauce
¼ cup Appleton White Rum

PREPARATION
1. Heat oil in a skillet and sauté veal until browned.
2. Add sauce and cover until cooked and veal is tender.
3. Add black pepper and salt with white rum and stir.
4. Bring mixture to slight boil and remove.
5. Drain and serve with sauce of your choice.

jamaican jerked
pork chops. ©

LITTLE LONDON PORK STIR FRY
A great recipe we got from the family of Mr. Chin site manager of Get Jamaica.Com

INGREDIENTS
1 package uncooked noodles
1 tbsp vegetable oil
1 lb pork tenderloin
or loin cut into thin slices
¼ cup garlic, minced
4 cups potatoes and carrots cubed
1 cup Jamaican pork broth
1 tbsp cornstarch
2 tbsps water
¼ tsp salt
¼ tsp black pepper
¼ cup grated cheese

PREPARATION
1. Cook noodles according to package instructions.
2. In a large frying pan or wok, heat oil over medium-high heat.
3. Sauté pork slices until lightly browned on both sides. Add garlic, prepared vegetables, herbs and stock.
4. Cover and simmer for about 5 to 7 minutes or until vegetables are tender-crisp.
5. Add cornstarch and water mixture to pan, stirring constantly until mixture comes to a boil and is thickened.
6. Season with salt and pepper to taste.
7. Toss with noodles and cheese. Serve immediately.

GREEN GROTTO PORK CHOPS IN APPLETON WHITE RUM
Pork is not pork without white rum to go along with it. Delicious does not do this recipe justice

INGREDIENTS
4 pork chops smoked
2 tbsp vegetable oil
½ cup onion diced
¼ cup garlic minced
¼ cup escallion diced
1 cups Appleton white rum
¼ tsp allspice
¼ tsp black pepper
¼ tsp salt
¼ tsp nutmeg powder.
1 tbsp. Jamaican sweet pork sauce
½ tbsp scotch bonnet pepper diced
2 cup orange juice
½ cup coconut juice

PREPARATION
1. Clean pork Chops of excess fat.
2. Cover chops with seasonings and white rum and marinate for 1 hour.
3. Mix black pepper, nutmeg and salt together and rub over drained chops.
4. Place chops in 2 tbsp. olive oil.
5. Allow chops to brown for 4 minutes on first side and 3 minutes on the other side.
6. Add water, sauce, scotch bonnet pepper and simmer for 25 minutes.
7. Add 1 ½ cups of orange juice and coconut milk and the rest of the marinade mixture of white rum, escallion, onion and garlic.
8. Allow to continue to simmer.

YALLHAS BRAISED PORK CHOPS

This is a oven braised pork chop recipe that is made from within your home, absolutely delicious.

INGREDIENTS

2 cups cane vinegar
3 tbsps vegetable oil
¼ cup garlic minced
4 boneless pork chops
½ cup onion diced
¼ tsp salt
¼ tsp black pepper
2 cups ripe pears cubed
¼ cup red wine
2 tbsps honey

PREPARATION

1. In a small saucepan, bring cane vinegar to a boil over high heat until the vinegar is syrupy and reduced.
2. Heat the oil in a large skillet over medium-high heat and sauté garlic until brown.
3. Lay the pork chops in and cook until the underside is browned. Remove and reserve the garlic cloves chops are fully browned.
4. Turn the chops, tuck the onion wedges into the pan and continue cooking until browned.
5. Season with salt and pepper. About halfway through browning the second side tuck the pear wedges in between the chops.
6. Stir the red wine vinegar and honey together in a small bowl until the honey is dissolved. Pour the mixture into the skillet and bring to a vigorous boil.
7. Return the garlic cloves to the skillet if you have removed them. Place the skillet in the oven and roast until onions and pears are tender and the juices from the pork are a rich, syrupy dark brown, about 30 minutes.
8. Once or twice during roasting, turn the chops and redistribute the onions and pears. Remove skillet from the oven.
9. Place a chop in the centre of each warmed serving plate. Check the seasoning of the onion-pear mixture, adding salt and pepper if necessary.
10. Spoon the pears, onion and pan juices around the chops. Drizzle the cane vinegar reduction around the edge of the plate.

HANOVER GOLDEN PORK CHOPS

A great recipe from the garden parish of Hanover. As sweet as you like recipe.

INGREDIENTS

2 rib loin pork chops
½ cup melted butter
¼ cup onions
¼ cup escallion
1 tsp. garlic power
¼ tsp. black pepper
¼ tsp. salt
2 tbsps. Jamaican sweet pork sauce
1 cup Jamaican Fruit Sauce

PREPARATION

1. Mix all seasoning together and season pork chops.
2. In a heavy skillet brown pork chops on either sides with melted butter.
3. Add Jamaican sweet pork sauce. Cover and leave to simmer for 45 minutes.
4. Remove and dredge with fruit sauce and Serve hot.

KINGSTON SPICY BRAISED PORK RIBS
A great braised pork recipe from two chefs in the capital.

INGREDIENTS
4 lbs pork spare ribs
¼ tsp salt
¼ tsp black pepper
¼ cup vegetable oil
½ cup onion diced
½ cup garlic chopped
1 cup tomatoes mashed
½ tbsp thyme leaves
3 cups hot water
1 cup Jamaican sweet pork sauce
¼ cup escallion chopped
¼ cup chopped parsley
¾ cup grated cheese

PREPARATION
1. Cut the rack of spare ribs between the bones into single ribs and season the rib pieces with salt and pepper.
2. Heat the vegetable oil in a large braising pan over medium heat.
3. Add as many of the ribs as will fit without touching. Cook, turning occasionally, until browned on all sides.
4. Remove the ribs, drain on a baking sheet lined with paper towels. Repeat with the remaining ribs.
5. Adjust the temperature throughout the browning so the fat in the pan is sizzling.
6. Pour off all but 4 tablespoons of fat from the pan. Add the onions and garlic and caramelize.
7. Stir in the tomatoes and thyme. Bring to a boil, scraping the pan to loosen the brown bits stuck to the bottom.
8. Tuck the spare ribs into the tomato sauce, season lightly with salt and pepper and bring to a boil.
9. Adjust the heat to simmering and cook until the ribs are fork-tender.
10. Ladle some of the hot water into the casserole to keep the ribs covered with liquid.
11. Sprinkle cheese over ribs and serve.

DOUBLE JERK PORK CHOPS
Absolutely jerky, we saved this recipe for last as the most spicy and herbed pork recipes we have.

INGREDIENTS
3 large pork chops
2 tbsp Jamaican hot pepper sauce
1 tsp salt and black pepper
½ tsp cinnamon
½ tsp allspice
¼ cup onion, minced
2 tbsp sugar
2 tbsp pepper, red, minced
2 tbsp hot pepper jelly
¼ cup escallion chopped
1 cup rice, cooked

PREPARATION
1. In a shallow container, place the hot pepper sauce. Add pork chops, one piece at a time, turning to coat.
2. Sprinkle salt, cinnamon and allspice over the pork chops. Place the pork chops in a single layer in a large shallow baking dish. Bake at 400 F, basting twice with pan juices for 45 minutes or until the pork chops is fork tender and then serve hot.

JAMAICAN BAKED PORK CHOPS
An exquisite Jamaican recipe that is as tasty as pork recipes can be.

INGREDIENTS
1½ lbs boneless pork loin, cut into slices
¼ cup vegetable oil
3 tbsps butter
3 tbsps flour
2 tsps salt
½ tsp dried thyme leaves
½ tsp black pepper
3 cups milk
5 cups potatoes sliced
½ cup onions, thinly sliced
¼ cup grated cheese

PREPARATION
1. In large frying pan brown meat in a small amount of hot oil.
2. Remove meat from pan, drain and place in a casserole dish.
3. In large saucepan melt butter over low heat and blend in flour, salt, thyme and pepper.
4. Gradually stir in milk. Cook and stir over medium heat until mixture boils and thickens.
5. Remove from heat and stir in potatoes and onions.
6. Pour vegetable mixture over meat in casserole and bake covered, in 350 degrees F oven for 30 minutes.
7. Remove cover and stir to combine meat, vegetables and sauce.
8. Return to oven and bake, uncovered for an additional 30 minutes. Remove from oven.
9. Sprinkle cheese over casserole and broil until golden brown.

SLIGOVILE BARBECUED PORK RECIPE
Absolutely a peach recipe from the hills of Sligoville, delicious with the barbequed sauce.

INGREDIENTS
1 lb pork loin de-boned
1 cup **Get Jamaica Pork Marinade**©
½ cup soy sauce
¼ cup white vinegar
¼ cup tomato sauce
¼ cup honey
2 tbsp Appleton V/X rum
¼ cup garlic; minced
1 tsp sugar
¼ cup chicken stock

PREPARATION
1. Split pork loin in half lengthwise.
2. Place in pork marinade to cover and marinate overnight in refrigerator.
3. Preheat oven to 400F. Place wire rack above roasting pan.
4. Place meat on rack and bake 40 minutes in oven.
5. Remove and let cool well.
6. Slice pork thinly and arrange on platter.

MAY PEN BREADED PORK
A great breaded pork recipe absolutely delicious when fried in seasoned vegetable oil.

INGREDIENTS
1½ cup small sized pasta elbows
1 cup chopped potatoes
1 cup chopped sweet potatoes
3 cups grated cheese
3½ cups cubed cooked ham
2 eggs beaten
¼ cup garlic chopped
¼ cup onion diced
¼ cup escallion diced
¼ cup flour
4 cups milk, hot
½ tsp salt
½ tsp black pepper
½ tbsp scotch bonnet pepper
½ tsp nutmeg powder
½ cup breadcrumbs
½ cup grated cheese
½ cup butter, melted

PREPARATION
1. Cook vegetables and pasta add small amount of butter and set aside.
2. Dip ham cubes in egg and dip in bread crumbs and set aside.
3. Sauté garlic, onion and escallion in melted butter and add breaded ham cubes until browned and remove pork and add more garlic.
4. Cook until fragrant but not brown, whisk in flour and milk and bring to a boil.
5. Reduce heat. Return ham and seasonings and simmer until sauce is properly cooked.
6. Remove sprinkle cheese over ham and serve with pasta and vegetable mixture.

Cooking Tip
One popular Jamaican pork recipe is the Jamaican ham recipe. This is usually baked and sometimes the bone is in the meat as well. To prevent the bone from burning place the bones down in the baking dish and inject fat in the end of the bone.

PRIORY JERK-BQ PORK STRIPS
A favorite jerk-bq recipe with pork strips seasoned in herbs.

INGREDIENTS
12 pork strips
2 tbsp soy sauce
2 tbsp rice wine
2 tbsp sugar
½ cup garlic minced
¼ cup Jamaican jerk-bq sauce
1 tsp allspice
1 tsp garlic powder
1 tsp onion powder
3 tbsp honey
3 tbsp Boiling water

PREPARATION
1. Put the strips in a bowl with the jerk-bq sauce, seasonings, soy sauce and wine and mix well to coat them thoroughly.
2. Marinate overnight in the refrigerator. Remove the pork from the sauce and baste the strips with the sugar mixture.
3. Use curved skewers to hang the meat from the top shelf of the oven over a large pan filled with water to a depth of ¼ inch.
4. Roast the pork at 350F for 45 minutes, basting occasionally with the honey. Increase the heat to 425F and roast for 20 minutes.
5. When the pork is cool cut it into ½-inch slices. Arrange the pork slices on a platter.

Cooking Tip
Pork must be well cooked as it carries a large amount of ecoli. Be sure that the pork is well cooked before serving. It is always bets to place the pork in a pressure cooker and cook before cooking down with seasonings. This makes the pork very delicious and soft when eating.

KINGSTON STYLE ROAST PORK
A less popular method of roast pork that uses one main ingredient spice, tasty nonetheless

INGREDIENTS
1 boneless pork shoulder roast
½ cup soy sauce
1 cup onion and escallion diced

PREPARATION
1. Place soy sauce and onion and escallion mixture in blender and puree until smooth.
2. Cut pork roast in half length wise and place the halves in a large plastic bag.
3. Add to the pork the seasoning and marinate overnight.
4. Preheat oven to 350 Degrees and remove pork from the marinade and place in a shallow baking dish and cover with foil in a shallow baking dish.
5. Bake for 30 minutes and turn the meat and bake for one hour more.

BLUE MOUNTAIN BAR-BQ PORK ROAST
A Blue Mountain pork roast with barbeque sauce a delicious recipe with a special taste.

INGREDIENTS
3 lb pork roast
1 tsp onion powder
1 tsp allspice
1 tsp garlic powder
1 tsp nutmeg
1 tsp salt
1 cup Jamaican barbeque sauce
1 cup Jamaican Otaheite Apple sauce
½ cup sugar

PREPARATION
1. Combine allspice, onion powder, garlic powder, nutmeg, peppercorns and salt in food processor.
2. Pulse until spices are mixed.
3. Pat dry pork roast and press spices on fat cap of roast.
4. Preheat a oven at 325 degrees F and roast about 90 minutes.
5. During the last 30 minutes of roasting, combine apple sauce, barbeque sauce and brown sugar and coat top of roast.
6. Continue roasting until internal temperature is 170F.
7. Apply apple sauce mixture until all is used.
8. Remove roast from grill and cool and carve.

COOLIE TOWN CURRIED PORK WITH SWEET POTATOS
Another great curry recipe from the little district of Coolie Town in Westmoreland

INGREDIENTS
1 cup cubed sweet potatoes
1 lb pork cubed
½ cup onion diced
1 tbsp minced ginger root
2 tbsp vegetable oil
1 tbsp soy sauce
½ tsp salt
¼ tsp black pepper
1 cup chicken stock
2 tbsp curry powder

PREPARATION
1. Peel sweet potatoes and cut into ½ inch slices.
2. Heat oil and deep-fry sweet potatoes until golden.
3. Heat remaining oil and add ginger root and onion and stir-fry.
4. Add pork and brown lightly on all sides.
5. Stir in soy sauce, salt and pepper then add stock and curry powder and bring to a boil.
6. Add deep fried potatoes and simmer, covered, until pork is done.

JAMAICAN PORK MEATBALLS
A great pork recipe made into meatballs and braised to make a delicious meal.

INGREDIENTS
1 lb ham minced
¼ lb sausage meat
½ cup onion diced
½ cup parsley flakes
1 cup dry bread soaked in the milk
1 egg beaten
¼ cup milk
1 cup flour
1 cup **Get Jamaica Pork Sauce**©

PREPARATION
1. Combine meats, onions and parsley.
2. Add bread, egg, salt and pepper.
3. Form into small balls and roll in flour. Brown on all sides in fry pan.
4. Add Get Jamaica Pork Sauce© and stir till sauce thickens and meatballs are well cooked.
5. Serve hot

DUNCANS GRILLED PORK TENDERLOIN
A trip through the Duncan's community came up big with this recipe, a must try for all pork lovers.

INGREDIENTS
1½ lb pork tenderloin
1 cup JB White rum (**or substitute**)
¼ cup vegetable oil
2 tbsp lemon juice
1½ tsp honey
½ tsp allspice
¼ tsp black pepper

PREPARATION
1. Preheat grill and cut pork tenderloin crosswise into 1" medallions.
2. Place cut side down and flatten to ½" thick.
3. In medium bowl, whisk together the rum, vegetable oil, lemon juice, honey, allspice and pepper.
4. Place pork medallions in marinade. Turn and marinade at room temperature for 15 minutes or up to two hours in refrigerator.
5. When coals are ready, place medallions, cut side down, on grill. Cook over medium heat about three minutes, or until juices rise to the surface.
6. Turn and grill on other side three or four minutes, or until no longer pink.
7. Serve immediately.

LIGUANEA TERIYAKI PORK

This is a Jamaican teriyaki recipe we got from a small Chinese restaurant with a great Jamaican chef.

INGREDIENTS

3 lb boneless pork shoulder
1 cup Jamaican teriyaki sauce
3 tbsp sugar
3 tbsp Appleton white rum
1 tsp ginger minced
¼ cup garlic minced

PREPARATION

1. Pierce pork with fork and place in large plastic bag.
2. Combine other ingredients; pour over pork and marinate overnight.
3. Reserving marinade, remove pork and place, fat side down baking dish.
4. Brush thoroughly with reserved marinade. Cover pork loosely with foil paper.
5. Bake at 375 Degrees F brushing with reserved marinade.
6. Turn pork over cover and bake until entire pork is soft.
7. Remove and slice in serving portions and serve hot.

JAMAICAN PORK AND OTAHEITE APPLES

Jamaican pork seems to taste better when accompanied with Jamaican apples. We know you will love this recipe.

INGREDIENTS

1 tsp thyme
1 tsp minced ginger
½ tsp salt
¼ tsp black pepper
1 pork loin roast
4 otaheite apples cut in chunks
½ cup minced onion
3 tbsp brown sugar
1 cup Otaheite apple juice

PREPARATION

1. Combine herbs, salt and pepper; rub over roast.
2. Cover and refrigerate for several hours or overnight.
3. Bake, uncovered, at 325 for 1½ hours then drain fat.
4. Mix apples and onion with brown sugar; spoon around roast.
5. Continue to roast for 1 hour then transfer the roast, apples and onion to a serving platter and keep warm.
6. Skim excess fat from meat juices pour into a heavy skillet. Add apple juice and syrup.
7. Cook and stir over medium-high heat until liquid has been reduced by half, about 1 cup.
8. Slice roast and serve with gravy.

CLAREMONT HONEY AND BEER GRILLED PORK

We guarantee that you will love this recipe, it's a perfect blend of everything Jamaican.

INGREDIENTS

3 lb pork loin
½ cup Red Stripe Beer
½ cup garlic minced
½ cup honey
½ tsp salt
¼ tsp black pepper
¼ cup vegetable oil
1 tsp allspice
1 tsp onion powder
¼ cup escallion chopped

PREPARATIONS

1. Place all ingredients except pork in a blender and puree until smooth.
2. Pierce pork on all sides, place in a zip-lock bag, add marinade and marinate overnight. Grill for 1½ hours.
3. Start roast on high to brown for 15 minutes.
4. Turn heat to low and baste frequently with marinade.
5. Remove from heat and allow to rest before slicing.

JAMAICAN FRANKS AND PEPPERS

Jamaicans are big on frankfurters and this franks and pepper recipe is absolutely riveting.

INGREDIENTS

2 tbsp salad oil
1 lb frankfurters, quartered
¼ cup onion, chopped
¼ cup garlic, crushed
1 cup tomatoes crushed
2 tsp scotch bonnet pepper diced
½ cup grated cheese

PREPARATION

1. In a large skillet, heat oil over medium-high heat. Add the frankfurters sauté until browned.
2. With a slotted spoon, remove from pan and place on one side of serving dish.
3. Add onion and garlic to skillet sauté 2 minutes. Add tomatoes and scotch bonnet pepper.
4. Bring to boil then reduce heat and simmer covered.
5. Sprinkle cheese over rice.

OCHIE JERKED PORK
A little restaurant on a Friday night whipped up this great Jamaican jerk pork recipe.

INGREDIENTS
4 lb pork shoulder
½ cup Red Stripe Beer (**optional**)
¼ cup escallion finely chopped
¼ cup onion, finely chopped
¼ cup garlic minced
1 tbsp scotch bonnet pepper diced
2 tsp thyme minced
¼ tsp salt
1 tsp brown sugar
1 tsp allspice
½ tsp nutmeg minced
½ tsp cinnamon
¼ tsp black pepper
2 tsp cane vinegar
½ cup vegetable oil
1 cup Jamaican Jerk Pork Sauce

PREPARATIONS
1. Combine all of the ingredients except pork and vegetable oil and sauce in a blender and puree.
2. Place the pork in a roasting pan and coat with the marinade. Cover and marinate overnight.
3. Prepare a charcoal grill when the coals glow dusty red, push the coals to the sides and place a foil drip pan in the center arranging the coals around the pan to ride indirect heat.
4. Brush the meat with the marinade as often as possible for 1½ hours sprinkling with beer as well.
5. Add more coal and jerk. Remove the pork to a chopping board and chop with a cleaver into 1-inch pieces.

ST. ANNS BAY MARINATED PORK KABOBS
Pork kebabs are quickly becoming popular on the North Coast and these pork kebabs take center stage.

INGREDIENTS
2 cups plain yogurt
2 tbsp lemon juice
¼ cup garlic minced
½ tsp allspice
¼ tsp cinnamon
2 lb pork tenderloin
¼ cup onions diced
½ cup tomatoes
1 cup sweet pepper

PREPARATION
1. In a medium glass bowl, combine lemon juice, garlic, cinnamon and allspice and mix well.
2. Add pork cover and refrigerate for 6 hours or overnight.
3. Alternate pork, onions, tomatoes and peppers on eight skewers.
4. Grill over medium coals for about 30-35 minutes or until meat is cooked

MISS NORMA'S SWEET AND SOUR PORK
This is one of Miss Norma's great tasting special pork recipes, try it its delicious.

INGREDIENTS
¾ lb boneless pork
1 tbsp rice wine
1 tbsp soy sauce
½ tsp salt
1 cup sweet pepper
1 cup carrot diced
½ escallions diced
1 egg beaten
2 tbsp cornstarch
1 cup vegetable oil
1 cup orange sliced in segments
¾ cup chicken stock
1 tbsp soy sauce
½ tsp salt
1½ tbsp cane vinegar
1 tbsp sugar
1 tbsp tomato paste

PREPARATIONS
1. Cut pork into cubes and put into a bowl with the rice wine soy sauce and salt and marinate for 20 minutes.
2. Cut the green & red peppers into squares and peel and cut the carrot and escallions into 1-inch chunks.
3. Bring a pot of water to a boil and blanch the carrot in it for 4 minutes; drain and set aside.
4. Mix the egg and cornstarch in a bowl until they are well blended into a batter.
5. Lift the pork cubes out of the marinade, put them into the batter and coat each piece well.
6. Heat the oil in a deep-fat fryer or large frying pan until it is almost smoking.
7. Remove the pork pieces from the batter with a slotted spoon, and deep-fry them.
8. Drain the deep-fried pork cubes on paper towels.
9. Combine the chicken stock, soy sauce, salt, vinegar, sugar and tomato paste in a large saucepan and boil.
10. In a small bowl, blend together the cornstarch and water. Stir this mixture into the sauce and bring it back to a boil. Turn the heat down to a simmer. Add oranges and pork cubes. Mix well, and then turn the mixture onto a platter. Serve at once.

MISS NORMA'S SPECIAL CURRY PORK
Another of Ms. Norma's great tasting pork recipes

INGREDIENTS
1½ lb pork tenderloin
½ cup sour cream
1 tbsp curry powder
2 tbsp vegetable oil
2 tbsp soy sauce
4 bananas
¼ tsp salt
¼ tsp black pepper

PREPARATION
1. Season pork with salt and broil or fry until tender. Arrange pork in casserole dish with bananas or peaches. Add peach syrup if appropriate. In a frying pan, heat up curry slightly in olive oil.
2. Add sour cream and soy sauce stirring well.
3. Bring sauce to boil over medium flame and simmer for 5 minutes.
4. Pour sauce over pork and bananas in casserole dish and cook in preheated 375 oven until done.
5. Serve with white or brown rice.

CHRISTIANA'S PAPRIKA PORK
A great pork recipe using one great tasting spice in paprika

INGREDIENTS
1 tbsp paprika
4 pork chops, trimmed
2 tbsp margarine
2 tbsp vegetable oil
½ cup onions diced
½ cup garlic chopped fine
¾ cup dry white wine (**optional**)
2 tbsp sour cream
½ peppers for garnish

PREPARATION
1. Spread paprika on a sheet of waxed paper.
2. Rinse the chops under cold water, then dredge both sides of each wet chop in the paprika, making sure the entire surface of both sides is covered with paprika.
3. Heat butter and oil together in a large skillet. Add onions and sauté until they are soft.
4. Add the garlic and cook another 2 minutes, stirring occasionally.
5. Push the onions and garlic to one side and add the chops.
6. Brown chops on both sides, about 4 minutes each side.
7. Add more oil if needed. Stir in wine and bring mixture to a boil over high heat; reduce heat to low, cover and simmer the chops a minimum of 10 minutes on each side depending on their thickness.
8. Remove the chops to a serving platter and keep warm.
9. Stir together the onions, garlic, and juices left in the pan. Increase the heat and cook, stirring constantly, until the mixture is the consistency of a thick soup.
10. Reduce the heat and add the sour cream and mix well. Pour the sauce over the chops, garnish with the pickled pepper and serve hot with egg noodles or boiled potatoes.

OROCABESSA PORK WITH FRUIT SAUCE
A great tasting pork recipe blended with a great tasting fruit sauce.

INGREDIENTS
3½ lb pork shoulder de-boned and cubed
½ cup Appleton white rum
½ cup orange juice
½ cup water
¼ cup lemon juice
1 tbsp orange peel
1 tsp ginger minced
2 golden apples
1 orange peeled
1 cup Jamaican fruit sauce
4 cup Hot cooked brown rice

PREPARATION
1. Sauté pork in large frying pan until browned on all sides. Sprinkle with Appleton white rum stirring to sauté herb. Add orange juice, water, lemon juice, orange peel and ginger.
2. Cover and simmer until pork is very tender.
3. Remove meat to serving dish. Apples and orange pieces to pan.
4. Cover and simmer about 10 minutes, just until apples are soft.
5. Spoon fruit and juices over pork. Serve with rice.

CASTLETON PORK CHOP SUPPER
A great pork recipe we got from two chefs in Castleton gardens a great tourist attraction.

INGREDIENTS
6 pork loin chops
½ cup flour
2 tbsp vegetable oil
2 tsp dried thyme
½ tsp salt
¼ tsp black pepper
2 cups potatoes cubed
1 cup carrots diced
½ cup onion diced
3 cups Jamaican beef broth

PREPARATION
1. Dredge pork in flour. Heat oil in a large skillet; brown the chops on both sides.
2. Sprinkle with thyme, salt and pepper. Peel potatoes and cut into ¾" cubes; add to skillet along with the carrots and onion.
3. Pour broth over all; bring to a boil.
4. Reduce heat; cover and simmer until pork and vegetables are tender.

SPICY PORK DUMPLINGS
Spicy dumplings go well with almost any meal you can think of.

INGREDIENTS
2 cups Jamaican dumpling dough
1 lb ground pork
¼ cup escallions chopped
¼ cup onions chopped
1 egg white
2 tbsp cornstarch
2 tsp salt
2 tsp soy sauce
¼ tsp black pepper
½ cup melted butter

PREPARATION
1. Knead dough well and separate into rectangles and flatten.
2. Mix all other ingredients in a bowl.
3. Drop an even amount of pork mixture on each dumpling
4. Close each rectangle and roll into a ball.
5. In a large skillet brown each dumpling in melted butter.
6. Place in a baking tin and bake at 375 degrees basting with melted butter to prevent burning.
7. Bake until done serve hot.

RUNAWAY BAY PORK STEAKS WITH PEPPERS
Steak dinners are popular on the North Coast again and with the scotch bonnet pepper adding flavor to the dinner.

INGREDIENTS
2 tbsp vegetable oil
1½ lb pork blade steaks
1 tbsp scotch bonnet peppers diced
½ cup garlic finely chopped
½ cup tomato crushed
½ cup Jamaican beef broth
1 cup water
½ tsp thyme leaves
¼ tsp black pepper

PREPARATIONS
1. Pork steaks should be cut ½ inch thick.
2. In large skillet, heat oil and brown steaks over medium-high heat.
3. Remove steaks, reduce heat to medium, into skillet, add peppers and garlic and cook 5 minutes or until peppers are crisp and tender.
4. Stir in tomato, then the beef broth blended with water, thyme and pepper and bring to a boil.
5. Return steaks to skillet and simmer, uncovered, stirring sauce occasionally until steaks are tender.

JAMAICAN PORK IN JUNE PLUM SAUCE
Absolutely wonderful is how we describe this recipe, the June plum sauce complements the sweet flavor of the pork

INGREDIENTS
2 lb pork tenderloin
1 tsp salt
1 tsp black pepper
2 tsp vegetable oil
2 tsp unsalted butter
¼ cup onion diced
1 tsp garlic minced
½ tsp thyme
¾ cup June plum juice
½ cup dry white wine (**optional**)
½ tsp salt

PREPARATION
1. Cut tenderloins into medallions, flatten slightly by hand and season with salt and pepper.
2. Heat oil in a skillet add medallions and brown on both sides and remove to a platter.
3. Heat butter add onions and garlic and sauté until softened.
4. Return medallions to skillet, sprinkle thyme and add June plum juice and wine, bring to a boil, reduce heat, and simmer until tender and sauce is thick.
5. Remove pork and serve hot with plum sauce.

PLAIN OL' JAMAICAN PORK ROAST

This regular Jamaican pork roast recipe is simple yet delicious.

INGREDIENTS

3 lbs pork roast
1 tbsp onion powder
2 tsp sugar
1 tsp allspice
½ tsp black pepper
¼ tsp salt

PREPARATION

1. Combine all seasonings and rub over surface of roast.
2. Spray bottom rack with no-stick spray.
3. Place roast on bottom rack. Pour 1 cup hot water into glass bowl.
4. Cook according to guidelines until internal temperature registers 160-170*F.

Remove roast from oven and cover with foil. Let stand 10 to 20 minutes before slicing.

MONTEGO BAY ROAST PORK SHOULDER

A sweet recipe that though used mainly at Christmas time is apt for picnic and sandwich meats recipe.

INGREDIENTS

2½ lb picnic ham shoulder
2 cup **Get Jamaica Pork Marinade©**
1 cup boiling water

PREPARATION

1. Marinate picnic ham in 1 cup marinade overnight.
2. Add boiling water to remaining marinade to make baste.
3. Place picnic shoulder on rack in shallow roasting pan.
4. Roast, uncovered, at 325 degrees F while roasting baste with marinade until done.

HOME MADE ROTISSERIE BARBECUED PORK LEG

As cooking technology becomes more popular we found a great rotisserie recipe for pork legs

INGREDIENTS

1 leg of pork
1 cup brown sugar
2 tbsp flour
1 cup Jamaican sweet sauce
¼ cup vinegar
¼ tsp cloves crushed

PREPARATION

1. Insert rotisserie rod through center of meat, place on rotisserie, and cook over coals that have burned down to red and glowing ash.
2. Roast until pork leg is cooked
3. Combine remaining ingredients and brush on roast frequently for last 30 minutes of cooking.

JAMAICAN SAUSAGE BISCUITS
A great sausage recipe blending between sausages and herbs

INGREDIENTS
½ lb sausage, cooked and drained
1½ cup biscuit dough
1 cup grated cheese
1 egg beaten
2 tbsp milk
¼ tsp salt

PREPARATION
1. Mix together biscuit dough and cheese then add sausage.
2. Mix liquids, then add to solid mixture.
3. Shape into small balls, flatten slightly.
4. Bake at 350 degrees F for 20 minutes on un-greased cookie sheet.

GREAT POND SPICY SAUSAGE DUMPLINGS
In great pond these sausage dumplings are king and go with many other recipes

INGREDIENTS
1 lb bulk sausage
½ cup onions chopped
1 pie crust
1 tbsp flour
½ cup water
¼ tsp salt
¼ tsp black pepper

PREPARATION
1. Make sausage into 12 balls and brown and cook thoroughly.
2. Wrap balls in dough made from pie crust.
3. Bake at 400° for 10 minutes.
4. While baking sauté onions in sausage grease until brown.
5. Add flour and water to make gravy.
6. Season to taste with salt and pepper.
7. Pour gravy over dumplings and serve.

MORANT BAY SPICED PORK ROAST
A Morant Bay recipe of spices and pork.

INGREDIENTS
3 lb pork roast
½ cup apple cider
½ tsp dried thyme
¼ tsp black pepper
¼ tsp salt
¼ tsp onion powder
¼ tsp garlic powder
¼ tsp allspice

PREPARATION
1. Place pork roast in tender cooker, add cider, sprinkle with seasonings and pepper.
2. Cover add indicator and cook on high for 30 minutes.
3. Serve hot.

OCHO RIOS SPICY PORK, BEEF AND VEAL KEBABS
Another sweet kebab recipe that is an absolute peach of a recipe enjoy every bite.

INGREDIENTS
2 lb pork or lamb cubed
¼ cup peanut butter
1 tsp allspice
½ tsp salt
1 tsp cinnamon
½ tsp black pepper
¼ cup onions chopped
¼ cup garlic minced
1½ tsp lemon juice
1 tbsp brown sugar
1 tbsp soy sauce

PREPARATIONS
1. Put all the ingredients into a large bowl, mix well, and cover.
2. Refrigerate overnight.
3. Put meat cubes on skewers, keeping as much of the onion mixture on them as you can.
4. Grill over hot coals, turning to brown each side, for 20 to 25 minutes or until meat is cooked through.

KITSON TOWN STEWED PORK WITH POTATOES
A district in the hills of St. Catherine stewed pork is a popular recipe and the best tasting recipe.

INGREDIENTS
4 lb pork shoulder cut into cubes
½ tsp salt
½ tsp black pepper
¼ cup vegetable oil
¼ cup onion diced
2 tbsp flour
2 cup white wine
¼ cup cane vinegar
4 cup Jamaican beef broth
½ tsp dried thyme leaves

PREPARATION
1. Pat the pork dry with paper towels and sprinkle with desired salt and pepper.
2. Heat the oil in a oven over medium-high heat on top of the stove.
3. Add the pork, without crowding, and brown well on all sides.
4. Remove the pieces to a plate as they are brown.
5. Pour off all but about 2 tablespoons fat.
6. Reduce heat to low and replace the pot on the stove.
7. Add the onion and add the flour and cook another minute, stirring.
8. Add the wine, vinegar and stock and bring to a boil.
9. Return the pork to the pot with any juices on the plate and add thyme.
10. Cover tightly and transfer the pot to the oven.
11. Cook until the meat is tender.

MAY PEN STUFFED BARBECUE PORK LOIN
A stuffed pork recipe that is to die for, try this recipe today.

INGREDIENTS
1 cup chopped sweet pepper
2 scotch bonnet peppers diced
¼ tsp salt
¼ tsp black pepper
½ cup sugar
½ cup onions minced
¼ cup garlic minced
1 tsp allspice
¼ cup escallion diced
1 cup Jamaican Ketchup
1 cup Jamaican Barbeque Sauce
3 tbsp soy sauce
2 tbsp Worcestershire sauce
2 lb de-boned pork loin

PREPARATION
1. Pat dry pork cut pockets into pork and season with black pepper and salt.
2. Mix the garlic, onion, escallion, cinnamon, allspice, ketchup, soy sauce, and Worcestershire sauce.
3. Stuff the stuffing into the pocket of the pork.
4. Close the open end of the pocket with tooth picks or poultry skewers.
5. Place the pork in a foil-lined roasting dish.
6. Pour 1 cup of the sauce over the pork, covering it completely.
7. Roast in a preheat 350 F. oven for about 45 minutes, basting 2 times and using half of the remaining sauce to baste each time. Remove roast from pan.
8. Cover with aluminum foil and let it stand for about 15 minutes before you slice it.
9. Heat pan drippings and sauce and serve along side of pork.

JAMAICAN JERK-BQ PORK BURGERS
A sweet and unusual burgher recipe but just as delicious.

INGREDIENTS
¼ cup escallions sliced
¼ tsp garlic powder
1 tbsp margarine
1½ lb pork
2 tbsp Worcestershire sauce
½ tsp salt
½ tsp black pepper
4 lettuce leaves
¼ onion diced
1 cup tomato sliced

PREPARATION
1. In a skillet, sauté onions with garlic powder in butter until tender.
2. Remove from the heat and combine pork, Worcestershire sauce, salt and pepper.
3. Shape into eight patties. Spoon onion mixture into the center of four patties to within ½-inch of edges.
4. Top with remaining patties; pinch edges to seal.
5. Grill, uncovered, over medium coals for 10-15 minutes, turning once, or until juices run clear.
6. Serve on rolls with lettuce, onion and tomato.

BLUEFIELDS PORK CUTLETS

On the outskirts of Sav-la-mar is a community where we got this great tasting recipe.

INGREDIENTS

8 boneless lean pork cutlets
½ cup grated cheese
1 egg beaten
1 cup bread crumbs
½ tsp onion powder
½ tsp garlic powder
½ tsp allspice
¼ cup vegetable oil
1 lemon

PREPARATION

1. Trim away any fat or connective tissues from pork and mix onion, garlic and allspice with breadcrumbs.
2. Between 2 sheets of waxed paper, pound each cutlet until flattened to about ¼ inch thick.
3. Trim cheese and ham to a size slightly smaller than cutlets.
4. Top four of the cutlets with a slice of cheese and a slice of ham. Cover with remaining cutlets and pound edges lightly to seal together.
5. Holding each sandwich together dip both sides in egg, then into bread crumbs to coat completely.
6. Place on waxed paper. In a heavy, 10-inch skillet over high heat, heat oil until rippling.
7. Lower heat to medium-high, add cutlets, and cover with a spatter shield if desired.
8. Cook until cutlets are cooked through. Remove from pan with slotted spatula, draining off oil, and serve hot, garnished with lemon wedges.

NEGRIL SPECIAL SWEET & SOUR PORK

A special sweet and sour pork recipe we got from a chef in Negril, finger licking good recipe.

INGREDIENTS

2 lb pork round
1¼ cup cane vinegar
¾ cup cornstarch
2 tbsp honey
¼ cup Jamaican cherry juice
2 tbsp soy sauce
¼ cup Jamaican pineapple syrup
½ tsp salt
5 pineapple rings chopped
1 sweet pepper chopped
2 tbsp sugar
¼ cup onion diced
¼ cup vegetable oil

PREPARATION

1. Cut the pork into irregular bite size pieces and place into pan with water to barely cover.
2. Add 4 tablespoons of the vinegar, bring to boil, reduce heat and simmer for 25 minutes then drain.
3. In a bowl, add the cornstarch, honey and soy sauce and mix very well.
4. Heat the oil in a large fry pan and fry the pork pieces until brown.
5. In a saucepan add the pineapple syrup, water, sugar, salt, cherry juice, remaining vinegar and bring to a boil. Add the pork pieces, cover and simmer for an additional 20 minutes, stirring occasionally.
6. Add the pineapple pieces and vegetables 5 minutes before cooking time is up.
7. Serve hot.

ANCHOVY CHICKEN AND PORK STEAK
We got this recipe from the district of Anchovy in St. James, it is a great blend of chicken and pork

INGREDIENTS
2 pork loin steaks trimmed
1 cup cubed chicken breast
2 tbsp soy sauce
1 tbsp white wine
2 tbsp molasses
1½ tsp ginger, grated OR
¼ cup garlic minced
½ tsp black pepper
½ cup melted butter

PREPARATION
1. Place pork and chicken in shallow dish then in a small bowl, whisk together soy sauce, wine, molasses, ginger, garlic and pepper.
2. Pour over meat turning meat to coat both sides.
3. Cover dish and allow meat to marinate.
4. Remove and in a large skillet cook chicken cubes in butter and set aside.
5. With paper towels, pat steaks to dry surface slightly.
6. Place steaks on greased grill over medium heat.
7. Add steak to platter and add chicken and garnish with parsley.
8. Serve hot.

HONEYWELL ROAST SUCKLING PIG
A sweet recipe from the hills of Honeywell a great hideaway for tourists.

INGREDIENTS
1 whole suckling pig
¼ cup cane vinegar
1½ cup carrots, chopped
1½ cup escallion, chopped
1½ cup onions, chopped
1 tbsp salt
1 tsp thyme
3 lbs yam
1 cup vegetable oil
2 whole scotch bonnet peppers diced
¼ cup cloves
2 cups breadcrumbs

Preparation
1. Rinse pig with vinegar and clean thoroughly.
2. Sauté, onions, garlic and escallion with breadcrumbs.
3. Boil yam until soft and mix with breadcrumb mixture

WALKERSWOOD SPECIAL TAMALES RECIPE
A tamales recipe delicious to the very last bite.

INGREDIENTS
4 lb Pork shoulder
6 cups water
1 tbsp scotch bonnet pepper diced
¼ tsp cinnamon
¼ cup garlic diced
¼ cup flour
¼ tsp salt
1 lb lard
½ cup Jamaican pork broth
1 pack corn husk

PREPARATION
1. Boil meat in water until tender. Remove the meat from broth, saving broth for dough and chile.
2. Chop meat into ¼ in. pieces and place in pan.
3. Dissolve scotch bonnet pepper in 1½ cups of the broth, and add to meat, add garlic, spices and salt, cook until done.
4. Cream lard in a mixing bowl. Add flour and mix.
5. Add enough of the broth to make the dough spread able with a table knife.
6. Rinse the husks and soak in water until pliable.
7. Spread the center portion of the husk with 2 tbs. of flour.
8. Top with meat mix and fold the sides of husks toward the center, the bottom up and the top down.
9. Tie each husk with a narrow corn husk strip.
10. Pour 2 in. of water into a large kettle and arrange the tamales on a rack above the water level.
11. Steam the tamales for about 40 min.
12. Serve hot

> **Cooking Tip**
> Use only as much scotch bonnet pepper to flavor recipes, don't try to flavor the recipe to your liking unless you are cooking for one.

NEGRIL WEST END SIZZLING PORK POCKETS
A great pork recipe that are delicious to the taste.

INGREDIENTS
2 tbsp lemon juice
2 tbsp Jamaican chicken broth
¼ cup garlic finely chopped
½ tsp black pepper
12 oz Boneless pork loin, cut into-thin strips
4 slices pita breads
2 cups chopped mixed lettuce

PREPARATION
1. In a medium bowl, combine the lemon juice, chicken broth, garlic and pepper.
2. Add the pork strips and toss to combine and marinate. Remove meat with a slotted spoon and discard marinade. Heat a large non-stick skillet over medium-high heat.
3. Stir-fry the pork for 5 minutes or until done. Open pita breads to form a pocket and fill each with an even amount of lettuce and pork strips.
4. Serve hot.

MOUNT CAREY SAVORY PORK AND VEGETABLES
Blending pork with vegetables has made a great tasting recipe.

INGREDIENTS
2 tbsp margarine
4 boneless pork chops
¼ cup escallion diced
¼ cup onion diced
½ tsp thyme leaves
1 cup Jamaican beef broth
2 tbsp water
½ cup potatoes chopped
½ cup yams chopped

PREPARATION
1. In skillet, in 1 tablespoon hot margarine, cook chops until browned on both sides then set aside.
2. In remaining 1 tablespoon hot margarine sauté escallion, onion and thyme until brown.
3. Add soup, water, potatoes and yam and heat to boil.
4. Return chops to skillet.
5. Cover and cook over low heat until chops longer pink and vegetables are tender, stirring occasionally.
6. Serve hot.

JAMAICAN PORK, SHRIMP AND LOBSTER RECIPE
A sweet blend between these sea foods and the ever delicious tasting pork.

INGREDIENTS
4 lb pork tenderloin
1 cups butter
½ cup whipping cream
½ tsp thyme
1 cup peeled small shrimp
1 cup lobster tails
¾ cup chopped escallions
½ cup chopped parsley
¼ cup minced garlic
¼ cup chopped onions
1 tbsp honey
2 tbsp Worcestershire sauce
1 tbsp scotch bonnet pepper diced
4 tbsp water
½ tsp black pepper
¼ tsp salt
¼ cup Jamaican hot pepper sauce

PREPARATION
1. Slice pork loin down center and season well with salt, scotch bonnet pepper and black pepper to taste.
2. Heat butter in saucepan and sauté onions, parsley, garlic and escallion for five minutes.
3. Add shrimp and lobster tails and sauté five minutes.
4. Place pork loin on foil and pour the above mixture down center. Tie with string to hold mixture in and fold up sides of foil.
5. Place on top of grill, cover, and add two handfuls wet mesquite chips to hot coals.
6. Prepare basting sauce by heating together butter, honey, Worcestershire sauce, and 4 cups water.
7. After loin begins to brown, baste every 10 minutes.
8. Remove and serve hot.

HIGHGATE ROAST PORK WITH GRAVY

This district in St. Mary is popular for chocolate, but this pork recipe that we picked up here is as popular there.

INGREDIENTS

½ cup water
1 tbsp Jamaican sweet pork sauce
1 tbsp flour
4½ lb pork roast, sliced cooked

PREPARATION

1. Add water to pork sauce to make ½ cup.
2. Stir flour into a small amount of the liquid until smooth.
3. Add remaining liquid.
4. Cook, stirring constantly, until thickened.
5. Serve over sliced roast pork.

WHITEHOUSE SCRAPPLE

This fisherman's village is has an absolutely great fish recipes and has now added this tasty pork recipe.

INGREDIENTS

4 lb pork scraps chopped finely
¼ tsp black pepper
½ tsp salt
3 whole cloves
½ tsp dried thyme leaves
2 cup cornmeal
¼ cup onion, finely chopped
¼ cup escallion diced
½ tsp allspice
¼ tbsp scotch bonnet pepper diced
½ tsp nutmeg powder

PREPARATION

1. Parboil pork scraps in water to cover then drain and discard water.
2. Return to pot with fresh water to cover, salt, black pepper, cloves and thyme.
3. Bring to a boil, cover and simmer until meat falls off the bones easily.
4. Strain stock and reserve.
5. Remove all meat from bones and chop; set aside.
6. Reheat stock; gradually add cornmeal, stirring constantly until thick.
7. Add meat, onion, scotch bonnet pepper, nutmeg and escallion; adjust seasonings with salt and pepper.
8. Pour into 2 greased loaf pans.
9. Slice and fry for breakfast.

JAMAICAN SAUCY PORK FAJITAS
Our in-house chef Doreen got the recipe in Mexico and amended it to have the Jamaican flavor.

INGREDIENTS
1½ lb boneless pork loin
1 tsp salt
¼ tsp black pepper
6 tsp vegetable oil, divided
1 cup sweet pepper sliced
¼ cup mango preserves
¼ cup escallions onions
¼ cup chopped onions
12 flour tortillas
¾ cup sour cream

PREPARATION
1. Toss pork with salt and pepper.
2. Heat 2 teaspoons oil in large skillet over high heat.
3. Add half of pork and cook, stirring, until brown, 1 to 2 minutes.
4. Remove with slotted spoon; repeat with 2 more teaspoons oil and remaining pork.
5. Remove from skillet. Reduce heat to medium.
6. Add remaining 2 teaspoons oil to skillet; cook peppers and onions, until tender, 10 to 12 minutes.
7. Return pork to skillet. Stir in salsa and preserves; heat through.
8. Remove from heat; stir in green onions and cilantro.
9. Place tortillas between dampened paper towels then bake at 375 Degrees F until hot and steaming.
10. Fill each tortilla with a scant ½ cup pork mixture.
11. Serve each with a dollop of sour cream.

PORTLAND BBQ PORK SANDWICHES
We got these pork sandwiches by Mr. Walkers place in Portland.

INGREDIENTS
4 lb Boneless pork roast
¼ cup garlic, minced
¼ cup onion, minced
½ tbsp salt and black pepper mixed
1 cup Jamaican barbecue sauce
1 tsp sugar

PREPARATION
1. Place the roast, garlic, and onion in a crock pot on high. Add the salt and pepper and a little bit of water.
2. Cook on high until you can easily shred the pork roast with a fork.
3. Remove the roast and shred the meat removing as much of the fat as possible and the bone.
4. Strain the grease in the crock pot, keeping any bits of garlic and onion left and throwing out the grease.
5. Place the shredded meat back into the crock pot, along with the bits of garlic and onion.
6. Pour the BBQ sauce over all until the meat is covered and mix well.
7. Continue cooking the pork in the crock pot for about three hours, on low.
8. Serve the BBQ pork on rolls.

JAMAICAN CROCKPOT PORK
If you are a crock-pot recipe lover this Jamaican pork recipe is perfect.

INGREDIENTS
1 boneless pork roast
15 whole cloves
½ cup onion diced
½ cup water
1 cup Jamaican barbecue sauce
1 tsp sugar

PREPARATION
1. Place onion slices into the bottom of a large crock-pot and dot roast with cloves.
2. Place roast in crock-pot along with the water. Cover and cook at least 8 hours.
3. Take roast from crock-pot, remove cloves and shred pork. Discard liquid and onions from crock-pot.
4. Place shredded pork, barbecue sauce and sugar in crock-pot and cover.
5. Cook at least 2 more hours and serve on toasted buns with slices of fresh onion.

FANTASY ISLAND PORK
An exquisite recipe from Negril, a delicious recipe

INGREDIENTS
5 lb Fresh ham
¼ cup escallions diced
3 tbsp vegetable oil
½ tbsp ginger minced
¼ cup garlic minced
5 cup hot water
1 cup soy sauce
1 cup rice wine
3 tbsp sugar
½ tbsp cinnamon powder
½ tbsp allspice
1 tsp salt

PREPARATION
1. Dry ham with paper towels.
2. Choose a heavy casserole or pot, large enough to hold the ham comfortably.
3. Heat the pot and then add the oil, ginger, garlic and scallions, and stir-fry in the pot for 2 minutes.
4. Push the aromatics to the side and brown the ham on each side.
5. Pour off the oil. Add all the braising liquid ingredients to the pot and bring the mixture to a boil.
6. Turn the heat down to a simmer, cover tightly and cook for about 4 ½ hours, turning the ham from time to time.
7. When the ham is tender, remove it strain the sauce, skim off any surface fat, and reduce the liquid until it is slightly thick.
8. Pour this over the ham and serve.

PORTMORE GINGER PORK

A great pork recipe seasoned with ginger.

INGREDIENTS

2 lb Pork, cubed
1 cup flour
¼ cup Jamaican chicken broth
¼ cup soy sauce
2 tbsp Appleton rum
¼ cup onion, sliced
¼ cup garlic minced
1 tbsp sugar
1 tsp ginger, ground
¼ tsp black pepper
1 cup rice, cooked
3 tbsp vegetable oil

PREPARATION

1. Dredge meat in flour, heat oil in large skillet. Add half of meat and brown quickly.
2. Remove meat and set aside. Pour off excess oil from pan. Combine chicken broth, soy sauce and rum.
3. Add onion, garlic, sugar, ginger and pepper. Place in a pan along with meat.
4. Simmer covered until meat is tender.
5. Serve over rice.

Cooking Tip
Ginger is a good ingredient that works well with pork and other ingredients such as beans.

LINSTEAD PORK LOIN IN MANGO SAUCE

A great mango and pork recipe sold on the outskirts of the Flat bridge in St. Catherine.

INGREDIENTS

4 tbsp butter
1 tbsp curry powder
4 cup mango diced
1 cup Jamaican pork broth
3½ lb boneless pork loin
1 cup Jamaican mango drink
¾ cup Jamaican mango chutney
¼ tsp salt
¼ tsp black pepper

PREPARATION

1. Preheat oven to 350 degrees. Place butter and curry powder in skillet.
2. Cook over medium heat for 3 minutes, stirring frequently. Add mango and stir to coat.
3. Add mango drink and broth and bring to a boil on high heat.
4. Place fat-side up, in a shallow roasting pan, using a slotted spoon, scoop up mango and place around the meat. Pour ¼ cup of drink-broth mixture over top of meat.
5. Place in the middle of a preheated 350x oven. Roast for 1 hour, uncovered.
6. Remove roast from oven and season with a little salt and pepper.
7. Spread chutney over the top of the roast, covering sides and ends.
8. Return to oven and roast, uncovered an additional 30 minutes.
9. Remove and slice and arrange pork slices on a platter.

NEGRIL PICKLED PORK
Pickled pork recipe is popular in Negril and possibly is one of the best recipes on the west end.

INGREDIENTS
1 tbsp escallion diced
2 tbsp Jamaican hot pepper sauce
½ cup cane vinegar
½ tbsp salt
¼ tsp black pepper
¼ cup garlic diced
2 lb boneless pork cooked

PREPARATION
1. Combine everything except the pork in a stainless steel pan and boil for 3 Min.
2. Cool and place in a refrigerator container and add the pork which you cut into 2" inch pieces.
3. Stir to remove bubbles.
4. Cover and refrigerate.

ST. JAMES OVEN BACON
A simple bacon recipe that can be easily prepared.

INGREDIENTS
1 lb sliced bacon

PREPARATION
1. Place bacon on a rack, in a roasting pan.
2. Bake at 400 degrees F for 15-20 minutes, cool cover and chill for 48 hours
3. Preheat at 450 degrees for 5 minutes until crisp.
4. Serve hot.

WESTMORELAND FRIED CABBAGE AND BACON
A special treat for cabbage fans, blending Jamaican spices and bacon.

INGREDIENTS
3 lbs cabbage head
½ lb bacon, sliced
½ cup water
1 tbsp sugar
1 tbsp salt
½ tsp black pepper

PREPARATION
1. Cut the cabbage into quarter. Remove any wilted and discolored outer leaves and cut out the core from the cabbage pieces.
2. Cut the cabbage into a large 1-inch dice.
3. Cook the bacon in a 4-quart pot over medium heat until crisp.
4. Remove the bacon to paper towels to drain.
5. Add the cabbage to drippings and cook without stirring until it begins to brown, about 3 minutes.
6. Add the water, sugar, salt, and pepper and cook covered until the cabbage is tender, about 20 minutes.
7. Crumble the cooked bacon into the cabbage and serve hot.

APPLETONS STIR FRIED PORK IN RUM SAUCE
Rum lovers delight! A perfect blend between pork and rum delicious.

INGREDIENTS
1 tsp rice wine
¼ cup garlic minced
2 tbsp Appleton rum
2 egg yolks beaten
¾ cup chicken stock
1 tsp water
½ cup cornstarch paste
1 cup bread crumbs
1½ lb pork loin boneless
3 tbsp vegetable oil
2 tbsp cooked rice
2 tbsp soy sauce
½ tsp sugar
2 tbsp warm water
1 tsp yeast
¼ cup grated cheese

PREPARATIONS
1. Use mortar and pestle to pulverize cooked rice and combine with sugar, yeast, soy and warm water.
2. Let stand in warm place for 30 minutes to activate yeast.
3. Slice pork butt across the grain into strips then heat vegetable oil in skillet until it begins to smoke.
4. Add some of pork to hot oil stir-fry pieces until they lose their pinkness repeat in batches until all pork is browned.
5. Next add garlic to skillet stir briefly. Pour in rice wine into paste with rice vinegar, rum and stock; bring to slow boil add pork slices.
6. Reduce heat, cover, and simmer. Remove pork, without sauce, to large platter.
7. Cool pork then heat deep-frying oil in skillet. While oil is heating, beat egg yolks with water; set out bread crumbs on platter.
8. Dip pork pieces in egg mixture, then bread crumbs, to thoroughly cover. When oil is at deep-frying temperature, 375 degrees slip in a slice of pork as a test: pork should lightly brown in about 1 minute.
9. Place 6 pork slices on Chinese strainer, and lower into oil, strainer and all.
10. Remove fried pork to warm platter, uncovered.

JAMAICAN PEANUT BUTTER AND PORK
A perfect blend of peanut butter and pork.

INGREDIENTS
¼ cup peanut butter
¼ cup yogurt
1 tbsp lemon juice
2 cloves garlic crushed
1 tbsp honey
1½ tsps cinnamon
12 pork leg shards

PREPARATION
1. Combine peanut butter with yogurt, juice garlic honey and cumin in a bowl mix well.
2. Brush shards with yogurt mixture.
3. Add shards to heated, greased griddle pan cook until browned on both sides and just tender.
4. Serve hot.

KINGSTON PEPPER PORK STEAK
Peppered steak is a great tasting recipe whether beef or pork. This Kingston recipe is delicious.

INGREDIENTS
1½ lbs boneless pork
1 tsp garlic powder
1 cup tomatoes
6 tbsp soy sauce
1 tsp Worcestershire sauce
2 tbsps cornstarch
¼ tsp pepper
1¼ cup water
1 cup sliced sweet pepper
1 cup chopped onion
½ cup escallion diced

PREPARATIONS
1. Cut meat across the grain into ½-inch slices, then slice again lengthwise.
2. Brown pork in non-stick skillet over low heat; add garlic, tomato, soy and Worcestershire sauces, pepper and 1 cup water. Cover and simmer mixture add green pepper, onion and escallion.
3. Cover and simmer combine cornstarch with ¼ cup water.
4. Add to skillet mixture, stirring until mixture thickens and meat is cooked. Serve hot.

DOREENS ROASTED PORK WITH STUFFED YAMS
A splendid recipe with roasted pork and Jamaican yams.

INGREDIENTS
2 cups yams or sweet potatoes diced
4 pork loin or rib chops
½ tsp salt
¼ tsp paprika
½ tsp garlic powder
½ cup orange juice
½ cup chopped otaheite apple
¼ cup onion diced
¼ cup escallion diced

PREPARATION
1. Heat oven to 350 degrees. Prick yams with fork to allow steam to escape.
2. Bake 55 to 60 minutes or until tender. Trim fat from pork chops.
3. About 30 minutes before yams are done, place pork in un-greased rectangular pan.
4. Mix salt, paprika, garlic powder and pepper; sprinkle half of the salt mixture over pork.
5. Turn pork; sprinkle with remaining salt mixture.
6. Pour ½ cup orange juice into pan. Cover and bake 30 minutes.
7. Cut yam lengthwise in half and scoop out pulp, leaving ¼-inch shell.
8. Mash pulp; beat in 2 tablespoons orange juice until light and fluffy.
9. Stir in apple, onion and escallion. Fill shells with pulp mixture.
10. Push pork to one end of pan place yams in other end.
11. Bake uncovered about 30 minutes or until pork is tender and yams are hot.

Cooking Tip
Soft yams and pork are a splendid combination especially when prepared well.

ST. BESS BEEF STUFFED PORK ROAST
A great St. Bess recipe of ground beef combined with pork roast absolutely delicious.

INGREDIENTS
1 boneless pork loin roast
½ lb ground beef
¼ cup chopped onion
¼ cup garlic minced
¼ tsp salt
¼ tsp black pepper
¼ cup bread crumbs
¼ cup grated cheese
1 cup Jamaican barbeque sauce

PREPARATION
1. Split meat lengthwise almost all the way to opposite side, then spread open flat.
2. Pound out to a 15 x 10-inch rectangle, about ¾-inch thick. Brush top with ¼ cup of the barbecue sauce.
3. Combine ground beef, onion, garlic, salt, pepper and an additional ¼ cup of the barbecue sauce.
4. Spread evenly over roast then sprinkle bread crumbs and cheese over meat.
5. Place on rack in shallow roasting pan and roast, uncovered, in 325 degrees oven for about 2½ hours.
6. Baste with additional barbecue sauce during roasting.
7. Remove slice and serve hot.

PINE HILL'S PORK ON PINEAPPLE
Pine Hill in St. Elizabeth served up this delicious recipe to us and we had to share this recipe with our readers.

INGREDIENTS
1 pineapple
1 lb Lean ground pork
¼ cup chopped onion
1 tbsp sugar
1 tbsp cane vinegar
1 tsp ginger minced
½ tsp salt
¼ tsp black pepper
1 cup sweet peppers diced
1 cup tomato crushed

PREPARATION
1. Pare pineapple. Cut crosswise into 6 slices.
2. Spray broiler pan rack with nonstick cooking spray then arrange pineapple on rack in broiler pan.
3. Cook ground pork and onion in nonstick skillet stirring frequently, until pork is brown then drain.
4. Stir in remaining ingredients. Heat to boiling; reduce heat. Simmer uncovered stirring occasionally until bell pepper is crisp-tender.
5. Set oven control to broil and broil pineapple with tops 4 to 5 inches from heat 5 minutes; turn.
6. Broil 3 to 5 minutes longer or until hot and bubbly.
7. Serve pork mixture on pineapple slices.

JAMAICAN PORK MEAT LOAVES
Meat loaves are delicious especially when made with pork.

INGREDIENTS
2 eggs beaten
¾ cup bread crumbs
½ cup milk
½ cup grated cheese
¼ cup onion chop fine
1 tbsp Worcestershire sauce
½ tbsp garlic salt
2 lb ground pork
¼ cup ketchup

PREPARATION
1. In a large bowl, combine eggs, crumbs, milk, cheese, onion, Worcestershire sauce, garlic salt and pork then mix well.
2. Shape into 10 individual loaves; place on a rack in a greased large shallow baking pan.
3. Spread ketchup over loaves; sprinkle with remaining cheese and seasoning.

JUNCTION MEATLOAF
A great recipe we found when we were traveling through the junction road top get to Golden Spring

INGREDIENTS
1¼ lb ground lean pork
6 strips bacon
¼ cup grated carrot
1 cup breadcrumbs
¼ cup onions diced
½ cup sweet pepper diced
¼ cup garlic crushed
4 tsp lemon juice
1 tsp lemon zest
¼ tsp dried thyme

PREPARATION
1. Mix all the ingredients very thoroughly with your hands and season well with salt and pepper.
2. Oil a 2 lb loaf tin, line with greaseproof paper and pack the mixture into the tin.
3. Press down the meat nicely and cover the tin with foil.
4. Stand it in a roasting pan and pour in enough boiling water to come halfway up the sides of the loaf tin.
5. Bake at 350 F for 1 hour then reduce temperature to 325 F remove foil lid and bake for a further 30 minutes.
6. Cool the cooked meatloaf for 30 minutes, then tilt the tin and pour off the juices.
7. Set aside in a cold place overnight before serving to allow flavors to blend and mature.

JAMAICAN GRILLED PORK IN BREADFRUIT
Try this recipe with the pork sauces soaked into the breadfruit.

INGREDIENTS
1 cup ground pork
1 tbsp allspice
1 small onion, chopped
salt and black pepper to taste
2 tbsps. cooking oil
2 tbsps. tomato paste
¼ cup water
1 breadfruit

PREPARATION
1. Scoop out heart of breadfruit.
2. Cook ground pork with seasonings, onion and tomato paste.
3. Drain off excess oil.
4. Stuff breadfruit with mixture, replace stem and roast in hot oven 425 degrees °F for ½ hour, then reduce heat to 350 degrees°F for another half hour.
5. Test to see if the breadfruit is tender with fork or skewer.

BALACLAVA FRICASSEED PORK
A proper recipe from the Shrimp parish, absolutely delicious.

INGREDIENTS
5 cups boneless pork chopped
¼ cup flour
½ cup diced carrots
½ cup diced potatoes
¼ tsp salt
¼ tsp paprika
¼ cup vegetable oil
2 tbsp Jamaican hot pepper sauce
3 cups water
½ tsp allspice
¼ cup onion, minced
2 tbsp sugar
¼ cup soy sauce
¼ cup escallion chopped

PREPARATION
1. Place pork in flour and brown in vegetable oil.
2. Place all other ingredients except carrots and potatoes and puree in blender.
3. Add puree and carrots and potatoes to browned pork and cook until pork and vegetables are soft.
4. Ensure that sauce does not dry out.
5. Remove and serve hot.

JAMAICAN BROWN STEW PORK RECIPE
Sweet brown stew recipe that we picked up in the Golden Spring area.

INGREDIENTS
¼ tsp salt
¼ tsp black pepper
¼ cup vegetable oil
4 cups pork shanks
½ cup onion finely chopped
¼ cup garlic minced
½ cup flour
1 cup tomatoes peeled and chopped
1 cup water
¼ tsp nutmeg
1 cup cooked potatoes cubed
1 cup cooked carrots diced

PREPARATION
1. Dredge pork in the flour and brown in skillet.
2. Season with salt and pepper cover with water and simmer until nearly tender.
3. Add all vegetable and other ingredients and continue to cook.
4. Add a little flour to thicken sauce.
5. Remove and serve with cooked rice hot.

Cooking Tip
When using salted pork ensure that the meat is boiled to remove all excess salt in the pork meat.

DUNNS RIVER BROILED PORK CHOPS
We got this recipe from a chef at the famed Sandals Dunn's River Resort.

INGREDIENTS
8 pork chops
¼ tsp salt
¼ tsp black pepper

PREPARATION
1. Broil chops on one side for a few minutes.
2. Season with salt and pepper on one side then broil on the other.
3. Once broiled serve hot

KINGSTON STYLE ROAST PORK
A less popular method of roast pork that uses one main ingredient spice, tasty nonetheless

INGREDIENTS
1 boneless pork shoulder roast
½ cup soy sauce
1 cup onion and escallion diced

PREPARATION
1. Place soy sauce and onion and escallion mixture in blender and puree until smooth.
2. Cut pork roast in half length wise and place the halves in a large plastic bag.
3. Add to the pork the seasoning and marinate overnight.
4. Preheat oven to 350 Degrees and remove pork from the marinade and place in a shallow baking dish and cover with foil in a shallow baking dish.
5. Bake for 30 minutes and turn the meat and bake for one hour more.

JAMAICAN FISH RECIPES.

jamaican fried fish with garlic. ©

PORT ROYAL STEAMED FISH WITH CRACKERS

Port Royal is renowned for its fish and seafood recipes and its most popular steamed parrot fish.

INGREDIENTS

2½ lb fish fillet
½ tbsp salt and black pepper mixed
¾ cup water
¼ cup melted butter
¼ cup coconut milk
¼ cup onion diced
¼ cup escallion diced
½ cup sweet peppers
½ cup tomatoes diced
½ tbsp scotch bonnet pepper diced
½ cup chopped okras
1 onion sliced
1 scotch bonnet pepper diced into rings
½ bag water crackers

PREPARATION

1. Season outside fish with salt and black pepper and allow to marinate and stuff cavity of fish with ½ seasonings.
2. In a deep skillet heat melted butter, and add fish and all ingredients.
3. Cover and allow to cook for until fish is done.
4. Add crackers atop and allow to soak.
5. Remove and serve hot.

RED HILLS ROAD JERK FISH

Jerk recipes are extremely popular and this jerk fish recipe is sublime.

INGREDIENTS

5 lbs fish fillet
2 cups tomatoes diced
¼ cup honey
¼ tsp salt
¼ tsp black pepper
1 cup Jamaican jerk sauce

PREPARATION

1. Scar the fish on both sides and marinate with the sauce outside and inside fish then cover in honey.
2. Place fish on hot grill 'till seared on both sides the set aside.
3. Place foil on grill, oil. Return fish onto foil pour in marinade and wrap allow to steam in juices for ½ hour.
4. Add the tomatoes, for 10 minutes then remove and serve with roast yellow yam, breadfruit and tomatoes.

KINGSTON STYLE BAKED FISH IN CURRY SAUCE
A great baked fish recipe from a prominent chef in Kingston absolutely delicious to the taste.

INGREDIENTS
4 fish fillets
2 tbsp lime juice
½ cup sliced tomatoes
½ cup onions sliced
¼ cup escallion diced
½ tsp dried thyme leaves
2 tbsp vegetable oil
¼ cup cane vinegar
¼ cup Get Jamaica curry sauce
½ cup cooked potatoes diced
½ cup cooked chocho diced

PREPARATION
1. Put the fish to marinate in some lime juice for about an hour.
2. Cut up tomatoes, onions, thyme and scallions and mix the with vegetable oil and a teaspoon of vinegar.
3. Cut into the fish so that some of the seasoning can go into the fish.
4. Put the fish in the oven at about 300 degrees for about half an hour.
5. Heat curry sauce and add cooked vegetables in the mean time.
6. When done pour sauce and vegetable over fish.
7. Serve hot.

Cooking Tip

When preparing fish, you can add a little lemon juice to make the fish meat firm. This prevents the fish from flaking easily especially when boiling the fish recipe. To avoid unpleasant odors when cooking fish you can also cover the fish with browned butter or lemon juice as well. This helps to restrict the strong odor that raw fish has. However after you have cut the fish and seasoned it there might be an odor left on the utensils the best way to remove the smell is to use ammonia. Ammonia not only cleans the utensil, kills micro bacteria but also totally kills the smell of the raw fish. Ammonia should not be used excess though as it has a strong smell that many find disturbing.

JAMAICAN GRILLED FISH WITH GARLIC BUTTER
This is an excellent fish recipe using garlic butter to enhance the sweet taste.

INGREDIENTS
1½ lb fish fillet
½ tbsp salt and black pepper mixed
¼ tsp onion powder
¼ tsp allspice
2 tbsps vegetable oil
½ cup Jamaican garlic butter

PREPARATION
1. Wash fish and pat dry and season with powdered seasonings then lightly coat fillets with vegetable oil.
2. When fire is ready, place fish on oiled grill cook until done.
3. Serve hot with garlic butter.

PORT HENDERSON ESCOVITCHED FISH
Port Henderson is a popular beach in Portmore with great fish recipes including this one.

INGREDIENTS
6 frozen fish steaks
½ tbsp salt and black pepper mixed
½ cup bread crumbs
½ cup vegetable oil
½ tbsp onion powder
½ tbsp allspice
½ tbsp scotch bonnet pepper
¼ cup escallion diced
½ tbsp garlic powder
½ cup Jamaican fish dry seasoning

PREPARATION
1. Mix breadcrumbs with dry seasonings,
2. Score fish and dredge in bread crumbs.
3. Heat a skillet and add vegetable oil.
4. Fry fish in vegetable oil until well done.
5. Serve and sprinkle fish pepper over the fish.

WHITEHOUSE BROWN STEW FISH
Whitehouse is a popular fishing village in Westmoreland and this is a tasty brown stew recipe from its archives.

INGREDIENTS
1½ lb fish fillet
½ tbsp salt and black pepper mixed
½ cup bread crumbs
½ cup vegetable oil
½ cup onion diced
½ tbsp allspice
½ tbsp scotch bonnet pepper
¼ cup escallion diced
¼ cup garlic diced
½ cup soy sauce
½ cup cooked potatoes chopped
½ cup cooked chocho chopped
½ cup Jamaican fish broth

PREPARATION
1. Prepare and fry fish coated with bread crumbs, set aside and then strain ½ oil from frying pan.
2. Sauté all other seasoning and then add fish and fish stock and soy sauce.
3. Add vegetables and simmer until flavors blend and sauce is thick.
4. Serve hot.

HELLSHIRE COCONUT SNAPPER
A great recipe we got from Screeches corner of the famed beach.

INGREDIENTS
6 snapper fillets
¼ pound breadfruit
1 tbsp butter
1 cup onion diced
2 cups sweet peppers
1 cup coconut milk
1 cup callaloo, diced
1 cup carrots, diced
1 cup flour
2 egg whites
½ cup garlic chopped
1 tsp thyme leaves
½ tbsp scotch bonnet pepper diced

PREPARATION
1. Season snapper fillets with salt and pepper. Crush the fish in the breadcrumbs.
2. Peel the breadfruit and shred. Place in a bowl and add a pinch of salt.
3. Add egg whites then cook in hot pan. Put aside and keep warm.
4. In a medium hot pan, cook callaloo with a little butter.
5. Add sweet peppers, thyme and onions and set aside.
6. Sauté onions, garlic, pepper and fresh thyme in a little butter.
7. Add the coconut milk and reduce to a creamy consistency, to coat the back of spoon.
8. In a medium hot pan, add butter and lightly pan fry the fillets for about two minutes per side or until done as needed.
9. Place breadfruit on centre of the plate. Add snapper and place callaloo on top. Spoon sauce around the plate.

LYME CAYE BAKED FISH
A fish recipe which is a perfect blend between jerk and barbeque.

INGREDIENTS
4 fish fillets
2 tbsp lime juice
½ cup sliced tomatoes
½ cup onions sliced
¼ cup escallion diced
½ tsp dried thyme leaves
2 tbsp vegetable oil
¼ cup cane vinegar
½ cup sweet potatoes diced

PREPARATION
1. Put the fish to marinate in some lime juice for about an hour.
2. Cut up tomatoes, onions, thyme and scallions and mix the with vegetable oil and a teaspoon of vinegar.
3. Cut into the fish so that some of the seasoning can go into the fish.
4. Put the fish in the oven at about 300 degrees for about half an hour.
5. Serve the fish hot.

ROCKY POINT STEAM SNAPPER AND CHICKEN
Rocky point has one of the most delicious combo recipes steamed chicken and fish with spices.

INGREDIENTS
3 skinned boneless
chicken breast
3 slices of snapper fillet
¼ cup onion diced
¼ cup escallion diced
¼ allspice
½ tsp scotch bonnet pepper diced
½ tbsp garlic
¼ tsp salt
¼ tsp black pepper

PREPARATION
1. Roll in fish and chicken in foil with all spices tightly.
2. Cook in boiling water.
3. Serve with steamed vegetables.

MILKY WAY BAKED SNAPPER
A great tasting fish recipe combining herbs and spices with fresh cows milk and snapper fillets.

INGREDIENTS
4 lb parrot fish fillet
¼ cup vegetable oil
¼ cup garlic minced
½ tsp nutmeg powder
¼ tsp salt
¼ tsp black pepper
¼ cup onion diced
½ tbsp
½ cup milk

PREPARATION
1. Mix all ingredients together then soak fish in milk for 20 minutes turning once.
2. Rub mixed ingredients on both sides of fish.
3. Bake for 10-15 minutes or until fish is flaky.
4. Garnish and serve with steamed vegetables.

DISCOVERY BAY FISH AND SHRIMP
A great tasting recipe from Discovery Bay blending fish and shrimp.

INGREDIENTS
¼ cup vegetable oil
¼ tsp salt
¼ tsp black pepper
¼ cup onion diced
¼ cup garlic diced
½ tbsp ginger crushed
½ tsp all spice
½ tsp scotch bonnet pepper diced
2 lb fish fillet
½ cup peeled and de-veined shrimp

PREPARATION
1. Season fish and shrimps with all the ingredients and marinate for 20 minutes.
2. Heat frying pan for 2 minutes, add 2 spoons of vegetable oil, add garlic and onion.
3. Stir fry for 2 minutes, add fish and shrimps and stir-fry cook.
4. Serve with steamed vegetables.

OCHO RIOS HONEYED FISH
A tasty recipe we got from off the beach coast in Ocho Rios

INGREDIENTS
2 lb. fresh water fish fillet
1 tsp salt
1 tsp black pepper
2 tbsp margarine
¼ cup escallion diced
¼ cup onion diced
3 tsps. honey
2 tbsps. orange juice

PREPARATION
1. Wash fillet, pat dry. Season lightly with salt and pepper.
2. Heat frying pan. Add butter and fish, and cook for about 1 minute.
3. Combine escallion, onion, honey and orange juice and pour over fish.
4. Cover and simmer until fish is tender.

FORT CLARENCE JERK-BQ FISH
A sweet recipe using a great tasting Jamaican jerk-bq sauce. Absolutely delicious.

INGREDIENTS
5 lbs tilapia fillet
2 cups tomatoes diced
¼ cup honey
¼ tsp salt
¼ tsp black pepper
1 cup Jamaican jerk-bq sauce

PREPARATION
1. Scar the fish on both sides and marinate with the sauce outside and inside fish then cover in honey.
2. Place fish on hot grill 'till seared on both sides the set aside.
3. Place foil on grill, oil. Return fish onto foil pour in marinade from dish and wrap tightly and allow to steam in its juices for about half an hour.
4. Add the tomatoes, for 10 minutes then remove and serve with roast yellow yam, breadfruit and tomatoes.

NEGRIL DRUNKEN FISH RECIPE
A sweet recipe, of great Jamaican rum and fish.

INGREDIENTS
2 lb fish fillets
2 tbsps lime juice
¼ cup Appleton V/X rum
½ tsp Jamaican sweet sauce
3 tbsps. butter
¼ cup escallion, finely chopped
¼ cup onion finely chopped
¼ cup sour cream
¼ cup parsley
½ cup flour
¼ tsp salt
¼ tsp black pepper

PREPARATION
1. In a non-stick skillet, heat butter over medium-high heat.
2. Dredge fillets in flour. Sauté on per side until crisp and highly browned.
3. Add salt and pepper while sautéing. When done, set aside and keep warm.
4. Add remaining more butter, lemon juice, escallion, onion and rum to skillet and continue to sauté briefly.
5. Add remaining ingredients except sour cream and parsley.
6. Simmer stirring then add in sour cream and pour over fillets.
7. Garnish with parsley and serve.

DOWNTOWN MACKEREL CAKES
A great tasting mackerel recipe straight from the tin and a favorite for many cooks and chefs in Jamaica

INGREDIENTS
1 pack of soaked oats
1 cup diced tomatoes
½ cup flour
1 tsp baking powder
4 mackerel steaks
2 eggs, beaten
1 cup water
¼ cup onion
½ cup Jamaican tomato sauce
¼ cup vegetable oil
¼ tsp salt
¼ tsp black pepper

PREPARATION
1. Sauté onion and tomato and set aside.
2. Mash oats and mackerel together. Add flour, baking powder, eggs and seasoning.
3. Mix to a smooth consistency then form into round cakes.
4. Heat oil in saucepan and fry the cakes until golden brown.

BLUE LAGOON BAKED STUFFED FISH
A great stuffed fish recipe from this major tourist resort.

INGREDIENTS
4 lb whole snapper
1 tbsp. salt
1 tbsp. black pepper
1 egg beaten
¼ cup breadcrumbs
1 tbsp. margarine
¼ cup escallion
¼ cup onion
½ tbsp scotch bonnet pepper diced
1 cup Jamaican fish stuffing

PREPARATION
1. Remove scales from fish and clean cavity in the usual way. Wash in cold water and pat dry.
2. Season fish with salt and pepper and fill cavity with stuffing.
3. Skewer into shape or sew with a needle and thread.
4. Put the fish in a greased ovenproof dish or baking tin, brush with a little beaten egg and sprinkle with breadcrumbs.
5. Put a few dots of margarine on top of the breadcrumbs and bake at 350ºF for 10 minutes then at 350ºF for 20-40 minutes.
6. Fish is cooked when the flesh flakes easily with a fork but is still moist.

JAMAICAN ONION ESCOVITCHED FISH
A top tasting recipe absolutely delicious to the taste. This is a premier recipe.

INGREDIENTS
6 frozen fish steaks
¼ cup vegetable oil
¼ cup onion diced
½ tbsp scotch bonnet pepper
¼ cup escallion diced
¼ cup onion butter
2 cups sliced onion

PREPARATION
1. Score and season with seasonings.
2. Preheat broiler and arrange fish steaks on broiler pan. Brush lightly with vegetable oil.
3. Place broiler pan with steaks about 4 inches below heat source and broil until flesh is barely opaque when tested with a fork or done to taste.
4. Arrange fish steaks on serving plates.
5. Serve with onion butter.

DOCTORS CAVE BEACH COCONUT FISH TIES
A great tasting fish recipe from the premier beach in Montego Bay.

INGREDIENTS
4 fish fillets
¼ tsp salt
1 tbsp Jamaican fish dry seasoning
2 cups coconut shredded
¾ cup vegetable oil
2 egg whites, beaten
½ cup flour
1 tbsp Jamaican hot pepper sauce
1 tbsp Worcestershire sauce
½ cup honey
¾ cup ketchup
1 tsp soy sauce

PREPARATION
1. Season fillets with fish spice and salt to taste then heat oil in a skillet.
2. Roll fillets, hold with toothpicks to keep shape and dredge with flour.
3. Dip in egg white and coat with shredded coconut then fry until light brown.
4. Drain on absorbent paper. Remove toothpick.
5. Garnish and serve.

MAMMEE BAY FISH TARTS
From the community of Mammee Bay a great tart recipe.

INGREDIENTS
1 cup salt fish boiled and flaked
¼ cup margarine
2 cups dumpling dough
1 cup grated cheese
¼ cup escallion
¼ cup onion
¼ tsp black pepper
½ tsp scotch bonnet pepper diced

PREPARATION
1. In a skillet melt butter and sauté salt fish, escallion, onion, and black pepper.
2. Shape dough into squares and even spread salt fish mixture on each square.
3. Seal each square and return to frying pan and cook and drain on paper towels and serve hot.

MORANT POINT SALT FISH DUMPLINGS IN A COCONUT CURRY
This recipe is absolutely superb from the fishermen of Morant Point. Definitely a top ten recipe.

INGREDIENTS
½ lb salt fish
½ cup escallion diced
½ cup garlic diced
½ cup onion diced
½ tsp thyme
½ tbsp scotch bonnet pepper
¼ cup vegetable oil
1 tsp curry powder
½ cup coconut milk
1 cup flour
2 tsp baking powder
1 tsp salt
1 cup water to mix

PREPARATION
1. Soak or boil salt fish to remove excess salt then skin, bone and shred fish.
2. Sauté seasonings in oil without curry and set aside.
3. Mix flour baking powder and salt and add water to make a soft dumpling.
4. Divide into balls and place 1 tablespoon of salt fish mixture on dough and fold over to close sealing with water.
5. Place in lightly salted boiling water and cook. Remove from water and set aside.
6. Heat oil in a Dutch pot and sauté left over escallion, garlic, onion, thyme, and scotch bonnet.
7. Add curry to pot to cook and add coconut milk.
8. Season with salt to taste.
9. When boiling leave uncovered add salt fish dumplings and cook till sauce thickens.
10. Serve as a cocktail, a main course or as a side dish.

MISS NORMA'S SPECIAL FILLET FISH
One of Miss Norma's special fish fillet recipes.

INGREDIENTS
1 lb salt fish
1 cup hot water
¼ tsp black pepper
½ cup onion sliced
½ tbsp scotch bonnet pepper diced
½ cup tomatoes diced
¼ cup escallions diced
½ cup vegetable oil
1 egg beaten
¼ cup grated carrots
½ cup sweet pepper

PREPARATION
1. Soak salt fish overnight in hot water then skin, bone and flake.
2. Add onions, scotch bonnet pepper, escallions and tomatoes to salt fish.
3. Add vegetable oil to mixture to cook. Add black pepper while stirring.
4. Serve hot with cooked ackees or dumplings.

PUERTO SECO FISH BURGHER
From this famous beach on the North coast comes the famous burgher recipe.

INGREDIENTS
3 fish fillets
2 eggs beaten
½ cup chopped sweet pepper
¼ cup chopped onion
¼ cup escallion chopped finely
¼ cup garlic chopped finely
¼ tsp allspice
¼ tsp cinnamon
¼ tsp black pepper
¼ tsp salt
1 tsp vegetable oil
¼ cup bread crumbs
1 tsp Jamaican sweet sauce

PREPARATION
1. Combine all dry ingredients and coat after dipping fillet in egg.
2. Fry the fillet in the vegetable oil each side remove and then drain.
3. Add the fish sauce and place on buttered hamburger rolls.
4. Serve with regular hamburger condiments.

PORT ANTONIO BARBEQUE FISH

Barbeque fish is not that popular but this recipe was so delicious we had to include it.

INGREDIENTS
5 lbs fish fillet
2 cups tomatoes diced
½ tbsp garlic powder
½ tbsp onion powder
½ tsp allspice
¼ cup honey
¼ tsp salt
¼ tsp black pepper
1 cup Jamaican Bar-BQ sauce

PREPARATION
1. Scar the fish on both sides and marinate with powder seasonings the sauce outside and inside fish then cover in honey.
2. Place fish on hot grill till seared on both sides the set aside.
3. Place foil on grill, oil. Return fish onto foil pour in marinade from dish and wrap tightly and allow to steam in its juices for about half an hour.
4. Add the tomatoes, for 10 minutes then remove and serve with roast yellow yam, breadfruit and tomatoes.

JAMAICAN JERK FISH BURGHER

This is the common fish burgher recipe but using the reputed jerk sauce to coat the fish fillet.

INGREDIENTS
3 fish fillets
2 eggs beaten
½ cup chopped sweet pepper
¼ cup chopped onion
¼ cup escallion chopped finely
¼ cup garlic chopped finely
¼ tsp allspice
¼ tsp cinnamon
¼ tsp black pepper
¼ tsp salt
1 tsp vegetable oil
¼ cup bread crumbs
1 tsp Jamaican jerk sauce

PREPARATION
1. Combine all dry ingredients and coat after dipping fillet in egg.
2. Fry the fillet in the vegetable oil each side remove and then drain.
3. Add the jerk sauce and place on buttered hamburger rolls.
4. Serve with regular hamburger condiments.

ST. ANNS BAY POACHED FISH
Sweet as can be the blend between poached fish and eggs.

INGREDIENTS
3 lb fish fillet
1 tbsp butter
¼ tsp salt
¼ tsp black pepper
¼ cup onion diced
¼ cup garlic dice
½ tbsp scotch bonnet pepper diced
1 tbsp flour
1 cup Jamaican fish broth
1 egg yolk

PREPARATION
1. Clean fish scar and add salt and black pepper. Poach the fish for 30 minutes.
2. Melt butter and add stock, then onion and garlic, return fish.
3. Add egg yolk and simmer for at least 15 minutes.
4. Serve hot with desired garnish.

COOLIE TOWN CURRY FISH
This is another in the series of the Coolie Town great curry recipes.

INGREDIENTS
1½ lb fish fillet
½ tbsp salt and black pepper mixed
½ cup bread crumbs
½ cup vegetable oil
½ cup onion diced
½ tbsp allspice
½ tbsp scotch bonnet pepper
¼ cup escallion diced
¼ cup garlic diced
1 tbsp curry powder
½ cup cooked potatoes chopped
½ cup cooked chocho chopped
½ cup Jamaican fish broth

PREPARATION
1. Prepare and fry fish coated with bread crumbs, set aside and then strain ½ oil from frying pan.
2. Sauté all other seasoning and then add fish and fish stock and curry powder.
3. Add vegetables and simmer until flavors blend and sauce is thick.
4. Serve hot.

DOWNTOWN SEASIDE ROAST FISH
In downtown Kingston this great recipe is prepared every Friday by the seaside.

INGREDIENTS
5 lbs fish fillet
2 cups tomatoes diced
¼ cup honey
¼ tsp salt
¼ tsp black pepper
¼ tsp allspice
¼ cup onion diced
¼ cup escallion diced
1 cup Jamaican sweet sauce

PREPARATION
1. Scar the fish on both sides and marinate with the sauce outside and inside fish then cover in honey.
2. Stuff inside of fish with escallion and onion then wrap fish in foil and place fish on hot grill and roast until prepare. Open and add tomatoes and serve.

JAMAICAN SNAPPER STUFFED WITH CRABMEAT
Usually seafood is stuffed with seasonings this recipe has stuffing's of crabmeat which enhance an already great taste.

INGREDIENTS
2 tbsp margarine
½ cup flour
¼ tsp salt
¼ tsp black pepper
2 whole snappers
1 cup cooked crabmeat
½ tbsp scotch bonnet pepper diced
½ tsp Worcestershire sauce
½ tbsp lemon juice
2 eggs beaten

PREPARATION
1. Scar the snappers and season with salt and black pepper dip in eggs then dredge with flour.
2. Fry in vegetable oil till just browned on the outside. Sprinkle sauce on the inside of the fish the lemon juice and stuff with crab meat and peppers. Wrap tightly in foil then place on grill and cook for at least 20 minutes. Remove and serve hot.

CLARENDON LEMON FISH
Clarendonians love this recipe, they are absolutely delicious with every bite.

INGREDIENTS
2 lb fish fillets
1 cup seasoned dry bread crumbs
¼ cup margarine melted
2 tbsp parsley flakes
2 tsp grated lemon peel
½ tsp garlic powder

PREPARATION
Cut fish into serving-size pieces and place in a greased baking dish. Combine remaining ingredients. Sprinkle over fish. Bake at 350 F. for 25 minutes or until fish flakes easily with a fork.

BORDER BAKED PARROT WITH JUNE PLUM SAUCE
Border is on the border between St. Bess and Westmoreland renowned for their fish and seafood recipes.

INGREDIENTS
3 lb snapper fillet
6 tbsp melted butter
¼ cup onions chopped
¼ cup garlic minced
2 tbsp Parsley
¼ cup wine
1 tbsp lemon juice
¼ tsp salt
¼ tsp black pepper
½ cup flour
1 cup June Plum sauce

PREPARATIONS
1. Place fish in baking dish or pan then brown garlic, onion in melted butter.
2. When brown, add parsley, wine and lemon juice then add sauce.
3. Pour sauce over fish sprinkle with salt, pepper, flour.
4. Bake covered 10 min. at 375 Degrees.
5. Uncover, basting with melted butter and dry white wine.
6. Bake for a few minutes then remove.

JAMAICAN BAKED FISH ON SCOTCH BONNET PEPPERS
A great recipe on peppers, not for the faint of peppery taste.

INGREDIENTS
3 tbsp vegetable oil
½ cup Jamaican fish dry seasoning
½ cup sweet peppers diced
¼ cup onion, sliced
1 tbsp cane vinegar
¼ cup scotch bonnet peppers sliced
¼ tsp salt
¼ tsp black pepper,
2 lbs fish fillet

PREPARATION
1. Preheat the oven to 400'F. Heat 2 tablespoons oil in a large nonstick skillet over medium heat.
2. Add the peppers and onion cook 10 minutes, stirring often.
3. Add vinegar and special seasoning and cook 15 minutes longer, stirring often.
4. Season with salt and pepper and 2 tablespoons parsley.
5. Spoon the vegetables over the bottom of a 9x9" baking dish.
6. Brush the fish with the remaining oil.
7. Sprinkle both sides with salt and pepper then lay the fish in the baking dish over the vegetables.
8. Bake for 20 minutes.
9. Garnish fish with remaining parsley.
10. Serve immediately.

coconut fried fish ©

RED STRIPE BATTER FISH FRY
You asked for more Red Stripe Beer recipes in our second edition review, so here is one more.

INGREDIENTS
1 cup flour
¼ cup onion
1 tsp salt
¼ tsp black pepper
½ cup beer
2 lb fish fillets

PREPARATION
1. Combine dry ingredients and add beer to get a sticky consistency for dipping.
2. Salt fish and dip in batter. Deep fry at 375 degrees until fish is golden brown and serve hot

SPICY SNAPPER FILLET
Another great recipe absolutely delicious with sweet tasting spices.

INGREDIENTS
2 tsp vegetable oil
1 cup cooked carrots diced
¼ cup escallions diced
½ tbsp ginger grated
1 tsp allspice
2 tilapia cleaned and scaled
¼ tsp salt
3 tbsp white wine (**optional**)
½ cup Jamaican fish stock
1 tbsp butter

PREPARATION
1. Preheat oven to 400 degrees F and rub a baking dish well with the oil.
2. Add the vegetables and whole spices, and toss to coat them lightly with oil.
3. Arrange in layers and season lightly with salt, and place on top of the vegetables.
4. Add the wine and 3 tablespoons of the stock.
5. Bake, rotating the pan once halfway through the cooking time until done.
6. Serve hot.

JAMAICAN FISH FILLET MOLD
A delicious recipe from the beaches of Fort Clarence in Kingston.

INGREDIENTS
1 cup chopped parsley
1 cup creamed cheese
½ cup dry white wine
¼ tsp salt
1 tbsp lemon juice
1½ lb parrot fish fillet, cooked
1 tbsp Jamaican jerk sauce

PREPARATION
1. Put parrot fish, wine, parsley, lemon juice and salt in food processor and chop.
2. Add jerk sauce and cream cheese and mix well.
3. Refrigerate overnight in a mold. Serve with crackers or on a bed of lettuce.

SCREECHIES FISH AND CHEESE
Screech on the Hellshire beach contributed this delicious recipe

INGREDIENTS
1½ lb fish fillet
¼ cup margarine
½ cup flour
¼ cup milk for stock
½ cup tomatoes chopped
1 tbsp chopped parsley
¼ tsp salt
¼ tsp black pepper
½ cup grated cheese

PREPARATION
1. Cut the fish into smaller cuts.
2. Melt the butter in a pan and stir in the flour.
3. Gradually add the fish and milk stock to make a smooth sauce.
4. Add the chopped tomatoes and parsley, season well.
5. Mix the sauce into the fish, then pile this mixture into two individual serving dishes.
6. Sprinkle the Parmesan over the top of the fish mixture and place under a moderate grill for 6-8 minutes or until the cheese is golden brown.
7. Serve hot.

LINSTEAD FISH FILLETS WITH BANANA
Linstead recipes have been an excellent addition to this book, this recipe is sweet with bananas.

INGREDIENTS
4 fish fillets
½ cup ripe bananas chopped
4 tbsp orange juice
2 tbsp gated orange zest
2 tbsp minced onion
2 tsp minced, scotch bonnet pepper diced
4 lime wedges

PREPARATION
1. Preheat the broiler and arrange the fish fillets and bananas on a lightly greased broiler pan.
2. In a small bowl, combine half the orange juice with the orange zest, onion, pepper
3. Add a pinch each of salt and pepper and spread evenly over fish and bananas.
4. Broil 4 inches from the heat source, without turning, until fish and bananas are browned.
5. Transfer to a serving platter. Sprinkle with the remaining orange juice.
6. Garnish with lime wedges.

steamed grouper and vegetables. ©

LINKS PON DI BEACH FISH FILLET
This party happens on the Hellshire beach every Sunday boasting some great recipes.

INGREDIENTS
1 lb white-fish fillets
¼ tsp vegetable oil
¼ cup soy sauce
1 cup water
2 tbsp cane vinegar
1 tbsp vegetable oil
¼ cup onion sliced
¼ cup escallion diced
½ cup sweet peppers diced
1 cup chopped tomatoes
1 tsp basil
½ tsp scotch bonnet pepper diced
½ cup cooked okras
1 cup cooked potatoes diced

PREPARATION
1. Sauté onion, escallion, sweet peppers, scotch bonnet peppers and tomatoes in vegetable oil.
2. Add white fish, cane vinegar, basil, soy sauce and tip water, continue to stir around until cooked.
3. Add cooked vegetables and okras and serve hot.

KINGSTON MIX UP AND BLENDER FISH
Aptly called the mix up and blender recipe, it is a mix up and blender of delight.

INGREDIENTS
¼ cup garlic diced
¼ tsp salt
1 tbsp paprika
¼ tbsp cinnamon
½ tbsp scotch bonnet pepper diced
1 tbsp lemon juice
¼ cup vegetable oil
2 lb whole fish, cleaned,

PREPARATION
1. Pound together the garlic, salt, paprika, cinnamon and peppers.
2. Stir in the lemon juice and vegetable oil.
3. Marinate fish for several hours.
4. Grill the fish for 4 minutes for each ½ inch thickness.
5. Baste with the marinade and serve at once

COVE TILAPIA IN SPICY SAUCE
From the cove beach in Westmoreland an absolutely delicious recipe

INGREDIENTS
4 lb fish fillets
1 egg white
2 tbsp cornstarch
2 cup vegetable oil
¼ cup garlic diced
¼ cup escallions diced
½ cup ground beef
2 tbsp soy sauce
2 cup Jamaican fish stock
2 tbsp rice wine
½ tsp onion powder

PREPARATION
1. Cut fish diagonally in 4 pieces and agitate the egg white and press between the fingers so that they jellylike part and the liquid part blend evenly.
2. Dip fish in the egg white and then coat with cornstarch and fry lightly in oil at 300F.
3. Heat the skillet and stir fry the beef until well cooked.
4. Add 1 tbsp soy sauce and stir in heated stock.
5. Add fried fish followed by rice wine and remaining soy sauce and cook.
6. Stir in cornstarch mixture to thicken and add onion powder.

PORTMORE FISH CAKES
A tasty treat for the Portmore citizen now enjoyed by many, a spicy recipe.

INGREDIENTS
1 cup fish flaked
¼ cup sweet pepper diced
2 tbsp minced parsley
¼ tbsp scotch bonnet pepper diced
2 tbsp minced onion
1 egg white
½ cup mayonnaise
1½ tsp lemon juice
1 tsp Worcestershire sauce
¼ cup garlic minced

PREPARATION
1. Preheat oven to 375 degrees F. Spray nonstick baking sheet with vegetable coating spray.
2. In large bowl, gently mix all ingredients and make cakes.
3. Shape mixture into circle, pressing flat. Place on prepared baking sheet.
4. Bake 20 to 25 minutes or until golden brown.
5. Serve hot.

DORREENS SPECIAL GRILLED FILLETS
Doreen has hit the nail on the head with recipe as sweet as you like.

INGREDIENTS
2 tbsp cane vinegar
2 tbsp lemon juice
1 tbsp vegetable oil
¼ cup garlic crushed
1 tbsp ginger crushed
¼ tsp black pepper
¼ tsp salt
3 lb fish fillets

PREPARATION
1. In a shallow glass casserole dish, combine vinegar, lemon juice, oil, garlic, ginger, and pepper.
2. Add fillets; turn to coat with marinade. Cover and refrigerate at least 2 hours.
3. Spray grill with cooking spray.
4. Preheat grill. Drain and discard any remaining marinade.
5. Grill fillets 4 minutes on each side until cooked through.

MISS NORMA'S CHEESY BUTTERFISH FILLET
Another top tasting recipe delicious to the taste.

INGREDIENTS
2 lbs fish fillets
¼ cup flour
¼ tsp salt
¼ tsp pepper
½ tbsp onion powder
½ tbsp garlic powder
½ cup Jamaican tomato sauce
1 egg beaten
1 cup bread crumbs
¼ cup vegetable oil
¼ cup grated cheese

PREPARATION
1. Rinse fillets and pat dry. Season flour with powdered seasonings.
2. Dip fish in flour, dip in beaten egg, then in bread crumbs.
3. Place in pan with a little vegetable oil and pan sear until lightly browned.
4. Place fish in a casserole dish or on a baking dish and top with tomato sauce and cheese.
5. Bake at 350° until cheese is melted and fish is moist.

PORT ROYAL FISH PIE
A port Royal recipe that has won many awards, it leaves your guests wanting more and more.

INGREDIENTS
2 cups flaked fish fillet
1 cup Jamaican fish broth
4 tbsp butter
1 cup wine
3 cup cold water
¼ cup onion sliced
1 cup carrot diced
½ tsp ginger minced
½ tsp cinnamon powder
½ cup grated peanuts
2 tsp sugar
1½ tsp salt
¼ lb butter
1 tbsp parsley chopped
¼ cup egg white
1 cup mixed fruits

PREPARATION
1. Ground peanuts and wrap the fish in a piece of cheesecloth and tie securely with string.
2. Cook gently for 30 minutes in stock, water, white wine, salt, onion and carrot.
3. Crush the fruits together and season them with the cinnamon, ginger, sugar and 1½ teaspoons salt.
4. Grate or grind the blanched peanuts and add to the fruit.
5. Now stir in the flaked fish, chopped parsley and 4 tablespoons melted butter.
6. Beat the egg white and stir it into the whole mixture.
7. Line pie dish with pastry and fill it with the fish mixture.
8. Cover with more pastry and crimp the edges. Make 5 or 6 generous slits in the top crust and place in a 350F. oven.
9. Bake for about 20 minutes, turn the regulator to 400^ F. and continue baking until it looks done, or for about 45 minutes in all.
10. Serve at once with white wine.

JAMAICAN BAKED FISH IN COCONUT CHUTNEY
A perfect blend of coconut chutney and a sweet baked fish recipe.

INGREDIENTS
¼ cup garlic chopped
½ tbsp scotch bonnet pepper diced
1 cup coconut flakes
¼ cup escallion diced
¼ cup onion diced
¼ tsp salt
¼ tsp black pepper
2 tbsp water
2 tbsp lime juice
¼ tsp allspice
2 tbsp vegetable oil
1½ lb fish fillets
4 lemon wedges

PREPARATION
In a food processor or blender, finely chop the garlic and peppers. Add the coconut, escallion, onion and lime juice. Process just to blend. Transfer to a bowl. Combine the oil and allspice. Place the fish in a foil-lined baking pan and brush with the oil mixture. Spoon some of the chutney on each piece of fish. Bake in a preheated 450-degree oven 12 minutes per inch of thickness of fish. Serve with remaining chutney and lime wedges.

APPLETON FISH FILET IN RUM SAUCE
Another one for my rum companions, true rum fish recipe delicious.

INGREDIENTS
6Jamaican cherries de-seeded
½ tsp soy sauce
½ tbsp salt and pepper mixed
3 tbsp Appleton V/X rum
2 lb grouper fillet
½ tbsp vegetable oil
2tbsp cold water
½ tbsp cornstarch

PREPARATION
Put the cherries in a bowl. Crush them with the back of a spoon. Stir in the soy sauce, salt, pepper, and sherry. Lay the fish filets in the sauce. Let them marinate about 4 hours in the fridge, turning occasionally. Remove the chicken from the marinade and dry with kitchen towels. Brush on ½ tbsp oil. Grill over hot coals till done, about 10 minutes. Meanwhile, mix cornstarch with 2 tablespoons cold water till smooth. In saucepan, mix the reserved marinade. Bring to a boil. Stir in the cornstarch mixture; stir constantly till sauce thickens. Remove the chicken from the grill; let rest on a cutting board for about 3 minutes. Cut crosswise into pieces about 1/2cm thick. Arrange the slices on two plates. Pour the sauce over.

Cooking Tip
Do not add excess rum to this recipe if you are a rum lover the rum is quickly absorbed by the fish meat which has a masking quality, of high alcohol levels.

DOWN TOWN FISH AND CABBAGE
A superb downtown Kingston recipe delicious as they say in every bite.

INGREDIENTS
3 lb fish filet
3 tbsp lemon juice
½ cabbage head chopped
1 cup sweet pepper diced
½ tsp thyme
4 tbsp vegetable oil
4 tbsp flour
¼ cup butter
½ tbsp salt and black pepper mixed

PREPARATION
1. Wash the fish, dry with paper towel and sprinkle with two tablespoons of the lemon juice.
2. Clean the cabbage and cut into small stripes blanch the cabbage in boiling saltwater for a couple minutes.
3. Mix the all other ingredients with the salt and pepper and beat in the oil.
4. Mix the cabbage with the peppers and mix in the marinade and arrange on a platter.
5. Cut the fish in stripes and roll in flour and fry in the butter until golden brown serve warm on the cabbage

PLAIN OLD JAMAICAN FRIED FISH
A regular fried fish recipe known to all Jamaican chefs and cooks.

INGREDIENTS
3 lb fish fillets
2 tbsp lemon juice
1 cup milk
2 cups flour
3 cup pancake mix
2 cup club soda
1 tsp basil
½ tsp black pepper
½ tsp garlic salt
¼ cup vegetable oil

PREPARATION
1. Cut fish fillets in half, making triangular shape. Cover with milk and lemon juice and refrigerate 3-4 hours.
2. Drain off milk and dip fillets in flour to coat each piece lightly. Let dry on a cookie sheet, making sure pieces do not tough.
3. Add oil to deep fryer or heavy pan to a depth of at least 3 inches. Heat oil to 425 degrees F.
4. Combine pancake mix, basil, pepper, garlic salt and enough soda to make a thick batter.
5. Dip floured fillets in batter and add to the hot oil one at a time. Fry 4-5 minutes.
6. Remove filets to cookie sheet, again, not letting them touch and keep warm in a 250 degrees F oven.
7. Deep fry remaining filets, keeping the depth of the oil at least 3 inches.
8. Serve hot.

GROUPER IN GET JAMAICA FISH SAUCE
Another great recipe blended with the best **Get Jamaica Fish Sauce**©

INGREDIENTS
1 cup sweet pepper, sliced
¼ tsp black pepper
¼ tsp salt
¼ tsp scotch bonnet pepper
1 lb grouper fillet
¼ cup onion slices
2 tbsp **Get Jamaica Fish Sauce**©
1 tbsp lemon juice

PREPARATION
1. Place sweet pepper in a 9-inch pie plate.
2. Cover with foil and preheat oven at 375 degrees F for 15 minutes.
3. Wipe pie plate. Quarter fish, arrange in pie plate, sprinkle with pepper and top with bell pepper and onion.
4. Bake for another 10 minutes until fish flakes easily.
5. Drain and cover.
6. Serve sauce with fish and garnish with lemon wedges.

FERN GULLY FRIED FISH WRAPPED IN BACON
In Fern Gully you will find a lot of Jamaican art and craft but we got a great tasting Jamaican recipe.

INGREDIENTS
3 lb fish fillets
4 strips of bacon
2 tbsp lemon juice
¼ cup escallion diced
¼ cup onion diced
1 cup milk
2 cups flour
3 cup pancake mix
2 cup club soda
1 tsp basil
½ tsp black pepper
½ tsp garlic salt
¼ cup vegetable oil

PREPARATION
1. Sauté bacon, onion and escallion in a skillet with oil.
2. Cut fish fillets in half, making triangular shape. Cover with milk and lemon juice and refrigerate 3-4 hours.
3. Drain off milk and dip fillets in flour to coat each piece lightly. Let dry on a cookie sheet, making sure pieces do not tough.
4. Add oil to deep fryer or heavy pan to a depth of at least 3 inches. Heat oil to 425 degrees F.
5. Combine pancake mix, basil, pepper, garlic salt and enough soda to make a thick batter.
6. Dip floured fillets in batter and add to the hot oil one at a time. Fry 4-5 minutes.
7. Remove filets to cookie sheet and add bacon wrapping the fish with them and warm in a 250 degrees F oven.
8. Deep fry remaining filets, keeping the depth of the oil at least 3 inches.

LUCEA PAN-ROASTED FISH WITH CORN

From the capital of Hanover on the west end of the island we got this great fish recipe from a fisherman.

INGREDIENTS
¼ cup escallion diced
2 tbsp chopped thyme
½ tsp salt
½ tsp allspice
½ tsp garlic powder
½ tsp onion powder
7 lb grouper fillet
¼ cup vegetable oil
½ cup stewed okras
1 cup corn kernels
1 cup white wine
2 tbsp lime juice
6 tbsp butter

PREPARATION
1. Preheat oven to 350-F, then mix all dry ingredients together then sprinkle over fish.
2. Divide oil between 2 skillets over heat. Add 4 fish fillets to each skillet and cook until brown.
3. Transfer fish to large platter. Place 4 fish fillets, browned side down a top vegetables in each skillet.
4. Bake until fish is cooked through. About 10 minutes. Transfer fish to plates.
5. Combine all vegetables and liquid in 1 skillet.
6. Add lime juice corn and butter and whisk over low heat until melted.
7. Season with salt and pepper.
8. Serve hot.

HOPEWELL ORANGE FISH FILLET

Hopewell is a small district popular for its spicy tasting recipes, this recipe combines fish and oranges.

INGREDIENTS
2 lb snapper
1 orange rind
1 tsp lemon juice
¼ tsp nutmeg crushed
4 tbsp butter
¼ cup orange juice
½ tbsp salt and black pepper mixed
¼ cup minced parsley

PREPARATIONS
1. Place fish in a single layer in large, thickly buttered baking dish.
2. Combine the remaining ingredients, except the parsley, and pour over the fish.
3. Bake at high for 10 to 12 minutes, or until fish flakes easily.
4. Let stand 5 minutes, then remove to a hot serving dish.
5. Pour any sauce remaining in the dish over the fish.
6. Sprinkle with minced parsley and serve.

ST. MARY FILET IN GRAPEFRUIT SAUCE

Fish and grapefruit, delicious to the core, this is another top ten recipe.

INGREDIENTS

1 cup grapefruit peeled and chopped
¼ cup grapefruit juice
1½ lb fish fillets
2 tbsp vegetable oil
¼ tsp salt
¼ tsp black pepper
1 tbsp cornstarch
½ tsp allspice

PREPARATION

1. In a large skillet, sauté the fish filets in hot oil until brown.
2. Salt and pepper the fish filets. Remove them from the pan and keep warm.
3. In the same pan stir in grapefruit juice and let the sauce come to a boil.
4. Stir in the cornstarch and cook till the sauce slightly thickens.
5. Add the grapefruit slices to the sauce and warm gently.
6. Serve hot with sauce.

JAMIACAN CROCKPOT JAMBALAYA

In our last edition our readers asked for more crock-pot recipes this is a taste of what is to come in our 4th Edition.

INGREDIENTS

2 cup diced boiled ham
½ cup onions chopped
¼ cup escallion sliced
½ cup sweet pepper diced
1 cup tomatoes chopped
¼ cup tomato paste
¼ cup garlic minced
1 tbsp minced parsley
½ tsp dried thyme
2 whole cloves
2 tbsp vegetable oil
1½ lb flaked fish fillet

PREPARATION

1. Thoroughly mix all ingredients except fish in crock-pot.
2. Cover and cook on low for 8 to 10 hours.
3. One hour before serving, turn crock-pot to high and stir in uncooked fish.
4. Cover and cook until fish is tender.
5. Serve hot.

OROCABESSA STEAM FISH IN OKRA
A better tasting recipe than most steam fish recipes, with a plethora of stewed okras.

INGREDIENTS
1½ lb fish fillets
1 tbsp vegetable oil
1 cup stewed okras
¼ cup garlic minced
¼ cup onions sliced
¼ cup escallion
½ tbsp lemon
½ tbsp scotch bonnet pepper diced
¼ tsp salt
¼ tsp black pepper

PREPARATION
1. In large skillet, heat oil over medium-high heat sauté onions, garlic, scotch bonnet peppers and escallion.
2. Place fish in skillet then season fish to taste with salt and lemon pepper.
3. Cover tightly and poach fish.
4. Serve each fillet smothered with okras.

PAN MAN FISH ROAST
A pan made gave us this tasty recipe at a travel halt outside of the Starfish resort in Trelawny.

3 lb fish fillet
¼ cup escallion chopped
¼ cup onion diced
¼ cup garlic diced
½ tsp allspice
¼ tsp salt
¼ tsp black pepper
½ tbsp scotch bonnet pepper diced
2 tbsp vegetable oil
4 tsp ginger minced
2 cup coconut milk
½ cup chicken stock
½ tbsp lemon juice
½ cup wine (**optional**)

PREPARATION
1. In a large oven-proof Dutch oven, sauté garlic, onion, escallions and ginger root in vegetable oil, until soft.
2. Add remaining ingredients and simmer for 15 minutes.
3. Add fish stir and bring to a boil.
4. Cover Dutch oven and place in a 450-degree oven for 10 minutes.
5. Serve hot.

RED STRIPE LIGHT BEER FISH FILLET
A switch from Red Stripe to the Red Stripe Light Beer delicious to the taste.

INGREDIENTS
2 lbs grouper fillet
3 cup cornmeal
1 cup flour
3 eggs beaten
¼ tsp salt
¼ tsp black pepper
1 cup Red Stripe Light Beer

PREPARATION
1.   Mix dry ingredients, add eggs, then add beer until batter is at desired consistency.
2.   Deep fry the fish and serve hot.

PORT MARIA FISH PUDDING
A pudding that's as tasty as possible with light cream.

INGREDIENTS
2 cup saltine crackers crumbs
1 egg beaten
½ cup melted butter
6 lb fish fillet poached
¾ cup light cream
¼ tsp Worcestershire sauce
¼ tsp black pepper
¼ tsp allspice

PREPARATION
1.   Mix together saltine crumbs and melted butter. Spread about ¼ of this mixture in an 8-inch pie plate.
2.   Scar fish season with allspice and black pepper and dip fillet in egg and drench in the crumbs.
3.   Mix until soft and add light cream, Worcestershire sauce and pour this into pie plate.
4.   Top with remaining crumbs and bake at 350 degrees for 45 minutes.
5.   Serve hot.

Cooking Tip
There are several ways to prepare fish however the best method is to devil the fish. To **devil** Jamaican fish recipes means to make the fish spicy by adding different seasonings or condiments to it. This can be done before preparing the fish or after. It is always advisable to do this after however. This is extremely important because if preparing a fish recipe for more than one person, you would like a person to add condiments to there liking. Some prefer hot and spicy foods while some prefer mild recipes, while others require no condiments at all.

TRELAWNY STIR FRY FISH FILLET
A stir fry recipe that's absolutely delicious from the garden parish.

INGREDIENTS
1½ lb snapper fillet
1½ tbsp soy sauce
2 tsp cornstarch
1 tbsp dry sherry
1 tsp ginger minced
¼ cup onion diced
¼ cup escallion diced
¼ cup garlic diced
¼ cup vegetable oil
½ cup sweet pepper diced
¼ cup Jamaican chicken broth
1 tbsp lemon juice
¼ tbsp honey

PREPARATION
1. Combine fish with soy sauce, cornstarch, sherry, ginger, escallion, onion and garlic.
2. Spray large skillet with nonstick vegetable spray. Heat vegetable oil over medium-high heat.
3. Add fish mixture and stir fry until fish is cooked.
4. Add all other ingredients after fish is cooked and cook.
5. Stir-fry for 1 minute.
6. Serve with vegetables.

PETERSFIELD BROILED FISH AND PLANTAIN
A broiled fish recipe with boiled plantain.

INGREDIENTS
1½ lb fish fillet
1 tbsp vegetable oil
1 tbsp lemon juice
2 cups chopped plantain boiled
½ cup flour
1 egg, beaten
1 cup bread crumbs
½ tbsp scotch bonnet pepper diced
½ tsp garlic powder
½ tsp onion powder
½ tsp allspice
½ tsp minced escallion
¼ lb butter

PREPARATION
1. Marinate cut pieces of fish for five minutes in lemon juice, salt and pepper.
2. Brush them with oil and broil to golden brown.
3. Season bread crumbs with powdered seasonings and escallion.
4. Peel plantains and dip the slices in flour, egg and bread crumbs.
5. Bake in a pan with butter then remove.
6. Serve plantains with fish hot.

YHALLAS POACHED FILLET SNAPPER
Poaching fish is quite popular in Jamaica as it can prepare the food quite quickly.

INGREDIENTS
2 fish fillets medium
¼ cup lemons juice
1 bay leaf
½ lb butter
1 tbsp flour
2 ea egg yolks
½ pt cream cheese
½ cup white wine
¼ tsp salt
¼ tsp black pepper

PREPARATION
Marinate fish fillet for 1 hour in the lemon juice and bay leaf. Sprinkle well with salt and coarse black pepper. Now roll the fillets, fasten with a toothpick to hold the roll, and place them in a deep frying pan. Cover with water and poach for 5 minutes. Strain water from fish and save. Melt butter, carefully mixing in flour until the hole thing is smooth and golden. Add strained fish stock. Boil for 15 minutes and strain the sauce. Season to taste with white wine and lemon juice. Blend in the cream and egg yolks. Serve with sauce.

> ### Cooking Tip
> To poach fish means to cook the fish slowly in hot liquid. The liquid must cover the fish entirely. This is almost like boiling only difference is that boiling requires a higher flame, so the liquid must be rollicking.

LITTLE LONDON FISH IN ORANGE MARMALADE
This little district contributed this big recipe that was absolutely delicious.

INGREDIENTS
1 cup tomatoes chopped
¼ cup onion grated
¼ tsp salt
¼ cup orange marmalade
2 tbsp Appleton white rum
¼ cup escallion diced
½ tsp cinnamon powder
½ tbsp scotch bonnet pepper
1¼ lb snapper fillets

PREPAPRATION
Place tomatoes in a saucepan with the onion and salt and cook over medium heat, 5 minutes, stirring occasionally. Add the marmalade and brandy and continue to cook, 5 minutes, stirring frequently. Add the escallion, cinnamon and scotch bonnet pepper and cook 5 minutes longer. Place fish in a skillet and add enough water to just cover the fish. Remove the fish and set aside. Bring the water to a boil then reduce heat and add the fish. Bring back to a simmer, cover and poach. Remove and drain off water. Place on a platter and pour the hot tomato orange marmalade over the fish. Serve hot.

CAVE HILL FISH IN GINGER SAUCE
The ginger sauce in this recipe is described as spicy and delicious, it enhances the great taste of the fish.

INGREDIENTS
2 tbsp rice wine
1 tbsp soy sauce
¼ tbsp allspice
½ tsp onion powder
½ tsp garlic powder
1 tbsp water
½ tsp salt
¼ tsp black pepper
1 tsp sugar
2 tbsp escallion diced
2 tsp vegetable oil
1 lb fish fillet
1 tsp cornstarch
3 tbsp ginger chopped
½ cup Jamaican sweet sauce

PREPARATION
Scar fish, then combine them with salt, black pepper, garlic powder, onion powder, sugar, cornstarch and season fish. Heat a wok or large skillet sauté escallion and ginger then add fish. Stir-fry until fish is white then add the sauce and continue to cook for 2 minutes. Serve hot.

> **Cooking Tip**
> To scar fish means to cut the fish slightly on either side. Just enough to touch the middle bone and to dab the fish in salt and black pepper. Only salt the fish to taste if this is freshwater fish.

DISCOVERY BAY SNAPPER AND SHRIMP
A great snapper and shrimp recipe, delicious to the last bite.

INGREDIENTS
4 lb snapper fillets
1 cup seasoned flour
2 tbsp vegetable oil
2 tbsp melted butter
1 cup shrimp, peeled, de-veined
½ tbsp lemon juice
¼ cup peanuts chopped
¼ tsp salt
¼ tsp black pepper

PREPARATION
1. Preheat oven to 150 F and dredge snapper in flour.
2. Heat oil in a large frying pan and add fillets then cook 3-4 minutes each side.
3. Season when turning fillets over then remove fillets from pan and keep hot in oven.
4. Add butter and shrimp to pan. Season and add all remaining ingredients cook 3 minutes over medium heat.
5. Remove red snapper from oven and serve with shrimp.

JAMAICAN FISH ENCHILADAS
A series of traditional Mexican recipes using Jamaican herbs and spices we got from some Mexican tourists in Montego Bay.

INGREDIENTS
8 lb grouper fillets
4 cup Water
¼ cup margarine
¼ cup flour
1 cup Jamaican chicken broth
1 cup sour cream
½ tbsp scotch bonnet pepper diced
¼ tsp salt
¼ cup vegetable oil
1 cup grated cheese
¼ cup escallion diced
¼ cup onion diced
¼ cup garlic diced
10 tortillas

PREPARATION
1. Bring 4 cups water to a boil in a large saucepan add fish and cook. Set aside.
2. Melt margarine in a small saucepan over low heat add flour, stirring until smooth.
3. Gradually add broth and water; cook over medium heat until mixture is slightly thickened.
4. Remove from heat, and let stand 5 minutes and stir in sour cream, pepper, and salt.
5. Pour ¾ cup sauce in bottom of a baking dish then add fish and all other ingredients.
6. Spoon fish mixture across center of each tortilla then roll up tortillas
7. Place, seam side down over sauce in dish and bake at 350 degrees until thoroughly heated.
8. Serve hot.

JAMAICAN FISH FRITTATA
Another Mexican recipe with Jamaican herbs and spices, Arriba!

INGREDIENTS
¼ cup butter
½ cup snapper fish fillet flaked
1 lb grouper fillet
¼ cup escallion sliced
¼ cup onions sliced
¼ cup garlic cloves, crushed
½ tsp scotch bonnet pepper diced
½ tbsp lemon juice
3 tbsp white wine
2 eggs beaten
½ cup tomatoes sliced
½ cup cheese shredded
½ cup sour cream

PREPARATION
In a skillet melt butter and sauté fish flakes, fillet and all other ingredients except tomatoes. Heat butter in a small omelets pan, add egg mixture when eggs have begun to set around the edge add seafood mixture. Work in mixture then place the tomato slices on top and sprinkle with shredded cheese. Place pan in 425 degree oven for 4-5 minutes. Remove to serving plate and add sour cream. Serve hot.

BLUEFIELDS FISH GUMBO
From the seaside of Bluefield's Westmoreland another delicious recipe.

INGREDIENTS
½ cup Jamaican beef broth
1 cup smoked ham cubed
2 bay leaves
½ tbsp scotch bonnet pepper diced
¼ tbsp salt
¼ cup diced cooked bacon
¼ cup flour
3 tbsp vegetable oil
3 cups okra
¼ cup onion chopped
½ cup sweet pepper diced
¼ cup escallion chopped
¼ cup garlic minced
1 cup tomatoes chopped
¼ cup Ketchup
¼ tsp thyme
½ tsp Worcestershire sauce

PREPARATION
Combine the stock, ham, bay leaves, pepper, and salt in a large kettle simmer, cover and cook 1 hour. Heat the bacon in a skillet and stir in the flour until absorbed. Cook until flour is dark brown. In a separate large skillet, heat the oil over medium heat. Add the okra, onions, sweet peppers, escallion and garlic and sauté until almost tender. Add the tomatoes, the catsup, Worcestershire sauce, and thyme. Reduce the heat to very low and simmer, covered, 1 hour. Serve hot.

SPECIAL JAMAICAN FISH THERMIDOR
Another special and unique Jamaican recipe to tantalize your senses.

INGREDIENTS
1 lb fish fillets
1 cup Jamaican sweet sauce
3 tbsp flour
¼ cup milk
¼ cup white wine
¼ cup shredded cheese
2 tbsp parsley
½ cup bread crumbs
2 tbsp butter
½ tsp paprika
½ tsp lemon juice

PREPARATION
Place fish in a skillet add lemon slice, onion and water to cover. Bring to a boil, then reduce heat and simmer for 4 minutes. In a small saucepan blend sauce and the flour then gradually stir in milk, lemon juice and wine. Cook while stirring constantly until thick and stir in cheese. Carefully, drain fish well and spoon mixture into a greased casserole. Combine bread crumbs, butter and paprika. Sprinkle over casseroles. Broil 1 to 2 minutes. Serve over your choice of rice or pastry shells. Serve hot.

JAMAICAN FISH TORTILLAS
These Mexican recipes keep getting better with every Jamaican herb added, absolutely delicious.

INGREDIENTS
¼ cup onion diced
3 tbsp butter
¼ cup parsley, chopped
½ cup cheese shredded
5 lb grouper fillet
¼ tsp scotch bonnet pepper diced
4 tortillas
3 tbsp butter
3 tbsp flour
3 cup milk
½ cup Jamaican white sauce

PREPARATION
Melt butter in saucepan. Stir in flour, then cook for 1 minute. Gradually stir in milk, then cook, stirring constantly, until bubbly thick. Stir in cheese and cayenne pepper. Preheat oven to 375. Grease a glass baking dish. Sauté onion in butter in skillet. Stir in parsley, cheese, and just enough white sauce to moisten. Stir in chopped fish and divide filling among tortillas, then roll up and arrange seam side down in a dish. Pour remaining white sauce over and cover with foil. Bake for 40-45 minutes. Serve hot.

MISS NORMA'S SWEET AND SOUR FISH
Ah! another masterpiece from Miss Norma, the Jamaican way to prepare the traditional Chinese dish.

INGREDIENTS
3 lb butterfish fillets
2 tbsp wine
¼ cup soy sauce
1 tbsp vegetable oil
1 tsp ginger minced
¼ cup garlic mashed
½ tsp MSG (**optional**)
1 egg beaten
¼ cup cornstarch
½ cup sweet pepper
½ cup carrots chopped
½ cup pineapple slices quartered
½ cup onion; quartered
¼ tsp Salt
¼ tsp black pepper
1 cup Jamaican sweet and sour sauce

PREPARATION
Cut fish into 1-inch cubes and place in baking dish. Combine wine, soy sauce, vegetable oil, ginger, garlic and ½ tsp MSG and mix well. Pour mixture over fish then marinate ½ hour. Mix together egg and cornstarch to form stiff batter, drain fish well and combine with batter. Deep-fry in skillet over medium heat until crisp and golden brown then drain on paper towels. In wok, or large skillet, heat 2 tablespoons oil. Add remaining ingredients and stir fry to 2-4 minutes or until vegetables are tender. Then add sweet and sour sauce and blend. Add fish, combine well and serve hot.

FALMOUTH CALLALOO STUFFED SNAPPER
From the capital of the garden parish, the sweet tasting callaloo and snapper.

INGREDIENTS
3 lb whole kingfish
¼ cup onion chopped
¼ cup escallion chopped
¼ cup sweet pepper diced
¼ tbsp scotch bonnet pepper
¼ cup garlic minced
¼ cup unsalted butter, melted
1½ cup diced cooked callaloo
2 eggs beaten
1 tbsp chopped parsley
1¼ lb slice boned ham finely diced
¼ tsp salt
¼ tsp black pepper
½ tbsp lemon juice

PREPARATION
1. Preheat the oven to 350'F.
2. In a skillet sauté the onion, escallion, sweet pepper, scotch bonnet pepper and garlic in ½ of butter.
3. Toss with the callaloo, eggs, parsley and ham seasoning to taste with salt and pepper.
4. Stuff the fish with the mixture, brush a glass baking pan with butter, and add the fish to the pan.
5. Mix the rest of the butter with the lemon juice, pour over the fish.
6. Bake for 30-45 minutes or until the fish flakes easily with a fork.
7. Serve hot.

> **Cooking Tip**
> This is an excellent recipe if prepared well to make this recipe perfect, check when the callaloo is cooked then remove the fish from the oven ensuring that the meat is white.

JAMAICAN FISH CAKES
Not exactly a fish recipe but the delicious taste and size of the meal gives you that big taste.

INGREDIENTS
2 lb snapper fillets
1 egg beaten
½ tbsp allspice
1 cup flour
2 tsp sugar
¼ cup vegetable oil
¼ cup curry paste
¼ cup onion chopped
¼ cup escallion chopped
¼ cup sweet pepper diced
¼ tbsp scotch bonnet pepper
¼ cup garlic minced
1 tsp grated lime rind
2 tsp paprika

PREPARATION
1. Remove bones from fish and blend all ingredients until smooth.
2. Combine in bowl with flour until batter is formed.
3. Roll fish mixture into a balls then flatten slightly.
4. In a skillet deep-fry fish cakes in hot oil until well browned and cooked
5. Drain on absorbent paper.
6. Serve hot.

LYME CAYE FISH FRITTERS
Lyme Caye the home of great fish recipes from the isle within the isle.

INGREDIENTS
½ lb snapper fish fillets
2 cups water
½ lb flour
¼ tsp black pepper
2 tomatoes chopped
3 stalks escallion finely chopped
2 tbsp margarine
1 lg chopped onion
2 cloves of garlic finely chopped
½ tsp scotch bonnet pepper diced

PREPARATION
1. Soak fish overnight, then boil and flake fish and set aside.
2. Sauté onions, tomatoes, escallion, garlic and pepper in butter then add to flaked fish.
3. Mix baking powder and flour and add codfish and seasonings to it.
4. Add small amounts of water stirring until you have a medium batter.
5. Remove and fry in saucepan in ½ inch oil until golden.
6. Serve hot.

Cooking Tip
There are several ways to boil a fish and to keep it from flaking, the first and more traditional method is to add line juice to the pot while cooking and the second is to tie the fish with cheese cloth then dip in boiling water.

MORGANS HARBOR FISH AND SEAFOOD DELIGHT
The home of Henry Morgan the famed pirate from the 1600's comes this delicious seafood recipe.

INGREDIENTS
1 cup water
½ cup onion sliced thin
2 cups milk
¼ tsp salt
¼ tsp black pepper
3 lb turbit fillet
½ cup Jamaican sweet sauce
1½ tbsp butter
1½ tbsp flour

PREPARATION
1. In a large skillet bring the water and onion to a boil.
2. Add the milk, salt, and pepper, and add the fish fillets.
3. Reduce the heat and cook for 5 or 6 minutes.
4. Turn off the heat and remove the fillets to a warm platter.
5. Over medium heat, reduce the poaching liquid by half until fish is tender.
6. Serve with sauce.

JAMAICAN SEAFOOD RECIPES

jamaican stir fried shrimp
jerk-bq sauce. ©

JAMAICAN LOBSTER RUNDOWN
A great tasting lobster recipe akin to what is known as mackerel rundown. Absolutely delicious.

INGREDIENTS
2 lb lobster tails
3 tbsp butter
5 cups coconut milk
¼ cup garlic, crushed
¼ cup onion chopped
¼ cup escallions finely chopped
½ cup tomatoes, chopped
½ tbsp thyme, finely chopped
½ tsp scotch bonnet pepper diced
½ tsp allspice
¼ tsp salt
¼ tsp black pepper

PREPARATION
1. Remove shell from lobster and cut into bite size pieces.
2. Bring coconut milk to a simmer in a sauce pan.
3. Add garlic, onions, tomatoes, thyme, peppers, and all spice. Simmer until coconut milk starts to thicken.
4. Mean while sauté lobster in hot butter until it starts to change color. Add coconut sauce and simmer until lobster is cooked.
5. Serve hot.

JAMAICAN JERK SHRIMP
A special Jerk recipe that was formulated using our in-house Jerk seasoning, watch out, this ones spicy.

INGREDIENTS
12 jumbo shrimps still in shell
½ cup Jamaican Jerk seasoning
1 cup June Plum Sauce
2 tbsp lime juice

PREPARATION
1. Wash shrimps in lime and water.
2. Pierce each one carefully several times with a large needle or very small skewer.
3. Cover in jerk seasoning. Place in refrigerator overnight.
4. Place shrimp on grill and baste with Plum Sauce until cooked.
5. Serve hot.

JAMAICAN JERK LOBSTER
This jerk lobster recipe can be used with a range of sauces but has proven to taste best with a light mango sauce.

INGRDIENTS
5 lbs lobster tails
½ cup Jamaican Jerk seasoning
1 cup Mango Sauce
2 tbsp lime juice
¼ tsp salt

PREPARATION
1. Pierce lobster tails with a large needle or very small skewer.
2. Cover in jerk seasoning and marinate overnight.
3. Place lobster on grill and baste with mango sauce until cooked.
4. Serve hot.

DIS YA ISLAND CRAB CAKES

These crab cakes are great this recipe we picked up on our way to Hellshire.

INGREDIENTS

1 lb. crab meat
1 egg beaten
¼ cup mayonnaise
1 tbsp. Worcestershire Sauce
1 tbsp. curry powder
¼ cup escallion, finely chopped
½ tsp scotch bonnet pepper diced
½ cup onion, finely chopped
1 tbsp parsley chopped
1 cup breadcrumbs
¼ cup salt
¼ cup black pepper

PREPARATION

1. Mix all ingredients together.
2. Make into bite-sized cakes and refrigerate for one hour.
3. Remove and heat oil in skillet.
4. Sauté crab cakes until done and drain on paper towel.
5. Serve hot.

JAMAICAN JERK CRAB

This recipe has a bit of extra spice added, as crab meat is not tasty without seasonings.

INGRDIENTS

2 cups crab meat
7 reserved crab back shells
¼ cup escallions minced
¼ cup onion minced
½ tbsp scotch bonnet pepper diced
½ tsp allspice
½ cup Jamaican Jerk seasoning
1 cup Otaheite Apple Sauce
2 tbsp lime juice
¼ tsp salt
¼ tsp black pepper

PREPARATION

1. Rinse out crab shells with limejuice and water.
2. Mix all ingredients together except apple sauce and marinate overnight.
3. Add a small amount of butter to each shell and evenly lay crab mixture in each.
4. Place each shell in oven and bake for 20 minutes and baste with apple sauce until cooked.
5. Serve hot.

Cooking Tip
When preparing lobster recipes that are fried or stewed use the small red lobsters or chicken lobsters. When grilling lobsters use the larger lobster.

JAMAICAN JERK CONCH
Jerk conch is not popularly prepared in Jamaica but is an absolutely tasty dish.

INGREDIENTS
2 cups conch meat cut in cubes
½ cup Jamaican Jerk seasoning
½ cup Jamaican Jerk Sauce
¼ cup escallions minced
¼ cup onion minced
½ tbsp scotch bonnet pepper diced
½ tsp allspice
2 tbsp lime juice
¼ tsp salt
¼ tsp black pepper

PREPARATION
1. Wash conch in lime and water. Pierce each cube and cover in jerk seasoning.
2. Allow conch to marinate in the jerk seasoning, then heat a skillet and brown the conch.
3. Add water and sauce then simmer for five minutes.
4. Remove and place in a baking dish and bake for another 15 minutes basting with the remaining sauce.
5. Serve hot.

JAMAICAN FRIED LOBSTER IN COCONUT SAUCE
Another great tasting lobster recipe, it cant get any better than this, just delicious to the core.

INGREDIENTS
3 lb lobster tails
¼ tsp salt
¼ tsp black pepper
¼ cup escallion chopped
¼ cup onion diced
¼ tsp allspice
¼ cup garlic minced
½ cup grated coconut
¼ tsp thyme
1 cup bread crumbs
½ cup frying oil
2 eggs
3 cloves garlic

PREPARATION
1. Bring a pot of water to a boil with ½ escallion, onion, garlic, thyme, salt and pepper.
2. Add lobster tails and blanch for 30 seconds then remove the meat from the shell, season with salt, pepper and allspice.
3. Add grated coconut to bread crumbs and toss until evenly distributed.
4. In a bowl, beat eggs, dip the tails in the eggs, then roll in bread crumbs.
5. In a skillet bring frying oil to heat and add remaining seasonings.
6. Fry lobster until golden brown.
7. Serve hot.

ST. THOMAS JANGA MOLD
The janga is actually the crayfish. The ever present relative of the shrimp it still is a tasty morsel for Jamaican cooks.

INGREDIENTS
1 cup parsley chopped
1 cup creamed cheese
½ cup white wine
¼ tsp salt
1 tbsp lemon juice
1 tbsp Jamaican jerk sauce
1 cup crawfish meat cooked
1 tbsp lime juice
¼ cup Worcestershire sauce

PREPARATION
1. Place crawfish in food processor add wine, parsley, lemon juice, salt, jerk sauce and Worcestershire sauce.
2. Add cream cheese and blend. Refrigerate overnight in a mold.
3. Serve with crackers or on a bed of lettuce.
4. Serve cold.

ST. BESS SHRIMP SALAD WITH PAWPAW
Papaw's mellow flesh and peppery seeds are good foils for shrimp in a piquant dressing.

INGREDIENTS
1 ripe pawpaw
¼ cup vegetable oil
1 tbsp cane vinegar
1 tbsp lemon juice
¼ tsp salt
¼ tsp escallion, thinly sliced
1 cup pear chopped
1 cup carrot shredded
1¼ cup peeled, cooked shrimp
1 head lettuce

PREPARATION
1. Peel, halve and scoop out seeds from pawpaw, reserving 2 teaspoons of the seeds.
2. Slice papaya thinly and set aside.
3. In blender or food processor, combine oil, vinegar, lime juice, salt and mustard; process until well-combined.
4. Add reserved papaya seeds; process again until seeds are the consistency of coarsely ground pepper.
5. Pour dressing into a medium bowl; mix lightly with onion and shrimp.
6. Add lettuce and pear with other greens.
7. Serve as is.

SPICY SEAFOOD SALAD
A great salad recipe using shrimp, lobster and fish, delicious in every bite and easy to prepare.

INGREDIENTS
½ cup fresh lemon juice
¼ cup garlic, minced
¼ tsp salt
¼ tsp black pepper
¼ cup vegetable oil
4 cups water
1 cup carrot, peeled and chopped
¼ cup escallion diced
½ tbsp lemon juice
1 cup shrimp peeled and de-veined
1 cup lobster cooked
½ cup fish flaked
2 tbsp minced fresh parsley
Lemon wedges, for garnish

PREPARATION
1. In a large bowl, stir together the lemon juice and garlic, and season with salt and pepper.
2. Slowly whisk in the oil until blended and set aside.
3. In a large Dutch oven, bring the water, carrots, escallion, sliced lemon and peppercorns to a boil over high heat.
4. Reduce the heat to medium and add the shrimp. Cook for 1 to 2 minutes, until pink; do not overcook.
5. With a slotted spoon, transfer the shrimp to a large bowl; set the bowl aside. Return the liquid to a boil and add the scallops.
6. Cook for 1 to 2 minutes, until just opaque; do not overcook. With a slotted spoon, remove the scallops and transfer to the bowl with the shrimp. Return liquid to a boil, add the squid, and cook for 30 seconds.
7. With a slotted spoon, transfer the squid to the bowl.
8. Return the liquid to a boil and add the mussels. Cook, covered, over high heat until most have opened, about 5 minutes.
9. Transfer the opened mussels to a plate and cook any unopened mussels for 1 minute longer. Discard any unopened mussels.
10. Remove the mussels from the shells and add to the bowl with the other cooked seafood.
11. Add the dressing and toss to coat. Cover and refrigerate, stirring occasionally, for about 3 hours, or until cold.
12. Remove the salad from the refrigerator 30 minutes before serving. Gently stir in the parsley and garnish the salad with the lemon wedges.

NEGRIL FLAMED SHRIMPS AND VEGETABLES
This is what we call feeling hot, this recipe can be mouth blistering but done right is a delightful taste.

INGREDIENTS
2 lb of Shrimps
¼ cup vegetable oil
¼ cup garlic minced
1 tsp. scotch bonnet pepper diced
¼ tsp black pepper
¼ tsp allspice
1 tbsp lemon juice
¼ tsp salt
2 tbsp parsley
3 potatoes uncooked
2 eggs beaten
2 tbsp whipping cream
¼ cup onion chopped

PREPARATION
1. Peel potatoes, grate them and dry them then whip the eggs with the cream add the allspice and the chopped onion.
2. Mix this preparation with the potatoes to make pancakes.
3. Bring to a boil a large pan filled with water add shrimp, the salt and pepper.
4. Allow to cook for 30 seconds, drain, then stir fry shrimps in a pan with olive oil, garlic and parsley.
5. Toss the ingredients then flambé the shrimps, sprinkle some more fresh herbs over the pan, then add the lemon juice.
6. Heat oil in a pan, place pancakes in and let them brown for 5 minutes, then return them, adding some butter, for five more minutes.
7. Serve hot

Cooking Tip
Flambé means to ignite the food by adding rum to the sauce pan and cooking until the flame or liquor runs out and the food is partially cooked.

APPLETON RUM CONCH

A sweet conch recipe, soaked in white over proof rum and marinated with chopped onion, garlic, escallion, ginger, thyme, salt and pepper and stir fry with an assortment of julienne vegetables and soy sauce. Absolutely delicious

INGREDIENTS
½ cup sweet pepper, diced
½ tsp scotch bonnet pepper, diced
½ cup carrot, diced
¼ cup onion, diced
1 cup conch, diced
¼ cup escallion, chopped
¼ tsp salt and pepper mixed
1 tbsp soy sauce
1½ tbsp. vegetable oil
1 sprig thyme
¼ cup over proof white rum
¼ tsp. chopped ginger

PREPARATION
Marinate conch with half of the chopped escallion, garlic and rum. Heat a frying pan or wok and add oil. Stir fry remaining portion of garlic and ginger with conch until tender, then add vegetables from 2 minutes. Add remainder of chopped escallion and soy sauce. Remove from heat and serve.

ROCKY POINT LEMON SHRIMP

From the fishing village on the South coast we got this great tasting shrimp recipe.

INGREDIENTS
¼ cup butter
2 cup shrimp, peeled and de-veined
¼ cup Appleton V/X
¼ cup whipping cream
1 tsp. tomato paste
1 tbsp. lemon juice
salt and freshly ground pepper
¼ cup minced escallion

PREPARATION
1. In sauté pan over medium heat, heat clarified butter.
2. Add shrimp; sauté 1 minute. Add bourbon and carefully ignite, shaking pan until flames die down.
3. Remove shrimp to warm platter. Add cream and tomato paste to pan.
4. Bring mixture to a boil; reduce until it is thickened and coats the back of a spoon.
5. Add lemon juice, escallion and season to taste with salt and pepper.
6. Return shrimp to pan to reheat.
7. Serve hot.

OCHO RIOS CURRY CONCH
A superb recipe from the resort town using lemon grass as an optional ingredient.

INGREDIENTS
2 cups conch
¼ cup onion diced
¼ cup garlic, chopped
¼ cup escallion chopped
½ tsp scotch bonnet pepper, chopped
1 sprig thyme
1 cup carrot diced
1 cup Irish potato cubed
¼ cup okra
4 oz. flour
1½ tbsp cornmeal
½ cup coconut milk
2 small pieces lemon grass (**optional**)
½ tbsp salt and pepper mixed
¼ cup water
1½ tsp. curry powder
1 tbsp. vegetable oil
1 cup Jamaican conch broth

PREPARATION
1. Clean and dice conch, marinate with a portion of chopped escallion, country pepper, garlic, salt, pepper and thyme.
2. Shape carrot, potato and okra as desired.
3. Mix flour and cornmeal with salt then add water to form a dough and make spinners.
4. Cook spinners, potato, and carrot separate from conch in a hot sauce pan. Add oil, curry, chopped pepper, garlic, escallion, and onion and allow to sauté.
5. Add milk, lemon grass and conch stock. Allow to simmer. Add salt and pepper to taste.
6. In a hot sauce pan add remaining oil and sauté marinated conch slowly until tender.
7. Strain curry sauce over conch and add okra. Simmer for two minutes and combine cooked carrot, potato, and spinners.
8. Serve hot.

POOR MAN'S LOBSTER
Actually lobster is not a poor mans meal but this recipe was crafted by fishermen.

INGREDIENTS
3 cups water
¼ tsp salt
¼ tsp black pepper
½ tbsp sugar
3 cups lobster meat
¼ cup melted butter

PREPARATIONS
1. Bring water, salt and sugar to boiling; remove from heat and add lobster.
2. Cover and let stand for 15 minutes. Drain carefully; pat dry with paper towels.
3. Place lobster on foil lined broiler pan. Butter generously and broil until lightly browned.
4. Serve immediately with melted butter.

KINGSTONS BAKED SHRIMP AND CURRY CRAB
Shrimp and crab baked and curried with a delicious taste.

INGREDIENTS
¼ cup butter
¼ cup escallion diced
1 tsp curry powder
3 tbsp flour
½ tsp salt
1¾ cups milk
1 cup sour cream
1 cup pasta shells cooked
1 cup shrimp cooked and chopped
1 cup crabmeat—fresh
½ cup bread crumbs

PREPARATION
Preheat oven to 350F. Melt three tablespoons butter in a saucepan over medium heat. Cook escallions, stirring constantly about 10 minutes. Stir in curry powder, flour and salt, mixing well. Add milk, increase heat and cook until mixture boils and thickens. Remove from heat. Stir in sour cream, pasta and seafood, and pour mixture into a buttered baking dish. Melt remaining tbsp of butter and combine with bread crumbs. Sprinkle crumbs over seafood mixture and bake uncovered about 30 minutes.

MISS NORMA'S SEASONED SHRIMP
Ms. Norma did us justice by putting together this recipe specially for the book absolutely divine. Thanks Ms. Norma.

INGREDIENTS
1½ cups shrimp boiled
½ cup Jamaican shrimp broth
½ tsp sugar
1 bay leaf
¼ cup sweet pepper
½ tbsp lemon juice
1½ cups water
¼ tsp nutmeg
1½ tbsp vegetable oil
¼ cup onion, chopped
½ tsp scotch bonnet pepper diced
¼ cup garlic, minced
½ tsp cornstarch
1 cup whole tomatoes, fresh
¼ cup diced escallion
½ cup tomato sauce

PREPARATION
1. In a stew pan, add water, salt, bay leaf, lemon and shrimp and cook over medium heat. When water comes to a boil, cover and cook five minutes. Sauté onion and garlic in oil until tender add tomatoes, shrimp broth, sugar, and bell pepper and simmer. Add sweet basil, nutmeg, red pepper and salt to taste. Cook a few minutes more. Make a paste with corn starch and 2 tablespoons water. Stir it into the sauce; stir and cook until it thickens. When ready to serve, add the boiled shrimp, parsley and green onion. Serve with cooked rice.

JAMAICAN SHRIMP JAMBALAYA
Jambalaya, absolutely a peach of a recipe blending shrimp and other herbs and spices.

INGREDIENTS
4 cups cooked rice
8 tbsp butter
1 cup chopped onion
1 cup chopped escallion
1 cup chopped sweet pepper
4 cloves garlic, minced
2 tbsp tomato paste
2 cups water
1 tsp. sugar
½ tsp. cornstarch
¼ tsp salt
¼ tsp black pepper
¼ tsp scotch bonnet pepper diced
2 cups shrimp
¼ cup parsley, chopped fine

PREPARATION
1. Melt butter in pot then sauté onion, celery, pepper and garlic until onion is wilted.
2. Add tomato paste, stirring constantly over low heat then add 1 to ½ cups of water and sugar.
3. Season to taste with salt, pepper and scotch bonnet pepper.
4. Cook uncovered over medium-low heat stirring occasionally and add shrimp.
5. Cook until shrimp are pink and cooked through and dissolve cornstarch in ½ cup water and add.
6. Cook another 2 minutes and mix ingredients with cooked rice.
7. Add escallion and parsley and mix again.
8. Serve hot.

Cooking Tip
Conch meat is usually very tough and needs to be softened by using a blunt object to beat before preparing it in any recipe.

RED STRIPE BEER SHRIMP
Another recipe for Red Stripe beer lovers, absolutely delicious, a great taste in every bite enjoy it today.

INGREDIENTS
4 cups shrimp peeled de-veined
2 cups flour
2 cups yellow cornmeal
2 eggs beaten
¼ tsp salt
¼ tsp pepper
¼ tbsp garlic powder
1 bottle Red Stripe Beer

PREPARATION
1. Mix flour, cornmeal, eggs, salt, pepper and garlic powder in mixing bowl.
2. Add enough beer, mixing thoroughly, to get the consistency of a thick pancake mix.
3. Pour batter over shrimp or fish and let marinate for an hour.
4. Deep fry at 370 degrees. Consistent hot grease will float the shrimp in a very short time.
5. Drop shrimp into hot grease, one at a time, to prevent them from sticking together.
6. Remove and place on paper towel to drain.
7. Serve hot.

PORTLAND CONCH FRITTERS
More great conch recipes, we've tried salt fish, crab and even banana fritters this conch fritter ranks with the rest.

INGREDIENTS
1 cup conch chopped
¼ cup onion diced
¼ cup sweet pepper diced
2 eggs lightly beaten
2 tbsp butter melted
8 tbsp flour
1 tsp baking powder
¼ tsp salt
¼ tsp black pepper
½ cup vegetable oil

PREPARATION
1. Chop conch in food processor then grate onion and pepper into conch.
2. Add eggs, salt and melted butter. Mix well.
3. Sift flour and baking powder into mixture. Blend until it is thick enough to spoon into hot oil.
4. Fry until golden brown on all sides.
5. Serve with seafood sauce of your choice.

SPICY SHRIMP IN GRAPEFRUIT SAUCE
This grapefruit recipe is one of a kind, the grapefruit was crafted in Jamaican by some wily botanists.

INGREDIENTS
1 cup grapefruit peeled and chopped
¼ cup grapefruit juice
1½ cup shrimp peeled and de-veined
2 tbsp vegetable oil
¼ tsp salt
¼ tsp black pepper
1 tbsp cornstarch
½ tsp allspice

PREPARATION
1. In a large skillet, sauté the shrimp filets in hot oil until brown.
2. Salt and pepper the shrimp filets. Remove them from the pan and keep warm.
3. In the same pan stir in grapefruit juice and let the sauce come to a boil.
4. Stir in the cornstarch and cook till the sauce slightly thickens.
5. Add the grapefruit slices to the sauce and warm gently.
6. Serve hot with sauce.

SPICY JAMAICAN CONCH CHOWDER
Conch chowder or soup is very popular dish, but we have made some alterations and spiced it up here.

INGREDIENTS
¼ lb salt pork
¼ cup onions chopped
¼ cup garlic crushed
½ cup sweet pepper—chopped
1 cup tomatoes chopped
½ cup tomato paste
2 cups hot water
1 tsp allspice
1 cup cubed conchs
1 tbsp cane vinegar
½ tbsp salt and black pepper mixed
2 tbsp Jamaican jerk sauce
2 cups potatoes peeled and cubed

PREPARATION
1. Soak the salted pork in water to remove some of the salt.
2. Dice the salt pork and fry in a large pot. Add the onions, garlic and green pepper.
3. Cook until tender but not browned. Add the tomatoes, tomato paste, hot water and poultry seasoning.
4. Cook over low heat while preparing conch.
5. Pound the conchs with a small mallet to break up the tough tissue.
6. Chop coarsely and add to the chowder. Bring to a boil.
7. Add the vinegar, salt and pepper and the barbecue sauce.
8. Bring to a boil again, cover, turn heat to low and simmer 2 hours.
9. Add potatoes and simmer until potatoes are tender, about 20 minutes.

SUPER SEAFOOD BLEND

As the name suggests it's a super blend of several great meats.

INGREDIENTS

4 tbsp flour
½ tsp black pepper
¼ cup cheese spread
1 cup cheese, shredded
½ tsp salt
2 cup milk
¼ tsp Tabasco sauce
¼ cup crabmeat cooked
½ cup cooked shrimp meat
½ cup cooked lobster meat
Hot cooked rice

PREPARATION

Combine flour, salt, pepper and 1 cup milk. Stir until smooth. Combine cheese spread and remaining milk in top of double boiler, cook over hot water until cheese melts. Add flour mixture and hot sauce to cheese mixture, stir until smooth. Add shrimp and crabmeat. Pour into a greased casserole dish and top with shredded cheese. Bake at 350 F. for 20 minutes. Serve over hot cooked rice.

Cooking Tip
Blending all seafood meat takes great care. Of the three most popular crustaceans the crab has the most distinctive taste and possibly is the least popular of the three. Bear this in mind when preparing this recipe.

JAMAICAN CRAB CAKES

An excellent crab cake recipe, you should try this one its absolutely delicious.

INGREDIENTS

1½ cup crabmeat
1 egg beaten
½ tbsp allspice
1 cup flour
2 tsp sugar
¼ cup vegetable oil
¼ cup curry paste
¼ cup onion chopped
¼ cup escallion chopped
¼ cup sweet pepper diced
¼ tbsp scotch bonnet pepper
¼ cup garlic minced
1 tsp grated lime rind
2 tsp paprika

PREPARATION

Place crabmeat and blend all ingredients until smooth. Combine in bowl with flour until batter is formed. Roll crab mixture into a balls then flatten slightly. In a skillet deep-fry crab cakes in hot oil until well browned and cooked Drain on absorbent paper. Serve hot.

MONTEGO BAY DRUNKEN CRAB
This MoBay recipe is typical of the resort town where rum is galore we called this recipe the drunken crab.

INGREDIENTS
1 lb crabmeat
1 pie crust
2 tbsp chopped parsley
4 tbsp Appleton white rum
½ tbsp salt and black pepper mixed
4 eggs, slightly beaten
1½ cup milk
½ tsp scotch bonnet pepper diced
1 egg white
½ tsp paprika

PREPARATIONS
Line bottom on pie pan, cover and refrigerate 1 hour. Preheat oven to 450 then mix crab with parsley, rum, salt and pepper. In separate bowl, combine eggs, milk and scotch bonnet pepper. Brush pastry with egg white, fill with crab mixture. Pour egg mixture on top and sprinkle with paprika. Bake for 10 minutes then reduce heat to 350. Bake 40 minutes longer until set. Serve in moderation and hot with rum taste.

Cooking Tip
When baking crab meat do not do so longer then 10-15 minutes, this will quickly burn the meat and most of the taste and flavor will quickly evaporate.

OCHO RIOS CRAB AND SHRIMP MELT
Another combo recipe that's at the top of our best seafood recipes. You have to try these today.

INGREDIENTS
1 cup shrimp, peeled
½ cup crab meat
¼ cup onion diced
¼ cup escallion diced
¼ cup garlic minced
¼ cup Jamaican hot pepper sauce
1 tbsp margarine
1 tsp lemon Juice
2 tbsp bread crumbs
1 cup shredded cheese

PREPARATIONS
1. Butterfly shrimp by cutting down the back remove vein and set aside.
2. Heat a skillet and sauté escallion, onion and garlic in the margarine.
3. When browned stir in lemon juice and bottled hot pepper sauce.
4. Toss with the flaked crab meat and fine dry bread crumbs.
5. Spread shrimp open. And in a baking tin bake at 350 degrees F for 20 minutes.
6. Remove and reduce heat to 275 degrees and sprinkle cheese on top.
7. Serve with lemon wedges

CURRIED CONCH WITH BANANA SAUCE
Another curried conch recipe that's more traditional but with a twist of banana sauce

INGREDIENTS
2 tbsps. vegetable oil
2 garlic cloves, finely chopped
1 tsp. curry powder
1 cup conch cubed,
¼ cup onion, chopped
½ cup potato diced
½ cup water
2 tbsps. Jamaican banana sauce
¼ cup grated ginger
¼ cup coconut milk

PREPARATION
1. In a frying pan, heat the oil and fry the garlic until golden brown.
2. Add the curry powder, stir to mix thoroughly, and cook for 1 minute.
3. Add the conch and stir well to coat the meat in the curry mixture.
4. Add the onion, potato and a quarter-cup stock, and stir-fry over medium heat until the potato is just cooked.
5. Stir in the banana sauce, ginger and coconut milk, and simmer gently until the sauce thickens.
6. Turn into a bowl and serve.

DEVILS BACK BONE LOBSTER
This recipe is from a small district in St. Catherine, absolutely delicious to the taste.

INGREDIENTS
¼ cup butter
¼ cup onion, grated
1 cup Tabasco sauce
1 tbsp lemon juice
2 cups lobster meat
4 tbsp flour
2 cup milk
½ tsp salt
¼ cup Appleton V/X rum
½ cup cheese grated

PREPARATIONS
1. This recipe is equally good with lump crabmeat, or using the frozen lobster tails; whichever is available.
2. Melt butter, add onion which has been grated along with onion juice.
3. Cook a few minutes until onion is tender. Add dried mustard, salt, then flour.
4. Slowly add milk and make your cream sauce.
5. Allow your sauce to thicken, stirring constantly, and then add all the other ingredients.
6. Serve this in flaky pastry shells.

FORT CLARENCE SEAFOOD CAKE
From the seaside to your table the chefs at the Fort Clarence beach crafted this perfect recipe

INGREDIENTS
1 cup cornbread crumbs
¼ cup onions diced
¼ tsp salt
¼ tsp black pepper
½ cup sweet pepper diced
¼ cup garlic cloves crushed
1 tbsp vegetable oil
1½ cup crabmeat
1¼ cup shrimp
1¼ lb fish fillets
¼ cup mayonnaise
1 tbsp lime juice
½ tsp scotch bonnet pepper diced
3 tbsp butter

PREPARATION
Cut onion into ½ chunks; sauté in 10 frying pan in hot olive oil until soft, about 4 minutes. Cut peppers into ½ chunks add peppers and garlic then continue cooking until peppers are almost tender. Coarsely chop shrimp and fish then onion and pepper mixture from heat and add seafood, mayonnaise and lime juice. Stir gently to prevent breaking up crab. Season to taste with salt and pepper. Shape into patties and coat both sides with cornbread crumbs. When ready to serve, heat 2 tbsp clarified butter in frying pan over moderately high heat. Sauté 3 cakes at a time until golden on both sides, about 2 minutes. Add more butter as necessary.

> **Cooking Tip**
> Do not use too much scotch bonnet pepper in this recipe as it can resonate through the entire cake recipe and make it inedible.

PORT ROYAL CURRY LOBSTER
This recipe from the home of Henry Morgan the famed pirate this recipe is absolutely delicious

INGREDIENTS
1½ tsp. curry powder
½ tsp. allspice
¼ cup vegetable oil
½ cup onion diced
¼ cup garlic diced
1 tbsp sugar
2 tbsp lime juice
½ cup **Get Jamaica Curry Sauce©**
2 tsp scotch bonnet pepper, diced
5 cups cubed lobster meat cooked
4 escallions, sliced thin
½ tbsp salt and pepper mixed

PREPARATION
In a large bowl, combine lobster and all seasonings and allow to marinate. Place in a skillet and brown, then reduce heat and add Get Jamaica Curry Sauce. Allow to simmer until cooked. Serve with potatoes and white rice.

ST. BESS PEPPERED SHRIMP
Peppered shrimps are a staple when driving through the parish of St. Elizabeth. Feel free to try this recipe its divine.

INGREDIENTS
1 tsp scotch bonnet pepper diced
1 tsp thyme dried
2 cups shrimp in shells
4 tbsp vegetable oil
¼ cup melted butter
¼ cup garlic crushed
½ cup tomatoes chopped
½ cup Appleton white rum
¼ cup onion chopped
¼ tbsp salt and black pepper

PREPARATION
1. Melt butter in oil and sauté onion and garlic until golden.
2. Add tomatoes and mix well then add all other ingredients and mix well.
3. Simmer for 30 minutes then add shrimp and simmer 15 minutes.
4. Remove shrimp still in shell and drain of oil.
5. Serve as is.

GINGER HILL SHRIMP IN GINGER SAUCE
Ginger is a contrast a their most famous fruit is the pineapple. Nevertheless ginger is also in abundance and makes a great shrimp recipe.

INGREDIENTS
2 tbsp rice wine
1 tbsp soy sauce
1 tbsp water
¼ tsp salt
1 tsp sugar
¼ cup escallion chopped
2 tbsp vegetable oil
3 cups shrimp raw peeled and de-veined
1 tsp cornstarch
½ cup Jamaican ginger sauce

PREPARATION
1. Combine shrimp with salt, cornstarch and 1 tbsp vegetable oil.
2. Heat a skillet, then add all other ingredients except sauce.
3. Stir-fry the mixture then add the ginger sauce ingredients and continue to cook.
4. Serve hot.

> **Cooking Tip**
> When preparing sauces to eat with seafood add a little extra salt if the recipe is used fresh water fish or canned seafood meat.

DORREENS SPECIAL LOBSTER
This is Doreen's special lobster recipe, you wont find this recipe anywhere else.

INGREDIENTS
1 cup lobster meat chopped
½ cup fillet fish
½ cup Red Stripe Beer
½ cup water
¼ cup onion diced
¼ cup escallion diced
¼ tsp salt
¼ tsp thyme
2 tbsp butter
2 tbsp flour
¼ cup cream
1 egg yolk
¼ cup garlic diced

PREPARATION
In a large saucepan, place beer, water, onion, escallion, salt, and thyme. Heat to boiling then add lobster and fish, cover, and simmer until fish flakes. Remove lobster and fish and drain well on paper towels. Boil stock to reduce and strain. In another saucepan, melt the butter. Stir in flour and add ¾ cup strained stock and the cream. Cook until thickened and add a little hot mixture to egg yolk and return to pan. Gently combine lobster and fish and sauce until cooked. A delicious recipe.

WHITEHOUSE SHRIMP AND LOBSTER IN WINE
This recipe from the Westmoreland fishing town was absolutely delicious. An excellent blend of wine and seafood.

INGREDIENTS
4 whole lobster tails
2 cups shrimp shelled and de-veined
¼ cup escallion
¼ cup onion diced
½ tsp garlic powder
4 cups water
¼ cup butter
½ cup flour
¼ tsp salt
½ tsp paprika
¼ tsp black pepper
2 cups light cream
1¼ cup white wine
5 parsley sprigs to garnish

PREPARATION
1. In large sauce pan bring water to a boil and add lobster and shrimp.
2. Return to boiling, reduce heat, and simmer, covered for 8 minutes.
3. Remove lobster and shrimp and set all seafood aside.
4. Melt butter in sauce pan and remove from heat then stir in flour, salt, paprika, and pepper.
5. Gradually stir in cream until smooth and bring to a boil, stirring. Reduce heat and simmer 5 minutes. Add wine and seafood and stir until combined. Cook over low heat until hot. Serve hot and garnish with parsley.

HELLSHIRE SHRIMP WITH CRAB SAUCE
Hellshire the home of the fried fish gave us this sweet shrimp recipe.

INGREDIENTS
1½ cup crab meat
4 cups large shrimp peeled and de-veined
¾ cup milk
¾ cup margarine
¼ cup flour
3 tbsp ketchup
¼ cup escallion diced
¼ cup garlic, minced
¼ cup onions diced
½ tbsp salt and pepper mixed
½ cup Jamaican bar-bq sauce

PREPARATION
1. Place crab meat, milk margarine, milk, flour, ketchup, escallion, garlic and onion in a food processor.
2. Blend until you have a batter then set aside.
3. Butterfly the shrimp and place shrimp in greased baking dish cut side up.
4. Place crab mixture in each shrimp, brush shrimp with margarine.
5. Bake at 350 basting with sauce until shrimp and stuffing is cooked.
6. Serve hot.

JAMAICAN SEAFOOD IN CREAM SAUCE
A wowser of a recipe with curry powder and sour cream.

INGREDIENTS
1 cup shrimp peeled and de-veined
½ cup lobster meat
½ cup crab meat
½ cup diced onion
½ cup vegetable oil
½ cup escallion minced
3 lg cloves garlic, minced
1½ cups milk
1 tbsp. cornstarch
1 cup Jamaican fish broth
2 tbsp. allspice
¼ tsp. curry powder
2 tbsp sour cream

PREPARATION
1. Spray large frying pan with vegetable cooking spray and place over medium heat.
2. Add seafood, onion, escallions, and garlic to skillet and cook over medium heat until onions slightly brown.
3. Stir together milk and cornstarch. Add milk mixture, fish broth, allspice and curry powder to skillet.
4. Increase heat to medium-high. Stir until sauce begins to thicken and seafood is no longer pink in centre.
5. Add sour cream product and heat
6. Serve over rice.

jamaican crab legs
baked.©

jamaican lobster tails
recipe ©

BLUE LAGOON LOBSTER MOUSSE

A superb recipe that you will definitely want to try and so easy to prepare.

INGREDIENTS

1 pack gelatin (lemon flavored)
1 cup hot water
2 cups lobster meat
½ cup escallion diced
1½ cup sweet pepper diced
½ tsp salt
1½ cup onion chopped
½ tbsp scotch bonnet pepper diced
½ cup mayonnaise
½ cup whipped cream
1 bowl vegetable salad

PREPARATION

Dissolve gelatin in hot water then add all ingredients except salad greens and blend. Pour into mold and when firm, un mold on salad. Serve warm.

ANNATTO BAY SWEET AND SOUR LOBSTER

The St. Mary town boasts this sweet recipe that is prepared quite easily and is absolutely mouth watering.

INGREDIENTS

6 lbs lobster tail
2 tbsp wine
¼ cup soy sauce
1 tbsp vegetable oil
1 tsp ginger minced
¼ cup garlic mashed
½ tsp MSG (**optional**)
1 egg beaten
¼ cup cornstarch
½ cup sweet pepper
½ cup carrots chopped
½ cup pineapple slices quartered
½ cup onion quartered
¼ tsp Salt
¼ tsp black pepper
1 cup Jamaican sweet and sour sauce

PREPARATION

Cut lobster into 1-inch cubes and place in baking dish. Combine wine, soy sauce, vegetable oil, ginger, garlic and ½ tsp MSG and mix well. Pour mixture over lobster then marinate ½ hour. Mix together egg and cornstarch to form stiff batter, drain lobster well and combine with batter. Deep-fry in skillet over medium heat until crisp and golden brown then drain on paper towels. In wok, or large skillet, heat 2 tablespoons oil. Add remaining ingredients and stir fry to 2-4 minutes or until vegetables are tender. Then add sweet and sour sauce and blend. Add lobster, combine well and serve hot.

> **Cooking Tip**
> Sweet and sour sauce used on fish and seafood recipes must be tempered as it will drown out the natural taste of other Jamaican seasonings used in the recipe.

MORGANS HARBOUR LOBSTER CAKES
The hotel is a great seafood fair with daily trips over to lime caye island. But lobster cakes were a gem of a recipe we had to include.

INGREDIENTS
3 cups lobster diced
1 egg beaten
½ tbsp allspice
1 cup flour
2 tsp sugar
¼ cup vegetable oil
¼ cup curry paste
¼ cup onion chopped
¼ cup escallion chopped
¼ cup sweet pepper diced
¼ tbsp scotch bonnet pepper
¼ cup garlic minced
1 tsp grated lime rind
2 tsp paprika

PREPARATION
Blend all ingredients until smooth except flour. Combine in bowl with flour until batter is formed. Roll lobster mixture into a balls then flatten slightly. In a skillet deep-fry lobster cakes in hot oil until well browned and cooked Drain on absorbent paper. Serve hot.

SPICY STEW SEAFOOD AND FISH COMBO
A perfect mixture of Jamaican seafood stewed together, then absolutely great.

INGREDIENTS
1 cup crabmeat
½ cup lobster cubed
½ cup shrimp
½ cup cream
¼ tsp salt
¼ tsp black pepper
½ tsp nutmeg
2 tbsp butter
2 tbsp flour
½ cup chopped tomatoes
1 cup cooked potatoes cubed
¼ cup onion chopped
¼ cup escallion chopped

PREPARATION
In a small saucepan combine the seafood and heavy cream and bring to a gentle simmer. Cook the seafood until soft then season with salt and pepper and nutmeg. Add the butter, seasonings, tomatoes, vegetable and flour and stir into the simmering stew. Serve hot.

> **Cooking Tip**
> When preparing a seafood combo, its sometimes better to prepare the meats in separate saucepans, to give your guest choice of meats instead of blending all three together.

GLORIAS STEAMED SHRIMP IN ORANGE SAUCE
Gloria's is a small but popular seafood restaurant In the Port Royal area and serves this tasty treat.

INGREDIENTS
2½ cups shrimp
½ tbsp salt and black pepper mixed
¾ cup water
¼ cup melted butter
¼ cup coconut milk
¼ cup onion diced
¼ cup escallion diced
½ cup sweet peppers
½ cup tomatoes diced
½ tbsp scotch bonnet pepper diced
½ cup chopped okras
1 onion sliced
1 scotch bonnet pepper diced into rings
1 cup cubed cooked potatoes

PREPARATION
Season shrimp with seasonings and allow to marinate. In a deep skillet heat melted butter, and add shrimp and all ingredients. Cover and allow to cook for until shrimp is done. Add cooked potatoes and allow to simmer. Remove and serve hot.

DOWN TOWN LOBSTER COCKTAIL IN SHELL
A scrumptious recipe with patty crusts acting as a shell

INGREDIENTS
6 Jamaican patty crusts
2½ cups chopped lobster meat finely chopped
1 cup Jamaican bar-bq sauce
1 tsp salt
¼ tsp dried thyme leaves
1 lg tomato chopped
½ tbsp scotch bonnet pepper diced
2 stalk escallion chopped
1 lg onion finely chopped
2 tbsp soy sauce
¼ tsp sugar
½ tsp allspice

PREPARATION
Sauté escallion, onions, thyme, pepper and chopped tomato in a frying pan. Add lobster in frying pan and fry until lobster is cooked. Add soy sauce, sugar, salt and allspice. Ensure that the lobster mixture is wet when placing it on the patty crust. Evenly spread lobster filling on each circle then and crimp with a fork the corners. Baste with sauce. Place in the oven then bake for approximately 20 minutes at 375 degrees basting with sauce. Serve hot.

Cooking Tip
When preparing seafood recipes with lobster and crab meat and you intend to reuse the shell ensure that the shell has been soaked in water and rinsed well with either limejuice or vinegar.

PELICAN SEAFOOD KABOBS

Pelican is an offshore restaurant and is a slice of heaven on the sea and this recipe fits that description as well.

INGREDIENTS

¼ cup garlic chopped
2 large onions
6 large sweet peppers, 3 red and 3 green
3 cups large boiled shrimp
8 cups lobster tails boiled and cubed
1 cup Jamaican sweet sauce
1 tsp. curry powder
¼ cup escallion chopped
1 tbsp thyme leaves
½ tbsp scotch bonnet pepper diced
¼ tsp salt
¼ tsp black pepper
1 tbsp. vegetable oil

PREPARATION

Season seafood with ingredients and allow to marinate. Slice red and green peppers and stick on each skewer. Allow to set for at least 10 minutes then heat the grill with one teaspoon vegetable oil. While grilling baste with fish sauce.

MIX UP AND BLENDER SEAFOOD ON ROTI

A great tasting recipe delicious and mouth watering in every bite, a true Jamaican recipe.

INGREDIENTS

1 cup shrimp grilled and diced
2 lb lobster Meat grilled and diced
½ cup butter
¼ cup flour
¼ cup vegetable oil
1 bunch pak choy
¼ tsp salt
¼ tsp black pepper
4 roti
¼ cup escallion diced
¼ cup onion diced
½ tsp garlic powder

PREPARATION

Sauté pak choy, escallion and onions in a large skillet with butter. Add diced seafood, sauté and add salt and pepper to taste. Mix remaining butter and flour to make a light paste and spread on roti. Spread seafood mixture on roti pin and place in and pre-heat oven at 375 degrees. Bake for 15 minutes then remove and allow to cool.

> **Cooking Tip**
> Conch meat is not usually prepared straight from the shell. This is basically because the meat itself is very tough and has to be tenderized. This is done by using a blunt object to pound the meat. This is a very arduous task and one which many cooks and chefs dislike. But if you take the time to do it you will see that the flavor of the conch meat is well wait the trouble.

SEASIDE SEAFOOD BLEND
A tasty treat that we know all seafood lover will delight in.

INGREDIENTS
1 cup shrimp cooked
1 cup lobster meat cooked
½ cup butter
3 cup tomatoes
¼ cup diced escallion
¼ cup garlic minced
¼ tsp salt
¼ tsp black pepper
½ tbsp paprika
2 cup cream

INGREDIENTS
Melt the butter in a large skillet and add the tomatoes, escallion, onions and garlic and sauté. Add the shrimp and lobster and continue to cook for another minute. Add salt and pepper to taste. Add the paprika and then the cream. Cook gently until the cream thickens, about 3 minutes. Serve hot.

COLLIE TOWN CURRY SEAFOOD
This coolie town recipe is a wonderful and blend of seafood with curry.

INGREDIENTS
2 tbsp vegetable oil
1 cup shrimp
1 cup cubed conch
1 cup cubed lobster meat
2 garlic cloves diced
1 tbsp curry paste
1 cup coconut cream
1 tbsp jerk sauce
2 tsp brown sugar
½ cup basil leaves
1 tbsp thyme leaves

PREPARATION
1. Pre-heat frying pan over medium high heat then add oil.
2. When oil is hot add seafood and stir-fry until lightly browned.
3. Remove to a bowl; set aside. Add garlic to frying pan and lightly brown.
4. Reduce heat and add curry paste then fry gently.
5. Stirring for 1 minute add coconut cream stirring constantly until smooth.
6. Add jerk sauce, basil and thyme leaves and the chicken.
7. Simmer together for 5-10 minutes or until seafood is done.
8. Add the basil leaves; stir together for 2-3 minutes. Serve hot

Cooking Tip
When currying Jamaican seafood, it is best to use a curry paste to flavor the stew. Unlike other meats you should neither season the seafood with the curry nor burn the curry powder and add the meat. Prepare the curry paste, set aside and then add when meat is cooking down.

JAMAICAN FRUIT BATTER FRY LOBSTER
Using Jamaican fruits in recipes adds color and great flavor, this fruit sauce recipe gave more oomph to the lobster.

INGREDIENTS
4 cups lobster meat cubed
2 cups flour
2 eggs beaten
¼ tsp salt
¼ tsp pepper
¼ tbsp garlic powder
1 cup Jamaican fruit sauce

PREPARATION
1. Mix flour, eggs, salt, pepper and garlic powder in mixing bowl.
2. Add enough fruit sauce mixing thoroughly, to get the consistency of a thick pancake mix.
3. Pour batter over shrimp or fish and let marinate for an hour.
4. Deep fry at 370 degrees. Consistent hot grease will float the lobster in a very short time.
5. Drop lobster meat into hot grease, one at a time, to prevent them from sticking together.
6. Remove and place on paper towel to drain.
7. Serve hot.

KINGSTON BARBEQUED SHRIMP
A Jamaican barbeque recipe that uses tasty St. Elizabeth shrimp.

INGREDIENTS
1 onion chopped
½ cup scallions chopped
2 garlic cloves
½ tsp thyme crumbled
1½ tsps salt
1½ tsps ground allspice (pimento)
¼ tsp nutmeg grated
½ tsp cinnamon
¼ cup scotch bonnet pepper minced
1 tsp black pepper
1 cup Jamaican barbeque sauce
2 tbsp soy sauce
¼ cup vegetable oil
2 cups shrimp

PREPARATION
1. Prepare the marinade by placing all the ingredients excepts shrimp in a food processor or blender and puree.
2. In a large shallow dish arrange the wings in one layer and spoon the marinade over them, rubbing it in.
3. Let them marinate, covered & chilled, turning them once and leave them overnight.
4. Arrange the shrimp in one layer on an oiled rack set over a foil-lined roasting pan, spoon the marinade over them and bake in the upper third of a preheated 450F oven, 30-35 minutes or until they are cooked through.

NEGRIL BAKED LOBSTERBALLS
These lobster balls is great to the taste with every delicious bites.

INGREDIENTS
1 lb. lobster meat cooked
½ cup dry bread crumbs
¼ cup milk
¾ tsp. salt
½ tsp. Worcestershire sauce
¼ tsp. pepper
¼ cup onion, chopped
1 egg

PREPARATION
1. Mix all ingredients, shape into twenty 1½ inch meatballs.
2. Place in un-greased rectangular pan and bake uncovered in 400ºF oven until done and light brown.
3. Serve with sauce of your choice.

SPECIAL JAMAICAN LOBSTER THERMIDOR
Another special and unique Jamaican recipe to tantalize your senses.

INGREDIENTS
8 large lobster tails
1 cup Jamaican sweet fish sauce
3 tbsp flour
¼ cup milk
¼ cup white wine
¼ cup shredded cheese
2 tbsp parsley
½ cup bread crumbs
2 tbsp butter
½ tsp paprika
½ tsp lemon juice

PREPARATION
1. Place lobster tails in a skillet add lemon slice, onion and water to cover.
2. Bring to a boil, then reduce heat and simmer for 4 minutes.
3. In a small saucepan blend sauce and the flour then gradually stir in milk, lemon juice and wine.
4. Cook while stirring constantly until thick and stir in cheese.
5. Carefully, drain lobster tails well and spoon mixture into a greased casserole.
6. Combine bread crumbs, butter and paprika.
7. Sprinkle over casseroles.
8. Broil 1 to 2 minutes.
9. Serve over your choice of rice or pastry shells.
10. Serve hot.

ST. BESS BAKED SHRIMP BALLS
Mixture of shrimp and seasonings to make great shrimp balls.

INGREDIENTS
3 cups shrimp peeled de-veined and cooked
½ cup dry bread crumbs
¼ cup milk
¾ tsp. salt
½ tsp. Worcestershire sauce
¼ tsp. pepper
¼ cup onion, chopped
1 egg

PREPARATION
1. Mix all ingredients, shape into twenty 1½ inch meatballs.
2. Place in un-greased rectangular pan and bake uncovered in 400ºF oven until done and light brown.
3. Serve with sauce of your choice.

PORTLAND BAKED CONCH BALLS
From Port Antonio comes this great conch recipe.

INGREDIENTS
2 cups conch meat
½ cup dry bread crumbs
¼ cup milk
¾ tsp. salt
½ tsp. Worcestershire sauce
¼ tsp. pepper
¼ cup onion, chopped
1 egg

PREPARATION
1. Mix all ingredients, shape into twenty 1½ inch meatballs.
2. Place in un-greased rectangular pan and bake uncovered in 400ºF oven until done and light brown.
3. Serve with sauce of your choice.

HELLSHIRE BAKED CRAB BALLS
From the coast line of Hellshire is the great recipe, absolutely delicious.

INGREDIENTS
3 cups crab meat
½ cup dry bread crumbs
¼ cup milk
¾ tsp. salt
½ tsp. Worcestershire sauce
¼ tsp. pepper
¼ cup onion, chopped
1 egg

PREPARATION
1. Mix all ingredients, shape into twenty 1½ inch meatballs.
2. Place in un-greased rectangular pan and bake uncovered in 400ºF oven until done and light brown.
3. Serve with sauce of your choice.

CONVERSION TABLES

Imperial to Metric Conversions

It is difficult to convert to metric measures with absolute accuracy. It is because of this fact that we have included a metric conversion table in our cookbook for the Third Edition©. It must be noted that this table is an approximate guide only. Different makes of cookers might vary and if you are in any doubt about the setting it is well to refer to the manufacturers guide.

All recipes in this cookbook use an American measuring cup, as the British measuring cup is slightly larger. Never mix metric and imperial measures in one recipe. Always use level measures.

Oven Temperatures

Farenheight	Celcius
200-250	110-130
250-300	130-150
300-350	150-180
350-370	180-190
375-400	190-200
425-450	220-230
450-500	230-240

Liquid Measures

Imperial	Metric
½ tsp	2 ml.
1 tsp.	5 ml.
1 tbsp	15 ml.
2 tbsp.	30 ml.
4 tbsp.	50 ml.
¼ pt.	150 ml.
½ pt.	300 ml.
1 pt.	600 ml.
1 3/4 pt.	1000 ml. (1 litre)

Dry Measures

Imperial	Metric
1 oz.	25 g
2 oz.	50 g
3 oz.	75 g
4 oz.	100 g
8 oz.	225 g
12 oz.	350 g
16 oz.	450 g
20 oz.	575 g
2 lbs and 3 oz.	1000 g (1 kg.)

Imperial	American cups
1 lb. butter or margarine	2 cups
1 lb. flour	4 cups
1 lb. castor sugar	2 cups
1 lb. brown sugar	2 cups
1 lb. icing sugar	3 cups
1 lb. rice	2 1/2 cups

JAMAICAN COOKING TIPS AND HINTS

This section of our cookbook is designed to assist you with the '*how to's*' of Jamaican cooking. There are a few essentials you should know before preparing Jamaican recipes and even if you do know a lot of these so called tricks of the trade there is nothing wrong with a little refreshers course.

TIPS

How to season and prepare poultry.
- Let the poultry meat to defrost naturally.
- De-bone the poultry meat.
- Clean and wash the poultry meat properly.
- Always use key seasonings.
- Use a poultry tenderizer.
- Allow the seasoned poultry to remain overnight.
- Store the seasoned poultry in the refrigerator in an air tight container.

How to season and prepare beef, veal and mutton.
- Allow the beef to defrost naturally.
- Clean and wash the beef properly.
- When cutting beef cut along main veins
- Always use key seasonings.
- Use a beef tenderizer.
- Allow the seasoned beef to remain overnight.
- Store the seasoned beef in the refrigerator in an air tight container.

How to season and prepare fish and shellfish.
- **How to cleaning the fish**

To clean and scale the fish means that you must use a fish scalar (or substitute that with a sharp knife or potato peeler), a table, a cutting board and a few sheets of old newspaper. Hold the fish by the tail and with the blade scrape off the scales working towards the head.
- **How to gut fish**

To gut the fish means that you make an incision through the belly of the fish. Grasp the end of the intestine nearest to the head and pull it away along the length of the slit. Then cut the intestine at the tail end. Trim the fins on the fish, starting with the back fin, the tail fin and totally remove the gill fins.
- **How to de-bone the fish.**

After gutting and trimming the fish, insert a de-boning knife close to the backbone at the tail end and cut the flesh from the bone, working towards the head and keeping the knife as close as possible to the bone. Small bones that stick to the flesh or are embedded in it, must be removed with tweezers or fingers. Next you can fillet the fish by splitting the fish on both sides. Once you have de-boned the fish you can carve the fish into filets that you would like.
- **Always season the fish with garlic, black pepper and salt**
- **Preparing Shrimp**

The most popular types of shellfish eaten in Jamaica are shrimps and lobsters. If you have received shrimp the first thing is to twist off the head and remove the shell. Remove the vein or the intestine out of the center back. Rinse the shrimp off with lime and water.
- **Preparing Lobster**

Set a gallon of water in a heavy pot to boil. When the water is bubbling place the lobster in a boiling pot then quickly cover allow to return to a boil for only 7 minutes then remove the lobster. Split the tail of the lobster then twist off the head. Remove the insides (the liver and stomach). Remove the claws and then crack then open and using a spoon remove the flesh from inside the claws.

- **Preparing Crab**

Set a gallon of water in a heavy pot to boil. When the water is bubbling place the crab in a boiling pot then quickly cover allow to return to a boil for only 7 minutes then remove the crab. Crack the hard back of the crab and remove any edible meat discarding the rest. Remove the crab claws and then crack then open and using a spoon remove the flesh from inside the claws.

HINT: Keep the crab and lobster shells by cleaning with lime juice, water and vinegar to use in recipes

How to prepare Coconut Milk

To prepare coconut milk get a dry coconut, this is different from regular coconuts. Grater the meat in the coconut on a fine grater. Place each ¼ cup of grater coconut to ½ cup of water. Place in a blender and puree. Remove and strain the liquid of the coconut dregs. Pour in a measuring cup or jar for use in recipes.

How to prepare Curried Recipes

There are two manners in preparing curried recipes first you can **SEASON** the meat, fruit or vegetable with the curry powder or you can **BURN** the curry. This means adding the curry powder to the pot and sautéing with other seasonings before adding the meat. The latter technique is favored as seasoning with too much curry powder is known to cause tummy aches.

HINT: Using Indian curry is always best to capture the real curry taste

How to season with Scotch Bonnet Pepper

To season **MEAT** with this pepper dice the pepper finely and rub all over the surface of the meat. Allow to marinate overnight. In **SOUP** recipes drop a whole hard scotch bonnet pepper in the soup while simmering for not longer than 10 to 15 minutes, any longer you risk the pepper bursting and making the meal inedible.

HINT: Scotch bonnet pepper is best used in a marinade especially with thyme and pimento which heighten the taste.

How to prepare Conch

Conch is the least used shellfish in Jamaica. Please note that the we DO NOT advise removing the conch from the shell yourself. There is a poisonous element in the conch shell as a natural defense mechanism. Please purchase your conch directly from your local supermarket or fish mart and season and prepare much like chicken.

Baking Tips and Hints
- Always use fresh ingredients especially fruits when baking Jamaican recipes
- Always ensure correct measurements, i.e. don't use American cups when you should be using an English cup
- Ensure that the right baking powder is used, i.e. single or double acting.
- Add the sugar to the recipe slowly and not quickly.
- When adding egg or egg yolks do not beat all eggs at once.
- Always add the cake flavoring to the creaming mixture and not to the batter.
- Always sift flour with salt and seasoning including baking powder.
- Ensure that egg whites are well blended with batter as it will give cake a raw taste.
- Always grease baking pans and tins with unsalted oil or margarine.
- The cake is done when it shrinks from the sides, has bounce on the top and when a cake tester comes up dry.
- Dark tins give darker cakes while light tins give lighter color cakes.

Bread Tips and Hints
- To cut bread easily use a hot knife.
- To make bread crumbs use dry bread and place in a dry bag and crush with rolling pin
- To freshen bread rolls place in air tight bag and place in hot oven for 15 minutes
- To make garlic bread soak bread slice in garlic butter and bake for 15 minutes.
- Toast bread first then apply butter or cheese.

HINT: You can easily substitute garlic in garlic bread for any other seasoning such as cinnamon, onion or pimento.

Fruit, Vegetable and Seasoning Tips and Hints

- Peel onions under water to keep from affecting the eyes
- To extract juice from onion cut slice from the root end and scrape out juice.
- Don't sauté seasoning too long they will lose flavor.
- To restore sweetness to vegetables add sugar to boiling water
- Cook vegetables for no longer than 35 minutes, longer they lose texture, vitamins and minerals
- Peel oranges and grapefruit easily by letting them stand in boiling water for 3-5 minutes.
- Peel potatoes, bananas, sweet potatoes, chochoes and other tubers before cooking.
- To keep vegetables and fruits from discoloring sprinkle with lemon juice
- To peel carrots easily by immersing in boiled water for a few minutes.
- To peel a tomato easily dip in boiling water then in cold water, then break skin and peel.
- To prevent stain when preparing vegetables rub a small amount of oil on hands
- To remove vegetable stain use a small amount of lemon juice when washing hands.
- To keep vegetable lighter in color when boiling add milk to boiling water.
- To make vegetable darker add sugar to boiling water.

HINT: One spoilt vegetable can spoil an entire meal, always get the most fresh vegetables at your disposal.

Chicken, Fish and Meat (Pork, Beef, Veal & Mutton) Tips and Hints

- To make fish firm while cooking add lime juice to mixture.
- To reduce raw fish smell use browned butter or lemon juice.
- To remove fish odors from utensils soak in ammonia and water for a few minutes then rinse well.
- To prevent fish from breaking apart when steaming place in foil paper.
- Flour chicken and other meats easily by placing flour in a plastic bag and shaking well.
- To keep bacon from curling snip ends or cook on racks.
- To deep soak ensure meat is fully immersed in marinade.
- Deep soaking is only recommended with pork recipes.
- Using crown roast bones in regular soup recipes can give added flavor.

Jamaican Cooking Technique Tips and Hints

- There are ten (10) food preparation techniques used in Jamaican cooking, frying, roasting, boiling, steaming, braising, broiling, baking, barbequing and jerking.
- FRYING involves cooking food in at least 1 to 1½ inch high oil under a high flame. Using a coating prevents the food from being easily burned. A mild version of frying is sautéing
- ROASTING involves placing the food in an oven and roasting at a low temperature for a long period of time. The higher the temperature the more juices are extracted and the more fat is reduced in the meat.
- BOILING food means placing the food in water that is already boiling and keeping that temperature over a period of time until food is cooked.
- STEAMING is used to cook the food by generating heat in a pot using liquid to generate the steam under a medium flame.
- BRAISING means to sear the food by browning on either side then to cover tightly and cook slowly in a marinade or normal water. Stewing is a popular method of braising.
- BROILING means the food is prepared with exposure to direct heat whether by coals, under a direct flame or in a broiler electrical unit.
- BAKING means to place the food in an enclosed area and cook in a high temperature, using no marinade while being prepared. This results in most of the fat being evaporated and leads to a dry meal.
- BARBEQUEING involves the same baking procedure but the food is constantly marinated to prevent drying and to achieve a desired taste. The secret of barbequing is the marinade.
- CURRY involves preparing the braising technique, however the curry flavoring is added to derive a new taste.
- JERKING is the most famous of all Jamaican cooking techniques and involves grilling a method of broiling using coals. The secret of jerking is in the marinade used to season the meat and in the beer used to marinate the chicken while grilling.

When to use which cooking technique:

- CHICKEN—frying, roasting, boiling, braising, broiling, baking, barbequing, curry and jerking.
- DUCK—roasting, broiling and baking.
- TURKEY—roasting, broiling, baking and jerking.
- BEEF—roasting, braising, broiling and jerking.
- VEAL—roasting, braising, broiling and jerking.
- MUTTON—braising, curry and jerking.
- LAMB—broiling, roasting and braising
- PORK—roasting, braising, steaming, broiling and jerking.
- RIBS—roasting, braising, broiling, barbequing and jerking.
- FISH—frying, roasting, steaming, braising, broiling, baking, barbequing, curry and jerking.
- CRAB—roasting, braising, baking, barbequing, curry and jerking.
- SHRIMP—frying, roasting, boiling, braising, broiling, baking, curry and jerking.
- LOBSTER—roasting, boiling, braising, broiling, baking, curry and jerking.
- CONCH—braising, broiling, baking curry and jerking.
- LEAFY VEGETABLES—boiling and steaming.
- HARD VEGETABLES—boiling and steaming.
- GRAINS—boiling and steaming.

You can get more Jamaican cooking tips and hints when you visit our website at *www.getjamaica.com*.
Get Jamaica Recipes

INDEX

Browse through this index by recipes, search by ingredients and popular dishes, to find the recipe quickly.

978-0-595-47957-3
0-595-47957-X

www.ingramcontent.com/pod-product-compliance
Lightning Source LLC
Chambersburg PA
CBHW080353060326
40689CB00019B/3993